TWENTY-SIX OUT OF EIGHTY-EIGHT AIN'T BAD

WALKING THE SHIKOKU PILGRIMAGE ROUTE

KEITH SHORTRIDGE

Copyright © Keith Shortridge, 2021

All rights reserved.

No part of this book may be reproduced in any form or by any electronic or mechanical means, including information storage and retrieval systems, without permission in writing from the author, except by reviewers, who may quote brief passages in a review.

ISBN 978-0-6452548-0-8 (Electronic Edition)
ISBN 978-0-6452548-1-5 (Paperback Edition)

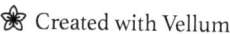 Created with Vellum

For my Elaine, who was there for all of this stroll through Shikoku, and for Holly and Tom, who were waiting for us when we got back.

1
THE FIRST TEMPLE (MONDAY APRIL 9)

We find the first temple, Ryōzen-ji, easily enough. It's the pilgrim shop we can't find. The temple is easy, because Elaine has the White Bible with its detailed maps, and the signs from the train station at Bando are clear enough that even we have managed to follow them to the temple.

But before we can go to the temple we have to go to the shop. More accurately, we can't go to the temple because at the moment we're just a pair of Westerners dressed in still rather unfamiliar hiking clothes and carrying nothing but backpacks. We need to be a pair of Henro - Japanese for 'pilgrim' - kitted out properly with conical hats, white jackets with traditional characters on them, sticks to walk with, and, most importantly, a book to record the temples visited on our pilgrimage.

That's the point: you need the book first, because you need to get it stamped when you go to the temple. You also need name slips, which you write your name on and leave at the temples. And a bag to hold the book and name slips; this is optional, but you have to carry them somehow. All of this is explained, with helpful illustrations, in the White Bible. What the White Bible also says is that you can buy all these at the pilgrim shop by the first temple, which it helpfully says is near the car park.

But we can't see the shop, and we can't even see the car park.

We really should stop calling it the White Bible, because this is asking for all sorts of potential religious confusion. It is in fact the small, mainly white, book called the "Shikoku Japan 88 Route Guide". Its web page says, "don't leave home without it", but that's a little too general, especially for literal-minded people like me. You don't need it to go down the road to the chemist. It ought to say: "don't even think about attempting the 88-temple Pilgrim route on the Japanese island of Shikoku without it". But that's not so catchy. And right now, as a guide it's proving a little inadequate. Fallen at almost the first hurdle. I mean, what's the point of telling you the shop is next to the car park, if you can't find the confounded car park?

We walk through the gate that leads to the temple. There's a proper sequence to follow at a temple, starting with bowing as you go through the gate, then washing your hands, then visiting the various parts of the temple in order. But the sequence ends with getting the book stamped, so we need the book. We look around. Each of these Shingon Buddhist temples has the same basic set of buildings, although the layout and the style of each temple varies considerably. But none of the charming wooden buildings here looks remotely like a shop. And there are certainly no cars, parked or otherwise.

Elaine leads us hopefully out into what turns out to be a fairly ordinary lane by the side of the temple. We walk up it a bit further, but it fails to reveal a hidden pilgrim shop. There isn't even a parked car. We pause. She looks more closely at the White Book (that's what we need to call it).

"There just doesn't seem to be a shop here. It's supposed to be obvious. Maybe there isn't one." There's a note of resigned failure here.

I pull out my iPhone and fiddle with the Japanese dictionary app.

"I think I know how to ask where the shop is. Shop is 'mise', so 'Henro-no mise-wa, doko desuka?' ought to be 'where is the Henro shop?'. I can go back and ask."

"If you knew that, why didn't you say so earlier?"

"I didn't know it earlier. I couldn't remember the word for shop. I just looked it up. I think I've got it right. I can try."

Elaine stays by the bags in the side street, and I go back to the temple. Somehow I'm not picking up an air of unquestioning faith in my ability here.

My first try isn't completely encouraging, but I think the chap I ask says something about not being Henro and so not knowing. Or something. I'm feeling my attempts to pick up a useful amount of Japanese haven't been completely successful. But then the second time I try, a lady helpfully points over to the other side of the temple, with a sort of 'go round that corner' gesture. She doesn't say anything. I suspect she can tell from the way I asked that I wouldn't understand if she did. I go around the corner. There, on the other side of the temple, outside the main block of the temple proper, are cars and even a couple of tour buses. All parked. And something that looks remarkably like a shop, with an array of conical hats, white jackets, and - probably - books. All you need to be a well-outfitted pilgrim.

I feel rather chuffed as I go back to fetch Elaine. She may have organised this whole trip, worked out all the details, understood the maps in the White Book (something I never truly master), and got us here almost flawlessly, but I found the car park. We all do our bit.

We return quickly through the temple, entering like tradespeople from the side street, around to the car park ("See? It was here all the time.") and into the shop.

This is clearly a Henro shop. You can tell from all the Henro stuff. It has numerous Henro conical hats, just as we expected, all with characters written on them - as far as I can see, all the same characters - and some time we must find out what they mean. (I assume they don't say: "this foreigner bought this hat thinking it says something meaningful; try not to laugh". Japanese people are trying them on, so presumably not. Unless they're all in on the joke.) It has a remarkable variety of Henro books, essentially just books of blank pages, ones you get stamped at each temple, but with elaborate covers and faint temple images interleaved with the blank pages. I hadn't realised they came in such a range of sizes. There are even scrolls, apparently used by the most serious of Henro, prepared to take the care required to hike them to each of 88 temples, unrolling and re-rolling them at each. Elaine picks a sensible, small book that won't load us down too much, or ask for too much care and maintenance. She also picks a pack of a reasonable number of white name slips (no colour choice here; when you start out your name slips have to be white) and a white messenger-type bag, also with the same presumably encouraging characters on it.

The full Henro kit - and outside the temple gates is a rather fetching mannequin showing it off - includes a complete white ensemble of white jacket and trousers, the conical hat, a staff, usually with a brocade cover with a small bell, and a brightly coloured scarf that gives you the air of a religious celebrant. (It is, apparently, a minimal version of a priest's robe, so that's not surprising.) We look at the hats, and try on a couple. They're straw, but they're stiff, and they rest on your head with a straw covered circle attached to the inside of the hat by a rather fragile looking support system. Since you seem to wear this most of the time, I assume it must be more comfortable than it looks.

It isn't. Actually, it's surprisingly uncomfortable, and insecure into the bargain. I assume my head must be the wrong size for it, and try another, which is equally uncomfortable but in a different way. A Japanese lady comes over from her desk and points at my pack and makes a number of rather fussy gestures I can't interpret. Misinterpreting ambiguous gestures is a speciality of mine. Actually, misinterpreting perfectly clear instructions is a speciality of mine, as has been pointed out at various times over the years. Fortunately, Elaine works out what she means.

"You have to put your pack on, so you can see if the hat catches on the pack when you move your head."

Which is a) nothing like what I thought the fussy lady had meant, and b) exactly what the fussy lady had meant. And when I get the pack on, the hat does indeed catch on the top of the backpack. I try another hat. More gestures.

"The single squiggle has to be at the front."

(The 'single squiggle', we discover later from the White Book, is the Sanskrit form of the name of the revered monk Kōbō Daishi. It's probably as well the Japanese lady doesn't seem to speak English.)

The hats are tricky. None seem to fit us properly, and all seem worryingly uncomfortable in various ways, quite apart from any tendency to get into arguments with the top end of my backpack. But we *have* got a stamp book and our name slips, which is the minimum we need to complete a formal visit to the temple. So we take those to the lady at the desk, who does something complicated with the front of the stamp book, takes our money, and doesn't seem particularly bothered that we don't appear to have bought hats.

And now we're pilgrims. Henro. Somewhat half-hearted as far as having all the proper gear goes, but Henro. Of a sort. It's time to visit our first temple.

We go back into the car park, and enter the temple properly. All temples have roughly the same layout, we've learned from the White Book. There's a reasonably imposing entrance gate, in this case with lanterns and cloths hanging down from the solid wooden cross piece. It looks old and weathered. The neatly clad mannequin just by the side of the gate modelling the full Henro outfit, all in white with a conical hat that she evidently finds comfortable, with a staff and orange scarf, is a more modern touch, apparently there to silently rebuke the less-completely-clad Henro. Inside, there will be a washing place, a main hall and a secondary hall, and an office.

There is a clear sequence to be followed when visiting a temple. Fortunately, Elaine has read it up and knows the sequence, at least in theory. I follow her. Outside the main gate, you bow, then you find the washing place. This turns out to have running water together with a collection of ladles. You wash your hands and mouth, and then move on to what the White Book calls the main hall, but which we think of as the main temple building. This is a wooden building with stairs leading up to it, and lanterns and cloths hanging from it, rather like the main gate, but here serving as the introduction to a rather dark interior, with rows of rather dim lanterns hanging from the roof. But before we go there, we have to prepare our name slips.

We sit down in the courtyard and Elaine explains what we do with the name slips. You leave one at each of the two halls of the temple, having written on them your name, address, the date, and a wish. We share out a few of these - two for each temple we hope to reach today - and start writing. I write our names, 'Sydney, Australia', the date, and try to think of a wish. This is always hard, and what I'm really wishing for is time to think of an appropriate wish. Finally, I write 'Tranquillity', which seems to me a really nice thing to wish for, something I personally am extremely keen on, and which has the minor advantage of being fairly short and easy to write. We collect our sets of name slips, and Elaine seems surprisingly happy with my wish. I suspect she was worried I'd wish for something Kōbō Daishi might think inappropriate.

There's a bell high up near the roof, with a substantial bell rope hanging down. Etiquette is that you ring this once. It looks an imposingly big bell, and I can imagine setting it going like a fire alarm with too vigorous a tug. Cautiously, I pull it just a bit. It is surprisingly heavy, and all I get is a slight 'ding'. I suspect having another go is probably not the thing to do, so I'll settle for that. At least I didn't have every head in the temple turn around to see what was going on. I realise that I'm in the middle of something I know almost nothing about, but which most of the other people here take very seriously. Elaine manages a slightly louder 'dong', but still not enough to attract attention.

The faintly lit interior of the building appears rather sparse and I feel I shouldn't be staring into it. I'm not entirely sure of my role here; I'm not a worshiper, I'm not really a tourist, or at least I don't think I am, but I don't think I should be just a detached observer either. Later I realise I hardly remember anything of what was inside, other than the lanterns and candles lit by other pilgrims. I'm intrigued by what I'm seeing on this trip, but I don't understand it all yet.

A proper pilgrim will now put their hands together and recite the appropriate sutras. Neither of us are up to that; we don't know the words. They are, helpfully, listed in the White Book, but I've not yet found a translation and I'm not happy reciting something when I don't know what it means. But it's apparently acceptable to just stand with hands together, head bowed slightly, and at least be respectful to the temple deity, and I settle for that. There is a donation box, where we each put a ¥100 coin.

We repeat this at the second hall. We have now visited our first temple; somewhat uncertainly, not yet comfortable with the etiquette and the process, but fascinated by it all, and at least feeling that we can see how this is all done, and that we'll learn more as we go on. And having done our first temple, we can get our book stamped. I look up the Japanese for 'stamp': 'inkan'.

The office is easy enough to find, but when we show the lady there our new stamp book and say 'inkan' in a hopeful way, she looks at it and gestures that we don't need to do anything; it seems the lady in the shop has already stamped it for us. So that's what she'd been doing with the book.

Out of the temple gate, turning and stopping to bow as we go.

We take photos of each other next to the white-clad mannequin, who turns her nose up at our incomplete costumes.

One temple down, eighty-seven to go. Elaine takes the White Book, checks the map, and points out the road we have to head down. What's more, just over the road from the temple we've just left, there's what looks as if it might be a coffee shop. We feel strangely drawn to that.

There's a small group of shops there. One might indeed be a coffee shop, or at least some form of cafe, but it's deserted and looks comprehensively closed. But close to it is another Henro shop. It looks somehow more welcoming and less official than the one at the temple, and we are conscious that we really aren't yet properly kitted out. It won't hurt to look.

Inside, almost immediately, we see an even bigger range of the conical Henro hats. What's more, when we look at them, each one has that bare and uncomfortable head ring covered with padding and a chin-strap to keep it on. This makes all the difference! These feel comfortable. It still takes a deal of trying on the various hats before we're happy, but we end up with two that actually fit comfortably. (And which don't catch on the backpacks - we did learn something useful at the temple shop, after all.) The hats have plastic rain covers, which I reluctantly agree will probably be useful.

Encouraged by that, we look at the rest of the Henro kit. We each pick a Henro jacket, opting for the rather lighter, sleeveless ones, more like Henro waistcoats. All white, but with a vertical line of characters going up the back. They also have a convenient number of pockets at the front, reminding me of the utility vests worn by fishers and photographers out in the great outdoors. Except that ours have less baggy pockets and the bright white has a feeling of purity that befits a pilgrim. Checking the White Book, I find that it too mentions purity and innocence when describing the 'hakui' or white vest, except that it dampens the party by adding that 'in the past, it also held the meaning of a death shroud, symbolising that the pilgrim was prepared to die at any time'. Well, in all honesty, not this Henro.

We also pick a couple of staffs. These are wood, about 130cm long, with a square cross-section, and have the same lettering on them as the back of the jackets. These aren't going to be all that comfortable to hold, but you also get the brocade covers with the small bells to go over the handles. Elaine picks a red cover and I pick an orange one. They're rather cheerful. (And the White Book doesn't say anything about the covers, so I can keep feeling cheerful about them. Probably the bells warn people that whoever's coming might die at any time, but if so I don't wish to know that.)

Now that feels much more like it. With my white jacket, conical hat sitting reasonably comfortably on my head, messenger bag slung over my shoulder, staff in hand, all adorned with these characters we really must get translated some time, and with the small bell tinkling as I stride forward, I actually feel as though I'm a part of something, a tradition that's existed over a thousand years. Oddly, I feel as though I don't stand out any more, although in all honesty, an obvious Westerner in Henro clothing probably stands out even more. Maybe it's more that I feel I'm making an effort to be part of this, and maybe people will accept this.

And we set off down the road to the second temple, Gokuraku-ji.

The Henro hat and our two pilgrim staffs.

Ryōzen-ji, the main hall.

Elaine outside Ryōzen-ji, with mannequin.

Keith outside Ryōzen-ji, clutching the messenger bag.

Lanterns hanging from the entrance gate to Ryōzen-ji

2

ORIGINS

I don't even remember when Elaine first mentioned the Shikoku pilgrimage. It's been "something we should do sometime" for some years now.

The first time Elaine went to Japan, it was on her own, it was for a conference, and she came back quite enthused.

"It's the closest I've been to being on a different planet, but it's manageable. The signs are all incomprehensible, the language is a complete unknown, but you can survive there."

'Survival' being the most minimal of minimum requirements for visiting a country, this sales pitch verged on the unconvincing, but she did make it sound, well..., interesting. What made it tractable, apparently, was that there were a few English signs, some people did speak English, and the trains ran on time.

The directions she'd been given to her hotel included "from such and such a station, go to platform 5 and get on the train that arrives at 6 minutes past 7. Not the one that arrives at 4 minutes past, not the one that arrives at 9 minutes past, but the one at 6 minutes past. Get out at the 4th stop, turn left on the exit from the station, then first right and there will be a hotel with this sign", followed by a set of Japanese characters that presumably were the name of the hotel.

Wondering what on earth would happen if this went wrong, she'd gamely taken the 7:06, turned left and then right, and ... there was the sign she'd expected, and inside were people she knew. On this basis, she was claiming Japan was manageable.

So we all went.

Our first family trip there, the two of us and our two young children, Holly and Tom, was for my 50th birthday. As I put it at the time, "I'm being taken to Japan with the idea that I should start the second half of my life in a country where I can't read the writing and don't even know the word for 'beer'". I discovered a few things about Japan on that trip:

1) There are indeed signs in English. All the train stations have their names in English as well as in Japanese. Kyoto has a lot of signs in English. Tokyo has fewer.

2) Just enough people speak just enough English that you can just about manage, particularly in hotels.

3) Ticket machines at stations have a button that you press to get instructions in English. Working out which button this is isn't always easy.

4) Cherry blossom season is lovely.

5) The word for 'beer' is 'beer'. Actually, it's 'bīru', but it's pronounced 'beer', because the final 'u' is almost silent.

6) I really like Japan.

Moreover, Japan is relatively close to Australia (you have to remember that not that many places are particularly close to Australia) and because it's almost a straight North-South flight, there's no jet lag.

We kept going back to Japan. We'd visited Kyoto, Tokyo, the old capital at Nara, and had gone up into the hills at Takayama, but all of these were reasonably large urban centres. We'd not spent much time in the countryside. We had developed a hard-to-explain fondness for Tokyo Disneyland, or rather for Disney Sea, which is next door to the main Disneyland park and has, unsurprisingly, a 'sea' theme including a section that reproduces a North-East US coast port, and another that captures some of the elegantly dilapidated feel of Venice

(Elaine called it "just like Venice, but without the flooding and the sinking into the Adriatic"). But we'd had glimpses of the country outside the cities, and wanted to see more.

And at some point, Elaine came across the 88-temple Shikoku pilgrimage.

"There's an island in Japan, on the Inland Sea, with eighty-eight temples, and a pilgrim route that goes to each one in turn. That might be an interesting thing to do, one day."

I don't remember, but I suspect I nodded, noncommittally. I do a good non-committal nod. Eighty-eight temples sounded a lot, but I imagined they were fairly close together. I assumed it was quite a small island.

"It's one of the more remote parts of Japan. It would be a way of seeing a bit of the country, outside the big cities."

"I can't see Tom and Holly doing it. They were 'temple-ed out' after a morning in Kyoto. And that was only about six temples."

"We could do it, just us, when they're old enough to be left at home."

"Well, it's an idea."

And it was an idea that stuck around. It stuck around much longer than other ideas for holidays. Much longer than her suggestion that it might be interesting to visit North Korea.

"Visiting North Korea would be a completely different experience."

"In the sense that it would be unpleasant, thoroughly controlled and spied upon by a totalitarian government."

When she was a teenager, Elaine went on a trip to the then Soviet Union, and every so often a residual yearning for uncomfortable travel seems to surface. Maybe it's some sort of penance for having access to the Qantas first class lounge. So far, we've not gone to North Korea.

Eventually, a number of things came together to draw us to Shikoku. Tom and Holly exchanged schools for universities, I left my job, in what I described as a "phoney retirement", and Elaine ended one fairly high-profile job and had a month's break before starting on another. And towards the end of a gap year in Europe, Holly walked the pilgrimage to Santiago de Compostela.

Holly's pilgrimage came as a surprise to us all, not least to Holly, who ended up doing it not out of any religious or even exercise-related conviction, but just to accompany a friend who would otherwise have had to do it by herself. I used to claim, unfairly, that she would take a taxi to the local coffee shop, and I had been sceptical that she would walk the best part of 1000km from France over the Pyrenees and into Spain. But she managed it splendidly, to our surprised admiration.

Obviously then, a stroll around a Japanese island would be something the two of us could do easily. We'd have time to prepare, get fit, learn some of the language - none of which Holly had had time to do. This couldn't be too hard. We started to plan seriously.

At least, Elaine started to plan seriously, and I did my bit by generally agreeing with her.

The roots of the Shikoku pilgrimage begin with the monk Kūkai, now known as Kōbō Daishi, who was born in 774 on Shikoku, and who founded the Shingon school of Buddhism. He also established many of the 88 temples on the island, as well as a separate retreat on the mainland at Mount Kōya, where he died, or at least entered into a state of eternal rest, in 835. The pilgrimage route runs around the island of Shikoku, visiting each of the 88 temples, and optionally a number of others, and is now a long-established tradition.

Elaine learned all of this well in advance; I eventually picked up most of the background in the initial couple of days we spent on the mainland at Kōyasan (Mount Kōya). What did become clear even to me in the planning state was that Shikoku was not a tiny island you could walk around in a week or so, as I had vaguely imagined.

I always think of Japan as having three main islands: Honshu, the main island, in the middle, Hokkaido in the north-east, and Kyushu in the south-west. Bear in mind that I did badly in geography at school. When you look closely at the western end of Honshu, you see that part of it is in fact a separate, fourth island, and this is Shikoku, the smallest of the four main islands of Japan. Shikoku is, apparently, the 50th largest island in the world, and the pilgrimage around it covers about 1,200km and usually takes between 30 and 60 days to complete. Our constrained schedule only had about three weeks for walking, and we were not likely to be the fastest of the pilgrims. We were more likely to be amongst the slowest.

But we could start by doing a bit of it. We began to prepare.

3

SYDNEY TO OSAKA (THURSDAY APRIL 5)

We started our pilgrimage the way all pilgrims should, in the first-class lounge run by Qantas at Sydney International airport. This is not somewhere that lets me in when flying by myself, but Elaine flies so much for work that one of the perks is a most superior frequent flyer card, and I'm happy to tag along to places above my station.

The lounge was more than happy to welcome people dressed in hiking gear, big boots and all, and we welcomed the French champagne. After all, we were going to be roughing it for the rest of the month.

The flight to Tokyo was late leaving, although we couldn't hear the announcement clearly enough to make out why. It seemed to have been saying something about the 'route'. We didn't really care much about the why of the delay; it's usually a late arrival from somewhere due to weather, or some fault the engineers have found in some vital piece of equipment such as a soap dispenser in the rear toilet. We cared much more about whether this would cause problems with our connection from Tokyo to Osaka, which was worryingly tight.

Actually, it was so tight it wasn't a connection anymore. It had been when we bought the tickets, but then Qantas contacted us and told us the flight out had been rescheduled by five minutes, and as a result our connection wasn't technically a connection because you need at least an hour between flights for a connection and this, now being only 55 minutes, no longer qualified. So we could choose to change our flights (their preferred option) or we could acknowledge the non-connection nature of our connection and just hope we made it, but if we didn't that wouldn't be their fault.

Since we had no luggage other than our cabin-baggage backpacks (one thing about being pilgrims is that you travel light, because you have to walk with everything you bring), we'd felt this wouldn't be a problem. And Elaine checked the arrival statistics for the Sydney-Tokyo flight and found it was usually on time. So Elaine had told Qantas we'd take the chance, and the system had recorded our rash decision, and then on a regular basis the system would keep forgetting it had done so, and Elaine would get another text about rescheduled flights and had to call up yet again to tell the system what it should have known already.

All of which had seemed fine in the planning stages, but was beginning to seem rash if the flight truly was going to be delayed. The real problem revolved around the fact that the flight to Osaka was about the only one that day that fitted nicely with getting to our first stop, at Kōyasan, to the east of Osaka, where we were booked in for two nights. We were discussing our fall-back options, most of which involved not getting to Kōyasan, or at least arriving a day late, when the flight was finally called.

Normally I have a complicated ritual on boarding an aircraft, involving extracting all I need from my backpack: noise-cancelling headphones, the glasses that focus properly on the screen in front, a book, a crossword, and a pullover because I always find aircraft too cold. But this time, we were travelling light, and I had none of these except the pullover. I did get the pullover out. We settled into our seats, which we'd chosen as close to the front of the aircraft as possible with a view to making as quick a dash as possible to the Osaka flight (Elaine thinks of these things), and tried to take advantage of the night flight by getting as much sleep as possible.

Although you'd not expect two adjacent seats to fall into two completely different climatic zones, Elaine found her seat too hot and I found mine unusually cold. So we swopped, and for the first time ever on a flight, I found myself overheating. First I dropped my pullover onto the floor and a little later I threw the supplied airline blanket on top of it. But then we did settle down, and must have slept passably well.

I woke to find breakfast being served and a helpful purser explaining to Elaine why the flight had been late taking off. A volcano had gone off near Osaka (cheerful news for those heading there, you have to admit) and Qantas had had serious discussions about cancelling the flight entirely. This had been the 'routing issue' in the hard-to-hear PA announcement. As it was, they'd decided to go, they'd even caught up a little, and were now only 15 minutes late. We asked if we would be able to make our not-officially-a-connection. There was a pause.

"Um," said the purser, who seemed to be struggling with finding a nice word for 'no'.

"We'll run?" I suggested, helpfully.

"Yes, that's what I'd advise."

We were first off the plane, in a rush. In hindsight, in too much of a rush, because my pullover was still on the floor under the discarded blanket, something I was to regret later. We scooted along the travelators, chafed at even the shortest of queues at immigration and customs, leapt on the bus to the domestic terminal, and just made the not-a-connection to Osaka, which helpfully had also been delayed.

Finally, we landed at Osaka's Kansai airport, built on an artificial island just off the coast in Osaka bay. Now we just had a train trip to Kōyasan to negotiate, and the adventure could start.

4
THE REST OF THE FIRST DAY - TEMPLE 2 TO TEMPLE 5 (MONDAY APRIL 9)

The road from temple 1 to temple 2 is fairly short (only 1.5 kilometres, according to the helpful chart in the White Book) and flat, which is just as well given that this is the first stretch we've walked with our full backpacks. Not to mention the full Henro kit, which isn't entirely what you'd call negligible. The white messenger bag is one more thing to have to remember. I take it for this leg. "We can take turns with the bag," says Elaine. We start getting the hang of walking with the staffs. They're fairly comfortable, although the brocade covers slip about a bit. We probably only really need these for the hilly bits; in the meantime, they're one more thing to carry, although they do have a most satisfying 'pilgrim' feel to them.

Elaine is following the route in the White Book, and I'm following Elaine. This is an efficient allocation of roles. She points out the Henro route markers, small red arrows, some with the silhouette of a pilgrim, at frequent points along the route. This pilgrim trail is a well organised one.

"They say if you go half an hour without seeing one of these markers, it's because you've lost the trail," Elaine says. I can see that could be a problem. I ask the obvious question: "How do you get back on a trail you've lost?"

At that point, apparently, modern technology will rescue you. Elaine has a map on her phone which has an overlay showing the pilgrim route. You can see where you are, and you can see where you should be. And then it's just a case of bringing the two together again. I find myself wondering what Kōbō Daishi would have thought of that. But then, I wonder what he'd have thought of a modern backpack and hiking boots?

We're just following a side road that leads through a village. Deep down, without thinking much about it, I'd imagined a pilgrimage as walking through untouched countryside, along tracks used only by walkers and horses. Actually, I realise I'm imagining the Canterbury Tales, with a disparate group heading across mediaeval England, from hostelry to hostelry, amusing themselves with bawdy stories. In fact, we're walking through a perfectly pleasant, modern, Japanese village, in a lightly built-up area. I decide my collection of bawdy stories probably aren't appropriate.

Japanese villages, I've noticed before, remind me of German ones, certainly the modern villages we've seen in southern Germany. Not that the Japanese villages go in for window boxes of geraniums, or look as if they're auditioning for the role of next Ravensburger jigsaw, but the houses do have a crisp, neat, not-much-nonsense look. They aren't the twee cottages of a magazine-ready English village, and they aren't the peasant huts that get ravaged in a Kurosawa movie. They're bourgeois, in quite a nice way.

They also have a lot of overhead cables. One of the first things I noticed about Japan, the first time we visited Kyoto, was how many cables ran overhead. It often strikes me that the Japanese in general don't care too much about the large-scale look of where they live, but do care about the small-scale; ugly overhead cables, yes, but individual doorways will be immaculate, with beautiful little details. Japanese beauty is intricate, and small-scale.

And, just to remind you you're not in Germany, they have temples. Suddenly, we reach temple 2, Gokuraku-ji, and it is a wonderful place, much larger than the first temple, with buildings nestling amongst trees and with a large open area near the entrance, where the washing place has an elaborate carved grey stone roof supported by carved grey stone pillars covered in what seem to be dragons.

There's a feeling of quiet and calm. Temples should all be like this. Around the back there are the halls, and the sun is shining brightly through the leaves of fall-coloured trees, which is confusing, given that this is spring, but which looks lovely. We visit the halls, leave our name slips, pause silently, and take our book to be stamped.

This is the first time I've watched the stamping process, and it's more elaborate, and much more satisfying, than I'd expected. It's not just a stamp on a blank page to tick off the visit, bang!, done, ¥300 please. There's a careful opening of the book and finding the proper page, three large red stamps on the page, and then, picking up a calligraphy brush, painstakingly dipping it in a black ink tray, they write something - I think these are Sanskrit characters - over the top of the stamp, with evident care and some pride, even though they must do this numerous times during the day. Then they take a piece of what I assume must be some sort of protective paper from where it was sitting over the previous temple's stamps, place it carefully over the new stamps and writing, and close the book. Then they ask you for ¥300, but most politely.

We've picked up a couple of small lunchboxes - rice and something - along the way, and we sit down in the open area by the washing place for lunch. We take a few photos of ourselves in our white Henro kit. A western-looking lady gets out of a car and comes over to us. She asks us, in English, where we're from; I suppose it's obvious we're not locals, despite the white Henro kit. Maybe she just heard us talking. We tell her, Australia, and she says she's from France, and they're going around doing some of the pilgrimage, but by car, because they don't have much time. She's our first 'car-Henro', and we feel quietly chuffed - not exactly proud, that would feel wrong, but happy with ourselves - when we say that we're doing it on foot. She says goodbye - she didn't have much time, after all - and we finish our lunch, pick up our staffs, and set off again.

The washing place at Gokuraku-ji, temple 2.

The upper temple at Gokuraku-ji,, temple 2.

Tree at Gokuraku-ji.

It's three kilometres to temple 3, Konsen-ji. We follow the road, looking out for the red arrow Henro markers along the way. Elaine turns out to be sharp-eyed when it comes to picking these out, which is just as well, because I'm not. They lead us through what feels like a long continuous village, although the houses are starting to thin out, and at one point we cross a fairly main road. Fortunately, the Henro route manages to avoid main roads as much as possible, and although we're walking on paved roads, there's hardly any traffic.

And then we come upon what could be a two-storey pagoda, a curving grey roof above a main structure of bright orange-red and white. Looking more closely, the bottom storey is actually a gateway, with small banners hanging down from the cross-beam. In front there's a pole with a highly convex mirror; we've seen a number of these on these narrow roads, providing a view for drivers around tight corners, but this one has a picture of two jolly looking Henro children low down on the pole. We seem to have reached temple 3.

(We think of it as temple 3, because the names aren't the sort of names that come naturally to either our tongues or our memories, and numbers are a convenient way of keeping track. It seems a bit cavalier, because they aren't just items in a checklist to be ticked off, and we're starting to realise that the temples all have their own characters.)

Konsen-ji is a colourful place. One building has a roof with a golden structure on the top shining in the sun, and the whole area is set against a background of small hills in the same variety of fall greens, browns, and even reds, that we've seen before. The red railings of a narrow could-not-be-anything-but-Japanese bridge lead across a tiny pond full of multi-coloured fish, and even the small metal incense burners outside the buildings are a bright orange.

Incense burners at Konsen-ji, temple 3.

The entrance to Konsen-ji, temple 3.

Other Henro at Konsen-ji, temple 3.

We're getting used to the sequence now, and are remembering to rinse both hands and mouth at the washing place, using the hands, not the ladle, to take the water to the mouth. We will have to work on the sutras, but we are starting to bow at the right places. Even if we aren't exactly authentic, we're at least showing respect for the traditions.

We aren't the only Henro who've come here on foot, although there don't seem to be many. We notice two, obvious from the staffs and conical hats, striding out some minutes before we leave, one all in white, the other in blue but with the same minimal white waistcoat that we're wearing.

It's now about half past three in the afternoon, and we have a decision to make at some point on the way to the next temple. The information office in Tokushima had booked us in to somewhere close to temple 5 for this evening. Temple 5, Jizō-ji, is about 5km due west of temple 3, with temple 4, Dainichi-ji, about 2km due north of temple 5. After temple 5 the pilgrim route heads south, which is why the usual route from temple 3 takes you about half way to temple 5, then cuts off to the north-west to temple 4, and then due south to temple 5. Do we have time to follow the normal route, given that it appears to be somewhat uphill to temple 4, or do we head directly to temple 5 and backtrack to 4 tomorrow morning?

This is the first choice we've had to make based on how far we think we're capable of walking. Other, that is, than Elaine's original decision to only try to get to temple 5 on this first day. As we walk, she explains that we're following a more leisurely schedule than most Henro. Most walking Henro apparently aim to take two days to get to temple 11. We, however, are going to take three, stopping at number 5 tonight, getting just past number 10 tomorrow, and on to 11 the next day. Temples are by no means equally-spaced, and it's nearly 10 kilometres between 10 and 11. She didn't plan for a long walk today, mostly, she reminds me, because she'd not been sure she'd get me out of bed early enough. I'm touched by the solicitous thought; unsure how I feel about her somewhat unwarranted lack of faith.

But I do already know why everyone aims to stop at temple 11. The path from 11 to 12 is notorious, and you want to set off fresh and early in the morning to tackle it. This is one of the notorious 'Henro-korogashi' sections of the route, a term the White Book translates as 'where a pilgrim falls down'. Temple 12 is at one of the highest points of the whole pilgrimage, and as if that weren't enough, you don't just slog your way up to it. Instead, you slog your way up to one peak, then down again, then up again, then down again, then, and only then, finally up to temple 12. I'm not actually scared of temple 12, but I am a little apprehensive.

However, that's in two days' time. Right now, we're feeling reasonably happy with our progress, and we really don't want to have to start a long walk tomorrow by backtracking to temple 4, so we decide we'll aim to get there today, so long as we keep making reasonable time.

We head on, through increasingly sparsely built-up country. Still, there are a number of houses, often rather larger now than we were noticing in the village streets earlier. We see a few that appear to be intended as throwbacks to an older style, with dark curving roofs with elaborate ornamentation running along the top and down the edges. The effect makes me think of a house wearing a Samurai helmet, and I start to see these as the Japanese equivalent of the Mock-Tudor half-timbered houses seen in England.

In the distance, we catch occasional glimpses of the two walking Henro we saw previously. They're keeping up a reasonable pace, but so are we. Every so often, we see them checking their route, pausing for a while before moving off again. Since this makes our navigation much easier, we start to catch them up, but awfully slowly.

The path now branches off to the right, away from the road and up a gradual slope into the hills. This is where we have to decide to try for temple 4 or not, but we've made good time, and the lads ahead are still showing us the way. We'll carry on following them.

The second half of the 5km between temples 3 and 4 does indeed climb, but does so fairly gently. The path is now just a track up the side of the hill, but it's a clear track, and our guides are in view most of the time. We keep a roughly constant distance for most of the journey; they don't quite pull ahead of us, we don't quite fall behind. (Back in Australia, we have just seen 'The Last Jedi', a large part of which is an extended pursuit sequence, with the forces of good maintaining an almost constant distance ahead of the forces of evil. It's an incongruous comparison, but the mind wanders on long walks. I must remember we are not heading for a Jedi temple.)

About 400 metres from the temple, our guiding pair pause as the path reaches a paved road, and we catch them up. We know it's 400 metres, because the one in full white turns to us and says, "400 metres".

There isn't much time to talk, because it's now about 4:40, and temples close at 5. I thought at first the two were Japanese, but they aren't. There is the usual basic exchange, as we hurry along the road.

"Where are you from?"

"Australia. And you?"

"We are from Taiwan."

We reach temple 4 at about 4:50.

Dainichi-ji, temple 4, is a is a slightly grey collection of steeply-roofed buildings in an open area off the road running up into the hills. As we walk in through the entrance and past the office building, a monk there says, in English:

"You must get your stamps quickly, because we are closing. Go in now please."

That's helpful of him. We reverse the usual order of things, and step into the office, which is fairly plain and business-like, with a young lady in blue robes sitting at a desk and a large ginger and white cat sitting on a set of new stamp books laid out for sale. As the lady gets out her stamps and calligraphy brush the cat takes an interest and walks up onto the desk and has to be pushed away. As we take our newly stamped books I gesture to my camera and the cat, and the lady nods and tries to hold the cat still for me. The cat, reluctant to perform, takes no interest in his moment of fame and wanders off.

At Dainichi-ji, temple 4.

Houses by the roadside, between temples 3 and 4.

The stamp office cat, at temple 4, Dainichi-ji.

Display of carved figures at temple 4.

A quick turn around the two halls of the temple, quick bows, putting of name slips into boxes, and we can leave the temple staff to shut the doors. There is a fascinating glassed-in gallery running around one of the buildings, with displays of carved figures that obviously have some significance, but we don't have a lot of time to look at them, or any way of finding out more about them.

On the way back down the road, past where we joined it and on towards temple 5, we talk a little with the Taiwanese lads. The one in white does most of the talking and his English is well-practised. This is his second time doing the pilgrimage; he's already done it once, as part of his training as a monk, although the previous year he did it in reverse.

Going in reverse is unusual, but is believed to confer greater spiritual benefits. Partly, this is because it's much harder, if only because the red guiding arrows that mark the path aren't easy to see from the other direction. And they point the wrong way, although presumably you allow for that. A nice thought is that it's believed by some that Kōbō Daishi still walks the pilgrimage, and because he does it in the usual direction, you maximise your chance of meeting him if you go the other way around. You'll certainly meet more other Henro if you try the reverse route, but you won't have so much time to chat.

Our trainee Taiwanese monk also tells us that on his last trip, he carried a sleeping bag and tent and camped out. This time, he's going around with his friend, and they've booked accommodation. His friend doesn't have time to do the whole pilgrimage, so he'll carry on alone after his friend leaves.

As we walk along the road, a local on a rather rickety-looking bike catches up with us and tags along for a while, chatting to the two Taiwanese in Japanese. I have no idea what they're saying, although at one point I hear 'Osotoraria', clearly something to do with us. Eventually he rides off and we continue on.

We're far too late to visit temple 5 tonight, of course, but we're going to arrive at the nearby accommodation comfortably before the expected 6pm. Our companions lead us straight to it, which is just as well, because it turns out to be an ordinary-looking house with no very obvious indication that it's a Henro lodging. However, as we stand outside, a lady appears, looks at Elaine and I, and says:

"Elaine?" with a very Japanese 'r' sound to the 'l'.

One advantage of standing out from the crowd is that you don't have to explain who you are to anyone who's had a booking and is expecting two Australians. On our first trip to Tokyo, we arrived in the area where we'd booked in, but couldn't work out where the hotel was, or indeed which street we were in - street signs are not written in English - so we walked around in increasing perplexity until a bike pulled up alongside us, and the girl riding it asked us, in English, if we were looking for the hotel. She had apparently been sent out to look for overdue lost foreigners, and had identified us immediately.

The lady leads us inside, we happily take off our boots and put on indoor slippers, and follow her up a steep wooden staircase. She makes a clear 'mind the beam' gesture that we should duck our heads. I nod to show I understand and bang my head on the beam as my head comes up. (During our stay, I and this beam develop a nodding relationship; I hit it three more times before we leave.)

Our room is a decent size, an advantage of the tatami mat and futon system. The lady shows us the shared toilet down the corridor, and the nearby couple of sinks. She looks at Elaine and asks:

"Furo?"

"Bath," Elaine says to me. I wasn't surprised she knew this word. She nods decisively to the lady. "Yes, and laundry." I reach for my iPhone and the Japanese dictionary app.

"Laundry is 'sentaku'."

The lady whips out a device that turns out to be a hand-held translator and types into it. She shows it to Elaine, who nods.

"I think it says the laundry is next to the bathroom."

Japan is an interesting mixture of tradition and high technology.

We're left on our own. Elaine locates the yukatas, we change into them, and she heads for the bathroom, taking our clothes. She comes back looking refreshed, but with damp clothes.

"The dryer looks complicated, but these should just dry overnight anyway. I reckon if you go down in your yukata and say 'furo' they'll show you to the bathroom."

I feel I know what I'm doing now, so I go down (hello, beam above the stairs) and indeed, the lady immediately points me to a small bathroom. In it there's a washing machine with our clothes still tumbling in it. This is obviously the same bathroom as Elaine used. Is this a private bathroom they use for people who might not know how to behave in a communal one? Is this the only bathroom and Elaine got some sort of private 'ladies only' time? How many others, and who, are about to walk in? I have a quick shower, dry with what appears a totally inadequate towel, and head back up, skipping the bath, which looks too hot for me anyway.

Supper is in a cosy communal room downstairs. When we go in, there are four people sitting at a large upright table, including the two Taiwanese, but we are pointed to a separate, low, table in the other half of the room. I have a lot of trouble with low tables; my limbs just don't bend in the right directions for them, particularly my right ankle after the great ice-skating injury (don't ask). I'd much rather have the high table. Next to us are a Japanese couple, already sitting comfortably. You're either born to these tables or you're not. The table is full of small bowls of food, and more keeps coming, all extremely tasty, not all of it identifiable. It's lucky we can both eat pretty much anything; I'd hate to have to explain a vegan diet in these circumstances.

"Konban-wa" we say to the other couple, 'good evening'. They say the same back. They're perfectly friendly, but it doesn't look as if they speak any English. Suddenly, I find I can remember none of the conversational Japanese from the Pimsleur courses, although we manage to get across that we're Australian:

"Osotoraria-jin desu."

After a while, I remember one conversational gambit. I know how to ask where someone lives:

"Doko-ni sunde imasu-ka?"

"Osaka."

That could be the start of a conversation, except that I can't think of anything to follow up with. I clearly need to work on this. Still, the food's excellent. We notice the people at the other table are drinking beer.

"Biru?" I ask hopefully of the lady as she brings out more food.

She nods, and holds up one finger, enquiringly, then two. I hold up two. Now there's a meaningful conversation.

Two huge bottles of beer appear on the table. One would have been more than enough for both of us. This is clearly a learning process. By the end of the meal, as we all leave, bowing our thanks, one bottle is mostly empty, and the other is untouched. But we tried.

Back in the room, we roll out the futons, hang up our wet washing, and quickly fall asleep. It hasn't been a long day, but it's been a busy one, and we seem to have survived.

5

OSAKA TO KŌYASAN (FRIDAY APRIL 6)

With time to spare at Osaka's Kansai airport, one's thoughts naturally turned to essential matters, namely trying to get a SIM card for one's iPad. At least, mine did, because Elaine hadn't weighed herself down with such unnecessary things. I had, because I'd also weighed myself down with a reasonably decent camera, and I wanted to be able to save backup copies of the photos onto something. It was only an iPad mini; fairly light, and copying photos didn't need an internet connection, but I thought one might be useful. And for that, I needed a Japanese SIM card.

We tried one hopeful-looking shop in the concourse. It had someone who spoke some English, and understood what I wanted, but didn't have it. "But maybe delivery 10 o'clock?" which sounded pretty implausible. I thought I should try somewhere else, and Elaine thought that I didn't need her while I chased after technical gadgets.

So, while Elaine went off in search of less important things, namely getting tickets for the train to Kōyasan, I joined a long queue that had formed in front of another shop that looked as if it might be selling what I was after.

One of us was rather more successful than the other, and it wasn't me. Elaine got the tickets. One the downside, she confessed she still had no idea of the route, but it looked as if the information office would open soon. I, meanwhile, reached the front of the queue only to find it was for something I didn't want, although I wasn't sure what - the fellow at the shop said 'literature' and 'reservation' and numerous other words that didn't appear to be English at all, and my attempt at Japanese (mainly 'SIM', iPad' and a hopeful 'desu-ka?' tacked on the end even if it didn't make sense there) didn't get the conversation any further.

With Elaine back, we found that the first shop we'd tried had now had its morning's delivery of iPad SIM cards (Kōbō Daishi understands the needs of pilgrims), and I got something suitable for a reasonable amount. In the end, I used it mostly to read Western newspapers on-line, which I suppose shows what a weak grasp I had of what was truly essential for a pilgrimage.

We headed off in search of breakfast and found somewhere selling a more than acceptable salmon set ('set' in Japan generally means with rice and miso soup). Unusually for Japan, the place selling it included nutritional information on the menu, and I was able to work out which number was the sodium content - I'm supposed to keep an eye on my salt intake. I knew Japanese food tended to be extremely salty, but this salmon set managed to contain, in one meal, more salt than I try to eat in two days. I learned from this; for the rest of our Japanese journey, I never again looked for nutritional information, and I didn't read it even if I spotted it by accident. As a result, I did perfectly well and enjoyed my food. (This is probably bad medical advice, but it worked for me.)

By now the information office was open, and a helpful chap wrote down our itinerary, which was just as well, because it certainly wasn't what you'd call direct. There were three trains, Kansai to Tengachaya, Tengachaya to Hashimoto, Hashimoto to Gokurakubashi, and then what was described as a 'cable car' to Kōyasan itself.

We set off.

Any countryside usually looks good from a train, at least on any sort of a decent day, with green fields and mountains and distant villages passing by. Towns and cities, on the other hand, don't look at their best from a train. You see the backs of everywhere: the back yards of houses, the car parks behind offices, the graffiti on the bridges. You shouldn't judge a city from a train. This is just as true of Japan, except that there isn't any graffiti, it not really being that sort of place.

Kansai airport being on an island, however, the train that takes you away from it does pass over the seriously long bridge that connects it with the mainland, which made for an interesting start, even if it was mostly grey girders rushing past and ending up as nothing but unwanted blurs on my photographs. Once on the mainland, however, we turned North and headed through the suburbs of Osaka, and were treated to the expected view of the backs of Japanese buildings.

Kōyasan is south-east of Kansai, but the route we took involved going north and a bit east to Tengachaya, then south and a bit more east to Hashimoto. We were travelling along two sides of a triangle. There was a more direct train that ran along the third side, but it was run by a different railway company.

Japanese railways are famous for their bullet trains and their punctuality, but they're run by a mishmash of over 100 different companies, and while many of these are part of the JR (Japan Railways) group, a lot of small ones aren't, and that third side of our triangle was run by one of these, which presumably is why JR had sold us tickets for this longer route.

Still, we had no need to hurry, having made our flight to Osaka. We managed the change at Tengachaya from the north-going train to the south-going train, although only just, realising with only two minutes to go that we were waiting on the wrong platform and dashing over to the other side of the tracks. The train south to Hashimoto moved away from the crowded suburbs and out towards more open country, and we noticed it had rather more Westerners on board. By the time we got to Hashimoto, there seemed to be almost no Japanese left.

This is because Hashimoto is the end of this line, and the main reason for coming to Hashimoto (although no doubt it's a lovely place in its own right) is to take the local train on to Gokurakubashi, which is itself little more than the entry point to Kōyasan. In fact, as far as I can make out, Gokurakubashi isn't a place, it's a station where you get out and transfer to the 'cable car' up to Kōyasan.

When we got out at Hashimoto, there was a general move down the platform, and a mixed collection of foreigners assembled at the end. Some of the group seemed to be dressed for hiking, with serious-looking backpacks and equally serious-looking outdoor wear. Others in the group were carrying more conventional suitcases. It was noticeably cool, and I was beginning to regret my missing pullover.

Up to this point, I'd not really understood where Kōyasan fitted in to all this. Elaine had described it as a sort of orientation for the pilgrimage, where we'd spend a couple of nights, and I'd envisaged it as being the starting point for the walk. I'd been a little surprised to realise it was on the mainland, well away from the pilgrimage route, although I was a bit reluctant to reveal the depths of my ignorance.

(This is how we usually work. Elaine likes to organise, and plan, and to know things. I'm happy to be organised, as long as I'm going to end up experiencing something new and interesting. I only need to know things if I'm going to have to make decisions, and then I need to know them in great detail. Experience has shown that if we both try to organise something, it doesn't work, because although we're both perfectly capable of organising something independently, our approaches to almost anything are totally incompatible. So we've learned not to try that, and things have almost always worked out pretty well. It does occasionally mean that I'm surprised to learn something about what we're about to do, and she's amazed that I could possibly not have known it.)

So as we waited I discovered some useful things: Kōyasan was the centre originally founded by Kōbō Daishi, the monk whose footsteps we would follow on the pilgrimage; it's a tourist centre in its own right, which is why not everyone was dressed for hiking; and it's noticeably high up, hence the 'cable car', whatever that would turn out to be. I had begun to worry about this cable car, which to me means one of those alpine things that swings worryingly between mountains. I don't care for cable cars: for one thing, they mean mountains, and that means cold, and I don't like the cold; for another, they mean cables, and we all have our irrational worries, and one of mine is that I don't trust cables. I even don't care for lifts, although I'm happy to use them, but that's because I know they have emergency brakes that stop them dropping to the bottom of lift shafts. Cable cars don't.

Still, cable cars aren't really a fear, just a bit of a worry, and once the small local train came and started to climb up through the hills I was able to enjoy the journey. Now this was countryside, and it looked lovely. The hills were a mixture of various greens, and we were running through remarkably narrow cuttings between them. It was getting cooler, though, and there was a hint of rain. We'd planned for rain, and had packed with that in mind, but packing for cold means packing a lot of heavy kit, and you can't do that if you're travelling light. A lot of the people sitting opposite us obviously had packed for the cold. There were heavy red and black-checked lumberjack shirts, and serious anoraks. That didn't look good. Especially when Qantas has your only pullover.

Gokurakubashi was indeed just a railway station with some lovely cherry trees close to the tracks and a small bright red bridge at one end and signs saying 'cable car' at the other.

"Oh, it's a rack railway!"

The track went up the mountainside at about 45 degrees and, inside, the carriages resembled steep flights of steps with seats on them.

"It must be pulled up by a cable. Oh, well, that's OK. It'll have brakes."

One slow haul later, we were finally at Kōyasan. Well, almost. Kōyasan itself is actually a bus ride or a decent walk from the cable car station, and we were discussing how we felt about the walk, when it started to rain and we realised we were 1000 metres up and cold. We huddled in a small shelter and struggled to put on rain jackets, then darted for the bus, which took us along a twisty road at exciting speed (it turns out you aren't even allowed to walk this road, which seems a wise precaution) and dropped us at what should have been the right stop for the temple we wanted.

Kōyasan has a number of temples that offer accommodation, and Elaine had booked us into one of these: Souji-in. However, it's not in the nature of a temple to have a sign that says 'Vacancies' and its name in neon outside. It wasn't at all obvious which of the various anonymous buildings set back from the road was the one we were looking for. We walked back and forth a while, trying to see anything that might be a sign.

"Does any of this say 'Souji-in'?"

"No, I think this is just another shrine. Let's try the next one."

"I think this might be it. At least it's a building with an entrance. Gosh, it's cold."

We passed through the roofed wooden gate, up a path, and into a most welcoming entrance hall. Someone, in robes and with some English, welcomed us, nodded when we said "Souji-in?", indicated we should take our boots off and put on house slippers, and sat us down in a pleasant ante-chamber. He said, "passuports?", took them, came back with green tea, and a few minutes later showed us to our room, pausing on the way to point out the garden, and the onsen. Elaine is extraordinarily fond of an onsen. Strictly, an onsen is a communal hot spring bath, and there's another name (sentō) for an indoor bath, but we just call them onsen. It's simpler.

The room was a traditional Japanese room, just as we'd expected: almost bare, opaque paper screens letting some light in from one wall, tatami mats on the floor, a small low table with low seats, and a cupboard that no doubt contained the bedding. It also had an air-conditioner, our own toilet and washbasin, a TV, and a number of power outlets. Quite a superior room, in fact.

The 'cable car' between Gokurakubashi and Kōyasan.

The station at Osaka airport.

Inside the train to Gokurakubashi.

The station at Gokurakubashi.

You can get Western style rooms in big hotels in Japan, but they tend to be cramped, and you realise how much space a Western bed takes up and how much bigger the room would seem without it. A traditional Japanese room is almost bare, with a number of futon sets of foldable mattresses and duvets that are only laid out at night.

Japanese travel light; where they stay usually provides a yukata for indoor wear, and we found these, together with warm jackets, in a box on the floor.

Elaine put on her yukata, trying to remember which side goes over which (the left always goes over the right), tying the belt around it in a bow, and headed enthusiastically for the onsen. Eventually she returned, looking relaxed and warm.

"It's just on this floor, and it's not too hot. You should try it."

"Er, yes. I probably should."

I had never gone to a Japanese bath. I don't care for excessively hot baths in the way the Japanese do. And I'd never felt entirely comfortable with the idea of communal baths. Everywhere else we'd stayed in Japan over the years had at least had a shower attached to the room, so one hadn't been necessary. But this room didn't, and I had been travelling now for over a day. Clearly, this was a plunge I was going to have to take.

"You could just have the shower. You don't have to commit to the whole experience."

If you've not been in a Japanese bath, there's a lot of etiquette. Japanese life has a lot of etiquette. Baths aren't for getting clean in and then lying in. ("Luxuriating in your own filth", as I once heard a warm English bath described.) In a Japanese bathhouse (as Elaine reminded me at this point) there is an outer room where you disrobe - or dis-yukata - then you take just a small towel - not a big one - into the main bathroom, where there are individual showers, which you use to get clean. Then, clean and thoroughly rinsed, you enter the large, and usually challengingly hot, communal tub. There are many potential breaches of bathroom etiquette, starting with bringing in a big towel, because you will inevitably get it wet, moving on to getting soap into the main bath through inadequate rinsing, which is thought horrific, and so on.

Trepidation is a wholly inadequate word on some occasions, and this was one. As it happened, the men's bathroom was completely unoccupied, so any minor breaches of etiquette went unnoticed. I showered, and rinsed, and got as far as gingerly putting a foot into the large, sunken, interior pool that was the main bath. It was hot; not as hot as I'd feared, but hotter than I'd have liked. Maybe tomorrow. For the moment, I was at least clean and warm. And nobody else had come in.

We went downstairs at the appointed hour for the evening meal, in yukata and house slippers, holding tightly onto the bannister to prevent the ill-fitting slippers from sliding away and tipping us down the stairs. Breaches of temple etiquette presumably include being found in a heap at the foot of the stairs, yukata undone, cursing the traditional Japanese slipper and its mismatch to Western foot sizes. Maybe there's some trick that involves curling up the toes to grip the slipper in some way. Whatever the trick might be, we didn't know it, and trying to climb stairs in slippers really brought this home.

The dining area was elegant. Black tables - at a height suited to ordinary chairs, thankfully - on immaculate tatami mats with painted yellow screen doors on all sides decorated with fanciful Japanese designs. We were directed towards the back of the room. Elaine left me there to get something from our room, and I sat down at the table at the far end of the screened-off area.

There were two places set, with chopsticks and a deep bowl about ten centimetres high, with deep cut-outs in its sides, and with something pink wrapped at the bottom, sitting in what could have been a silver cupcake wrapper. I looked at the something pink, wondering if it was some sort of appetiser; a small snack. There was writing on it. While I waited, wondering how it would taste, I tried to decipher the writing. It was all in kana, and I'd been learning those. I should be able to at least work out the sounds. This would be useful practice.

たべられません

OK, that's 'ta-be-ra-re-ma-se-n'. Ah, I know that: 'Cannot be eaten'.

I decided not to eat it.

I felt this was an achievement. I had actually managed to understand something written in Japanese, and had saved myself some embarrassment, not to mention potential poisoning. On the other hand, I had very nearly tried to eat what Elaine, once back, was quick to point out was the fuel pellet for an on-table heater for a bowl of food. She also pointed out that I was sitting at the wrong table.

We'd been directed not to the back of this room, but to another room at the back of this one, in which we found a table laid out for two, this time already with a selection of real food: small bowls of interesting items, all meticulously plated like something out of a food magazine, with small flowers adding decoration. It didn't appear to be a lot of food, but it looked exquisite.

A young monk came out and brought more small dishes. He spoke good English, and offered us drinks. Splendid. Two glasses of wine, white for Elaine, red for me. There was a small menu in English that listed over twenty different items, but we weren't asked to choose from them. We ate. Every dish was vegan, and it was delicious. I'll eat anything, but both Holly and Tom are vegan, and Elaine doesn't eat much meat or fish, all of which means we get our share of vegan food, but this was eye-opening. I had not realised you could get such flavours out of a purely vegan meal. Moreover, dishes just kept coming. We realised we didn't have to choose from the menu, because we were going to get everything on it. Most came in fairly small quantities, but some were more substantial, like the broth that was cooked on top of the stand with the lighted fuel pellet. Which I, fortunately, had not eaten.

We were tired and full when we returned to our room and found the futons laid out ready for us. It felt as if the trip was off to a fine start, although it also felt much colder outside than we'd expected. Maybe it would be warmer in the morning.

A section of the dining room at Souji-in.

This is not something to eat...

... but this is.

6

SECOND DAY - TEMPLE 5 TO THE UDON RESTAURANT OF THE SPIRITS (TUESDAY APRIL 10)

I wake up at 1am with a painfully sore throat, and the realisation that I drank precisely no water whatsoever yesterday. I normally drink very little water, even when out in the sun, yet somehow I never seem to feel thirsty. Elaine often tells me I must be a member of some lizard family, and there's some evidence for this - whatever system I have for internal temperature regulation seems pretty ineffective, and my preferred way of keeping warm is just to lie out in the sun and bask. This never worked out well in England, where I had to fall back on plan B, which involved a lot of warm clothes. This was one reason for moving to Australia, where the whole basking in the sun option worked much better.

But right now, my throat is complaining of serious neglect, and I'm hoping it's really nothing more than a lack of water. Elaine - who always has water handy - is woken by my coughing and finds me a water bottle. A couple of deep swigs help and I get back to sleep, but when we wake properly at 5:30 (we have a long day's walk ahead, and breakfast is at 6:00) I'm still feeling pretty uncomfortable.

As is Elaine. She woke with a swollen eye yesterday morning, and now it's back. She's read somewhere, probably on Google, that cedar pollen is a common cause of allergies, and Japan has more than its fair share of pollen. She takes another anti-histamine, and we hope for the best.

The clothes we washed last night aren't completely dry, but we pack them up anyway because we don't have much choice. We'll have to work out how to dry them this evening. At least we did bring one change of clothing each.

Down to breakfast, banging my head on the beam again, and we're seated at the same low table. I experiment with different sitting positions, but I'm clearly not built to sit either cross-legged or squatting on my heels. However, the breakfast is splendid, although I'd not rate cold fried egg any more than 'interesting', especially when it has to be eaten with chopsticks. It's hard to do that elegantly, and I fail dismally. The lady serving breakfast points at something on the table and says "Natto", as if that's all we need to know about it. I try some. Wikipedia says Natto is made from fermented soybeans and 'may be an acquired taste because of its powerful smell, strong flavour, and slimy texture'. I say Natto is gooey and stringy and served in its own pot and best left there unopened. I'm wiser now.

We pack our backpacks, pay, and walk down to the end of the street to temple 5. Jizō-ji is a lovely place, shining in the early morning sun, with cherry trees outside the office, and a large blue-green statue of Kōbō Daishi next to the rather small and straightforward building that acts as the gate. It seems almost completely empty; any others staying where we did have probably already been and gone while we were sorting ourselves out.

My throat is feeling a bit better, and with faith it's possible to believe Elaine's swollen eye is less swollen, but I can feel a dull ache in my heel. I've forgotten to do my calf-stretching exercises. I look around for a suitable wall I can stretch against, and end up with my shoes off, arms against someone's garden wall in the middle of a side street by the temple, pushing my legs back, 30 seconds at a time. It looks as if I've been stopped by an invisible policeman and am up against the wall being frisked. Elaine is looking around, wondering if she can plausibly pretend not to know me if anyone comes. Fortunately, no one does, and we set off again.

It's just over five kilometres to temple 6, Anraku-ji, along the sort of fairly modern village streets that we've seen before, complete with the usual comprehensive display of overhead cables. We stop to look into a small roadside hut. Outside is an interesting collection of two swivelling office chairs and three rusty folding chairs. Inside, there are tatami mats on the floor and mattresses and bedding piled up against the walls. This is a Henro hut, where the tired pilgrim without other accommodation can rest, overnight if necessary. It doesn't look particularly comfortable, but it looks much better than sleeping outside. There are many ways of travelling the Henro trail, and we realise we've not picked the hardest of them.

I buy a bottle of water from one of the many vending machines that can be found everywhere in Japan. I'm not going to repeat yesterday's mistake.

Anraku-ji is a big, open, temple with splendid gardens. There is cherry blossom on the trees, and a large courtyard with pools full of golden carp. However, first, we feel drawn to a coffee shop that we can see near the exit. We're the only people in there. Elaine asks for coffee ('kōhi'), which she gets, and I ask for tea ('kōcha'), which they don't have. Nor do they have ocha, or sencha, or any of the names for types of tea that I can remember. This really is a coffee shop. Normally, the only coffee I drink is decaffeinated, because ordinary coffee makes me twitch (Elaine's phrase is 'turns him into a werewolf'). But, a) I don't know the Japanese for 'decaffeinated', and b) I'm absolutely certain they don't have it, so just this once, I order ordinary coffee. It's nice and warm and appears to have no ill effects. Maybe it's on the weak side. The sun is falling on a couple of lovely cherry blossom trees outside the coffee shop, and I spend a while failing to take a photo that does them justice.

Back into the temple, and we spend a while walking around the grounds, looking at the flowers by the pool and the fish swimming under the stone bridge. The statue of Kōbō Daishi has a white bib, and white cloths hanging from his wrists and ankles, and someone has placed three oranges in front of him. Giving gifts to statues seems strange to us, but I imagine it's an interaction with them and what they represent, and better that than just looking at them and moving on, which is what we're doing.

An eye-catching yellow diamond-shaped sign in the courtyard, the size of the average road sign, has symbolic figures of a running Henro, with stick and conical hat, and a small child running alongside. Just what this means is unclear: 'don't let your children run into Henro and knock them over'?

Outside in the road, just around the corner from the temple, we pause by a sign we've seen a few times now. It's a vertical sign with a big red arrow, something we've come to associate with Henro signs, pointing up - presumably indicating 'ahead' - above two kanji characters that mean nothing to us. We've seen these from time to time along the road, always pointing the way we're going, so we're starting to assume these are Henro signs, confirming that we're on the right track. This one is on a post supporting one of the many convex mirrors providing a view around corners for drivers. We don't really need to know what the characters mean, but trying to find out would be an interesting exercise, and the dictionary app on my phone has some kanji look-up functions I've been meaning to play with. I'm wondering how these work when a Subaru wagon turns the corner and stops on the other side of the road.

A middle-aged Henro gets out and walks across to us. He must think we're lost - it's certainly true we don't understand the sign. But it isn't that. He gives us two cans of coffee and two bags of chocolates. This is our first Henro gift! Profuse thanks, "domo arrigato", bows, and we remember the etiquette is that we're supposed to give him one of our name slips. He bows, smiles, and goes back to his car. Again we have this feeling that, in some silly way, walking Henro (even us) outrank car Henro, and we've been acknowledged, accepted. And, deep down, I think I'd not really believed this stuff about being given gifts along the way, but it turns out to be completely true.

Running Henro and child sign at Anraku-ji, temple 6.

The entrance to Jizō-ji, temple 5.

A shelf outside one of the buildings at Jizō-ji.

Henro hut by the roadside between temples 5 and 6.

Cherry blossom outside Anraku-ji, temple 6.

The mysterious sign that confirmed we were on the right track. Or perhaps didn't...

I take a photo of the mysterious Henro sign as a translation project for later, we pack away the chocolates and the surprisingly heavy cans of coffee, and set off again.

Temple 7, Jūraku-ji, is only half an hour away. It's a small place, although near the entrance it has a large collection of small Jizō statues, all smartly bibbed in red. It also has an imposingly large and modern office block, which houses the stamp office. This block also has two large toilet areas, his and hers, and appears to be the accommodation wing for the temple. Using the toilets involves taking off our boots and putting on toilet slippers. We'd not expected that, and it slows things down a bit. Japanese tend to prefer shoes that can be slipped on and off quickly. Hiking boots can't. It has to be said the toilets are extremely clean; no mud from dirty boots.

We sit outside and drink some water and gratefully nibble at some of our car-Henro chocolates.

The countryside opens up a bit as we cover the nearly four kilometres to temple 8, Kumadani-ji. We walk along the road, under the power lines, past more of the mock-Tudor ('faux-Meiji'?) houses, and a number of other buildings in a pretty dilapidated condition. These do tend to reinforce the impression that the overall tidiness of an area is less important to the Japanese than the neatness of their own small areas. There's no sense that people with houses almost falling down are going to be visited by outraged neighbours complaining that they've ruined their hopes of being named 'Tidiest Village In Tokushima Prefecture'. One feels this would not happen in Southern Germany, where you could be ostracised for failing to trim the dead geraniums in your window box.

We walk past a number of what seem to be hand-painted warning signs illustrating a variety of potential disasters. A small pond has a picture of a child up to its shoulders in water, crying out something in Kanji. At another vending machine, we replace our water bottles and try a bottle of Pocari Sweat for the first time. This enticingly-named concoction is a well-known (and well-advertised) sports drink, and the name itself is just another example of how English words are often used in puzzling ways in Japan. We'd not tried it before, but it claims to replace all the nutrients you lose in sweat when you exercise, and it actually tastes much better than anything with 'sweat' in its name should. I'm not entirely sure I trust it, but it's more interesting than drinking plain water.

The final kilometre to temple 8 takes us up into the woods, and up rather a lot of steps. Kumadani-ji has an older feel to it, not recently rebuilt or painted in bright colours, but it sits comfortably in a lovely sylvan setting, old stones and old wood among the greens and browns of the trees. There are splashes of colour from the red bibs of a group of Jizō statues, one large and three small, as if in a cheerful family group.

Temple 8 to temple 9, Hōrin-ji, is a simple walk of about two and a half kilometres, mostly either level or slightly downhill. The countryside is getting much more sparsely populated now. We come to a reasonably large road intersection, with just one large, solitary modern brick house, two storeys and attic windows in a steeply sloping roof, that looks as if it had been lifted from a new housing estate and put down, a Dorothy no longer in Kansas, all by itself by the side of the main road. You feel there must be some sort of story behind such things - is it all that's left of a plan for some huge development that ran out of funds after just building the show house? - but you never find out these things.

Hōrin-ji has almost an 'outback' feel to it, the temple buildings surrounding a slightly parched dry earth courtyard, and an office with a wooden verandah. Looking back through the temple gates we can see a small isolated shack of a store with a striped green and white awning, and wonder if it has anything suitable for lunch. By now, however, it's early afternoon, and they don't seem to have anything left that we fancy. However, we've had a substantial breakfast, and some of our car Henro snacks, so we aren't really hungry yet.

Temple 10, Kirihata-ji, is four kilometres away. The helpful summary of the pilgrim route in the White Book shows its vertical profile, displaying how the height of the path rises and falls as you go from temple to temple. Up to temple 11 the profile is relatively flat, with a few occasional minor peaks here and there. Between 11 and 12, the 'Pilgrim fall down' section, the profile rises alarmingly in a sawtooth that goes up and down and up and down until it reaches temple 12, then drops again to temple 13. In comparison, the hill up to temple 10, which lies ahead of us now, looks a mere molehill.

Red-bibbed Jizō statues at Jūraku-ji, temple 7.

Temple #8, Kumadani-ji.

Red-bibbed Jizō at temple #8, Kumadani-ji.

A warning sign near the side of the road.

Why is this house all on its lonely own out here?

The courtyard at temple #9, Hōrin-ji

Small store seen through gate of temple #9, Hōrin-ji

Looks deceive.

For most of the way, the route follows a minor road, lined at first with houses, but these soon turn into fields and signs of cultivation, and the houses are scattered more widely. A number of fields are laid out with rows of plants that stretch across them under long half-cylinders of opaque white plastic, presumably acting as mini-greenhouses. One decidedly imposing faux-Meiji house stands next to a smaller house in serious disrepair, the roof completely collapsed on one side, in a not-unusual Japanese juxtaposition of aspiring elegance next to total neglect.

The road reaches a denser collection of houses with a number of shops, and the red Henro signs point us off to the right.

"According to Facebook, one of the shops here is a very good Henro shop, but I've no idea which one," says Elaine.

"Is there anything we actually need?"

"No, but it would still be interesting to know which one."

But none of the shops has a sign saying 'Recommended for Henro on Facebook', or if it does, it's written in Japanese. I don't see why we should expect anything else, but it does bring home how awkward it is not to be able to read, and reminds us that in Japan we are, quite honestly, functionally illiterate.

The road to the right is starting to climb, and we can see that it leads up into a worryingly steep hill. We start to make more use of our staffs as we work our way along and up. The road gets progressively steeper and the backpacks get unrelentingly heavier until, finally, we reach a car park. Not the temple, just the car park. The road carries on to the left, while for us a dispiritingly steep path leads forward, and eventually, when it would otherwise be impossibly steep, this turns into a flight of stone steps. At this point we begin to feel every kilo in the backpacks as we plod up, one step at a time.

It isn't a huge flight of steps, but we feel worn out when we reach the top. Unfortunately, all there is at the top is an apparently disused washing place with a few ladles laid across it. And - oh, surely not! - another, longer, flight of steps climbing off to the right. We sit a while, then struggle on.

"You go on, I'll catch you up."

She's determined to do this at her own pace without feeling she's holding me back. For once, I do go on ahead, although it's not as if I'm itching to be let free to bound on enthusiastically. I slog on, only a little faster than her, counting the steps as I go. I often count steps as I climb them; it gives me a feeling of progress, and quantifies the accomplishment when I finally get up there. But mostly it takes my mind off what a slog it is and how much I wish I didn't have to do it.

Two hundred and thirty-four steps later, each one an effort, I reach a level area and wait a few minutes for Elaine. And then there's another short climb of a mere fifty-six steps, each one counted, and finally we're at the temple.

We drop our backpacks with real relief, and look around. It is a lovely place, buried in woodland, with green trees enfolding the temples and with hills rising behind. But would it have hurt to put it just a bit lower down?

There's a group of about eight Henro that must have come on a bus. They're standing in front of one of the temple halls, with someone at the front reciting the sutras. Some Henro, but not all, are reciting along with him, and we see a bus driver standing at the back, occasionally mouthing a few words just to show willing.

We follow our own slightly cut-down ritual at each of the halls, ringing the bell somewhat diffidently, standing silently instead of reciting sutras that we still don't know, putting in coins and name slips, then we look for the office. Now that must be the office, but where is the entrance? We aren't completely illiterate; we recognise a couple of kanji, including the one for entrance ('iriguchi', 入口) and there it is on the door with an arrow (入口 ->) pointing to the right. But there isn't an entrance to the right. We walk over to the right of the building. There isn't another building that could possibly be an office. We go back to what we thought was the office, and see someone - the bus driver - going in, sliding the door with the sign *over to the right* in order to open it. We feel a little foolish. Unusually, we'd both misinterpreted a simple sign; usually that's my job.

The bus driver is standing there with a pile of eight books that he's obviously brought in to be stamped. He looks at us, with our one book, smiles, and gestures us forward, which is kind of him. Being a bus-Henro looks a nicely relaxed way to go on pilgrimage; someone recites the sutras for you, and someone else gets your books stamped. I can see the attraction.

Outside, we see another flight of steps heading up. There appears to be a pagoda on a higher level yet. Without our backpacks, we get up the 55 steps easily enough, and the panorama is worth it. The pagoda is large, old, wooden, and has something of a neglected air, but has been built on a clearing with an unobstructed view of the countryside, and we can see down to the plain we'd been walking along, and over to another range of high hills in the distance.

"That's where we're heading. Temple 11 is at the base of those hills, and we'll be there tomorrow."

"And temple 12 is at the top." Showing I'd been paying attention.

"There are several tops. Temple 12 is on the third of them, and we have to do one after the other. They do look high, don't they?"

Actually, they just look a long way away, and not particularly threatening. But we'll find out in two days' time.

As I try to take a photograph of the view, my camera battery flashes red briefly and shuts down. I'm sure it wasn't due to do that, and the spare batteries are in my backpack, fifty-five steps lower down. I take a couple of shots on my iPhone instead.

We collect our backpacks and work our way carefully down the many sets of steps. At the level part with the unused washing place we pause for a moment. The narrow road runs past here, in a series of hairpin bends, and we watch cars negotiating both the bends and the oncoming traffic, which is not easy on a winding road that isn't wide enough for two cars to pass, except at the bends. We leave them and their smell of burning brakes. This time I count the lowest set of steps, which I'd not done on the way up. Exactly 100, which makes it four hundred and forty-five steps from the car park to the pagoda, most of them lugging our backpacks. No wonder we feel tired.

As we walk down the road from the car park, we come across two familiar figures. The two Taiwanese lads are striding up towards the temple.

"They're setting a fair pace. They must be fit."

"Must be. Wait a minute, they don't have their backpacks. How did they manage that?"

We pause and greet them. Apparently, there is a shop down in the village that will look after your backpack for nothing while you visit the temple. Two hours earlier, that would have been useful information. We watch them saunter off, cheerfully unencumbered, up the path, heading for the steps.

In the village, we look closely at all the shops we pass. None give the slightest indication that they act as a Henro left-luggage office. Clearly, you have to have inside information here, and we didn't have it.

But we managed anyway, and we're going to be nicely in time for the accommodation that's been booked for us, about a kilometre and a half further on.

An inscription above the bell rope, Temple 10, Kirihata-ji

Two neighbouring houses, in quite different condition, on the way to temple 10.

Temple 10, Kirihata-ji

Pilgrims at Temple 10, Kirihata-ji,

Array of vending machines at Temple 10, Kirihata-ji,

The view from Temple 10, Kirihata-ji, across the valley towards temples 11 and 12.

We're looking forward to being able to put our feet up and get something to eat. The helpful lady at the tourist office at Tokushima station had booked us into what we assumed was a ryokan (the name had an 'R.' at the front, which should be a little up-market from an 'M.' for 'minshuku', where we were last night). She'd told us they didn't do meals, but that next door was an udon restaurant, and we're just in the mood for a decent udon. The note she gave us with the address also says '5pm'; we're not exactly sure what that signifies, but we'll easily be there by then.

At one of the temples, Elaine had noticed a sign on a bench advertising the udon restaurant; she recognised the name because it was in the White Book next to that of the ryokan. It appears to be well known, or at least it advertises widely, and along the way we've been seeing billboards with its distinctively jolly picture of a chap in a blue robe rolling out something or other. We should be able to find this, and a ryokan is usually easy to spot.

It should be on highway 12, which is a busy road, by Shikoku standards, with only a very few buildings scattered on either side. It could be any of those anonymous suburban stretches you find in the States. Well, it could if anonymous suburban stretches in the States had billboards in Japanese.

We've reached the point where the map on Elaine's iPhone says we ought to be, but there isn't anything remotely resembling a traditional Ryokan anywhere here. There is a somewhat undistinguished rectangular building in beige brick, with what might be an entrance surrounded in brown brick to relieve the monotony. This isn't what we'd been looking for, which was something cosily traditional. But maybe we ought to have been looking for an undistinguished building in beige brick, because in the distance, on the far side of a large parking lot, we can see a sign with a huge version of the chap in a blue robe, so maybe that's the udon restaurant.

There's a string of kana high up on the front and side of the beige brick building, and the last three are ホテル - 'ho-te-ru'.

"I think this is it. I don't know all of what that says, but it ends in 'hotel'."

"Maybe this really is it. Maybe it's more traditional inside. Let's try the door."

We go up to the door, which isn't locked. We go in. It isn't more cosily traditional. There's the most ordinary of ordinary corridors, with carpet tiles and doors leading off, and no sign of anyone. At one end, we find what is surely the reception desk of a hotel. With nobody there. Nor is there a bell anywhere to be seen. There's a brochure for the place, with pictures of facilities like washing machines. There's what might be a price list.

"One of these prices is what I was told a double room cost for the night," says Elaine. "I really do think this is it."

"Except that there's nobody here."

It's about 4:35.

"Maybe 5 o'clock means not before 5 o'clock."

"We don't have anywhere else to go. We could wait."

We wait until 5 o'clock. Nobody appears.

"I don't think there's anywhere else to stay for miles. This could be a problem."

Then at one minute past 5 o'clock a small Japanese lady appears from the other end of the corridor. She doesn't look surprised to see us. I say our names, and she says "passuporto". We hand them over, she copies them, and hands them back. She gives us a plastic key with '203' on it, and goes over to a door and mimics putting it in the key slot to open the door. Elaine shows her the brochure and points to the washing machine. The lady points upstairs and says 'ko-in', which sounds plausibly like 'coin'. As we head off, we see what is surely one more guest arriving; he looks local, he probably knew not to turn up before 5pm.

We find room 203, one floor up, and the key works. It's a small Western-style room with two single beds. But, delightfully, it has a bath and a shower!

"This is a business hotel," says Elaine. "It's not what we expected, but it will definitely do." Actually, it will do me nicely. "Now, do we have coins for the dryer? And where is it?"

We collect the stuff we need to dry, and locate the washing machines down at the end of the corridor. At this point we discover we have no idea how to operate the machines, and the instructions are written purely for locals. What's more, we're going to need more ¥100 coins. Elaine makes what may or may not be an informed guess as to which button selects dryer mode, puts in the damp clothes and a coin, and sets it going. It starts turning, and for all we know it might be drying.

"I can get some more coins," I say, in a show of confidence. "I'll ask the lady at the desk, and if she can't help I'll try the udon place."

But the lady at reception wasn't at reception. Nobody was. There still wasn't a bell. Maybe '5pm' doesn't mean 'from 5pm', it means '5pm on the dot or sleep in the car park'.

I'll try the udon place. I have a ¥500 coin, I'm sure they can change that. I go out from the hotel, and walk over to the udon restaurant.

It looks like an udon restaurant. But it's shut. Deserted, closed, not open, no customers, no udon, no ¥100 coins. That doesn't look entirely hopeful, and I'm beginning to wonder about our supper tonight. There's just a hint of light, no more, from somewhere right at the back. Maybe it opens later, but there's not much evidence for that.

I look around. There isn't anywhere else in reasonable walking distance, apart from a garage over the road. It looks as if it's still open. I dart across the busy road in a break in the traffic and walk towards the petrol pumps. A gnarled looking chap in overalls comes over; he's wondering why I'm here if I haven't a car. I hold up my ¥500 coin. How do you ask for small coins? I know what 'small' is - 'chiisai' -

because I looked that up after we were served such large bottles of beer last night.

"Chiisai koin?" He looks puzzled. What's the word for 100? I should know that. "Hyaku yen?"

His face lights up. He looks at my ¥500, holds up 5 fingers, and says, "Go", Japanese for five.

"Hai. Yes."

He reaches into a wallet, but can only find four ¥100 coins. I'd settle for that, but he walks over to the till, opens it, and passes me the full set of five. Lots of thanks, and I work my way back across the road to our room.

"Some good news, and some bad news. I've got some coins, but the udon place seems to be closed."

"Oh. Where are we going to eat, then?"

"I assume it's going to open later. Let's hope so. Anyway, how's the laundry?"

"I think I've worked it out now, but at first I couldn't get the dryer to stop. I couldn't find a stop button and I couldn't open the door. Eventually I pulled the plug out of the socket on the wall."

At least that had worked, and we do manage to get a fresh set of laundry in and going properly. That's the clothes problem solved, at least for today.

Supper is another matter.

We go out together to check on the udon restaurant. Still closed. By now you'd think it would be open for the evening. But it isn't. We go back to our room and wait a while longer. The laundry finishes. We go back to the udon restaurant.

There's still a faint light on somewhere inside, but no sign of life whatsoever. There are big windows, and we can see inside to the dining area, full of chairs and tables, all in darkness. It is very much a closed udon restaurant. And there doesn't seem to be anywhere else in the neighbourhood at all. Or even anyone to ask.

Then, as we walk around, we notice that between the darkened udon restaurant and the hotel there are a pair of sliding doors that seem to be open. There are no obvious signs anywhere near them, no indication of what lies beyond. It's really just an opening, a little bit like what might be the entrance to an anonymous ryokan that didn't want to advertise. We go through the doors, and inside is a desk, unattended, a few steps up to a wooden platform with a number of pairs of house slippers, and a set of shelves that contain a few pairs of shoes. In fact, this is how we'd expected the ryokan entrance to look, except that it, whatever it is, seems to be nothing to do with either the business hotel or the udon restaurant.

"Can you smell food?" asks Elaine.

"Yes, I can. From somewhere. Do you suppose this is some private dining room? Some sort of club?"

"It might be some sort of particularly anonymous restaurant. There's a button on the desk. It might be a bell."

"I just have no idea what this place is. Do you reckon we should press it?"

"Let's have one more look at the udon place, and come back if it's still closed."

The interior of the udon restaurant is still in darkness, and there's no more sign of life than last time we looked. As we go back to whatever the other place is, I try to work out what we might say there. "Is this a restaurant?" might be a good start, and I can manage that.

Back through the doors. There's still nobody there, so we press the button on the desk. From a very long way away, there is a very faint ding. We try it again. Another faint ding. And then the sound of someone shuffling along very quickly, and a slightly chubby, thirty-something Japanese lady in a kimono rushes in. She looks at us. I say the longest, most complicated Japanese sentence I've used so far:

"Kore-wa, restaurant desu-ka?" (This, is it a restaurant?).

A slightly puzzled nod, as if that was a funny question to ask. I had another sentence ready:

"Watashitachi-wa tabetain desu-ga." (We would like to eat.)

Another nod, as if that rather went without saying. She gestures in the general direction of the hotel.

"Ryokan?"

Our turn to nod. We are indeed from the ryokan. Well, the hotel, at least. She seems happy with that, as if explains what we're doing here. She points at the row of house slippers and indicates that we should follow her. We take off our shoes, put on slippers, and shuffle off awkwardly after her.

She leads us down a set of corridors with elegant polished wood floors, past what a row of which might be curtained-off private dining rooms, some clearly in use, and finally stops at the end of one long corridor, in front of an open doorway, beyond which we can see another room, too dimly lit to make anything out. There's a rack full of more sets of slippers. She changes hers and points to us, and we do the same. Whatever's in that next room, it's something that needs different footwear. We step through the doorway, down a couple of steps, onto a much more basic wooden floor and into the unknown.

There is more light than I'd thought. The far end of the room is dark, but there are lights on at this end; enough light to see that we're in a cavernous room, full of many tables, separated by wooden grills, laid out in two rows and with benches on each side. It could be the Japanese equivalent of a large American diner. To our surprise, we realise we're actually in the darkened, deserted, dining room of the udon restaurant. And, even though we're in it and may even be about to be fed, it still looks closed.

She points to the nearest table, bare except for a menu, one of those helpful Japanese ones with pictures of almost everything, and another button. She points to the menu, and then to the button. We nod, she seems happy that we know what to do, and scurries off at high speed towards the area off to one side where I'd seen the light earlier. I guess that's the kitchen.

"What on earth is going on?" I ask.

"I have absolutely no idea. But we seem to be in the udon restaurant, and we've been given a menu."

"But what did we just walk through? Why are we the only people here? Is this place really open?"

Not only do we have no idea, we have no idea how to ask either. But it does look as if we might get fed. We both pick the same tempura udon set from the menu, and gingerly press the bell.

There's an enormous 'dong!' from somewhere close by, and she shuffles back at the same high speed. We point to the picture of the tempura set on the menu, and hold up two fingers. She writes something down on her notepad. "Biru?" we ask, hopefully. She points at something on the menu, which has no pictures but might be the beer section. There seems to be a range of prices - different brands? Different sizes?

"Chiisai?" I say - I'm pretty sure that works for beer. She holds the flat of her hand just a little bit off the table, so it looks as if 'small' here could be quite small. There's a bit of putting hands at various levels above the table, and we seem to have compromised on two glasses, or maybe bottles of something, mid-sized. She shuffles off again, and we wait, with no idea what's going on.

"Maybe it's some sort of private dining club," says Elaine.

"For all we know, the place is closed this evening for the meeting of the local mafia - the Yakuza,"

"Maybe they just don't trust us to know how to sit at the other tables."

"In my case they'd be right."

From time to time, there's another loud 'dong!' and we see her rush-shuffling along to the steps up to the fancier corridor, change her slippers, head off towards the private diners, then come back, changing slippers yet again on the way.

"It feels like something from 'Spirited Away', where they end up in this strange bathhouse that caters to the spirit world. As if we're in the Udon House of the Spirits".

And now here comes our Spirit guardian, shuffling along to the table with the food and the beer.

If this is the Udon House of the Spirits, it serves extremely good udon. ¥1,000 for a tempura set with prawns, loads of vegetables, udon and rice, not-easily-identified-pickled-things, etc. And the beers are a reasonable half-litre size. We eat an excellent meal, sitting in the faint light at our end of this darkened dining room.

Finally, we ring the bell again and this time a different lady arrives to take our money. I try my most complicated bit of Japanese yet:

"Ashita-no asa, doko-de tabemasu-ka? Koko-ni?" which may or may not mean: "Where can we eat tomorrow? Here?". I can't have got it too far wrong; she seems to understand. I think she says they open at 11 (I hear the 'ju-ichi' for '11'), but there's a convenience store ('konbini') somewhere in the general direction of where she's pointing. Well, that will do fine. We head back the way we came, changing slippers as we leave the dining room, and then again at the entrance, where we pick up our boots from the rack.

We head back to our comfortable, if slightly cramped, room at the business hotel, and feel well-fed and satisfied, even if most of what has just happened is a complete mystery to us.

The Udon restaurant must be close. This is its sign.

And it appears this might be where we're staying.

With a helpful garage opposite.

Elaine in the otherwise deserted Udon restaurant of the Spirits.

The Spirits eat well at the Udon restaurant, and so did we.

7
COLD AND IN KŌYASAN (SATURDAY APRIL 7)

It was *not* warmer the next morning in Kōyasan.

We woke early, at about 5:15, having set an alarm so we could go to the Buddhist ceremony in the Meditation Hall. We'd been told this started at 6am, we were welcome to watch from the rows of chairs at the back, and we should wear ordinary clothes, not yukata. This was something of a pity, as the thick yukata jacket was warm, and my pullover was probably in Qantas lost properly. Still, I put on the rather thin rain jacket I had, and we headed gingerly down the stairs, not trusting the combination of our feet, the rather randomly-fitting indoor slippers, and the shiny wooden staircase.

Other guests were already sitting at the back of the hall. Most seemed to be Western. The room was small but deep, and the main area was elaborately decorated. A central rectangle between wooden pillars had a variety of different objects around it; small tables with metal candlesticks, bowls, lanterns and all manner of ornaments, and hangings coming down from the roof. The overall effect was of somewhere dimly lit, cosy, and full, in the every-surface-covered way that Victorian-era rooms are always crammed with assorted bric-a-brac. As we arrived and sat down, the main area was empty, but a few minutes later a procession of eight monks filed in and silently arranged themselves around the central rectangle.

Six of the monks wore black robes, with white messenger bags over their shoulders. One, who I assumed was the abbot, was in cream robes and sat at the front, with his back to us. The eighth, sitting on our right next to the young monk who'd served us at supper last night, was a lady dressed in yellow robes, with a full head of styled hair, in contrast to the shaved heads of the others.

A squat-looking monk on the left began to chant. He wore glasses, and I found myself thinking of him as 'Accountant monk'. Opposite him, on our right, next to 'Lady monk', was a large and powerful looking monk - 'Sumo monk'. The others were too hard to see clearly.

I'm not religious, but I appreciate ceremony, particularly when it has a feeling of something greater than the everyday, and religions do this well. I was reminded of a Latin mass, possibly because of the ethereal religious structure, possibly because I couldn't understand anything of what was being said. The chanting of the sutras continued, sometimes recited only by Accountant monk, sometimes with all joining in. Sometimes the chants would stop, and all you could hear was the quiet voice of the Abbot, talking on as if he hadn't noticed everyone else had finished. From time to time Accountant monk would shake a pair of reverberating cymbals. Most were reading the sutras from black books that had a concertina structure, which they moved through, backwards and forwards, with obvious familiarity. Lady monk was the only one reading from a conventional book. Sumo monk obviously found sitting on his heels uncomfortable, and kept shuffling slightly into a different position. He also had a cold, and from time to time would pull a tissue from his sleeve and wipe his nose.

In the middle of the ceremony, the young monk got up and worked his way through the audience, indicating a small flame and a box of powder just in front of the audience area, explaining that we should all get up in turn and sprinkle a pinch of powder on the flame. One by one we did so, bowing, sprinkling, and returning to our seats. It was a worryingly small flame, and I was afraid my pinch of powder might put it out, but it survived. What was the significance of this?

Participating in something you know almost nothing about raises so many questions.

Finally, the chants stopped, the monks filed out, the abbot got up, stood in front of the audience, looked as if he intended to say something, then realised this audience would probably not understand, smiled, and left.

Breakfast was in the same room as before, at the same table, and as excellent as before. I did find the slippery and fragile soft tofu an awkward thing to eat with chopsticks, and I'm normally good with chopsticks, a skill acquired during shared meals in Chinese restaurants with other students, where the most dexterous were the best-fed.

Back in our room, we thought it would be interesting to lay out the contents of our backpacks and take a pair of photos of 'what she thought was needed on a pilgrimage' and 'what he thought was needed on a pilgrimage'. It wasn't clear that the results reflected well on 'him', since 'he' had evidently felt the need for multiple electronic gadgets (camera, iPad, even an electric razor) all of which needed chargers, which in turn needed adaptors for the Japanese mains. 'Her' lower-tech pack looked much more Spartan and easier to carry.

What's more, 'his' didn't even include a pullover anymore.

We went out to see the town. Kōyasan was a neat, tidy, Japanese town up in the hills. The odd cherry blossom tree was dwarfed by tall conifers. The slightly drab shops were enlivened by brightly coloured signs, none of which we could read. But one thing that stood out about Kōyasan was that almost everyone in the street was a western visitor.

And they were all wrapped up as if on an Antarctic expedition and looking quite comfortable. We were wearing lightweight hiking trousers and just our thin rainproof jackets over our shirts, because that was all we had. I can't believe we looked comfortable, and we weren't.

I left the UK because I don't like being cold. Since then, I've lived in southern California and in Australia. Cold has not been something

I have ever sought out; I once drove through Death Valley in California in mid-summer trying to persuade my companions to turn off the car's air conditioning. (I failed.)

"I think we need to buy ourselves something warm. Look, this shop has scarves in the window." Even Elaine was feeling the cold.

Elaine bought a scarf. I didn't; it wasn't really my neck that was cold.

"Well, that helps. You didn't want a scarf?"

"What I need, I think, are gloves. It's my hands that feel it most. I'd have got gloves if they had them."

"They did. Didn't you see them?"

We went back and bought gloves.

At the information office in the middle of the town, we each bought a multi-temple ticket valid for most of the main temples in Kōyasan. Then we walked on.

"It is still bloody cold. The gloves help, but they don't really provide the basic warmth the body needs."

"We walked past a place that seemed to have down jackets."

We retraced our steps to a shop that sold padded down vests that looked as if they'd squash into something we could fit into the backpacks. Nobody in the Kōyasan shops spoke English, but we managed by pointing at what we wanted, they managed by showing us the prices on a calculator screen, and we gave them money (only a few places in Japan take credit cards; it's a cash economy). It all worked out perfectly well, and maybe we would start to feel warmer now.

After this unanticipated expenditure, we were a little bit light on cash, which is not a desirable thing to be in a cash economy. Something we learned many trips back was that all Japanese Post Offices have auto-tellers that accept international cards. We found the Kōyasan Post Office, and in the entrance we found the auto-teller. Elaine found the 'English' button, put in her Australian bank card, and followed the instructions. The machine turned her down: transaction rejected. She tried again. It turned her down again. I tried with my card, from the same bank. Mine worked, which was good from a being-able-to-buy-things-right-now point of view, but Elaine wasn't happy.

"So what's wrong with my card? I told the bank I was going to Japan. I went into my local branch specifically to do that, and they said it would be OK."

At that point, my phone buzzed. The bank had sent me a text confirming a card transaction in Japan. Carelessly assuming it was checking on my withdrawal, I replied 'Yes' as requested.

Then I looked again at the message.

"Oh. That wasn't about mine. It was about yours. It says a card ending in such-and-such has been blocked, and please enter 'Yes' to confirm it was OK. But my card doesn't end in that, and mine wasn't for that amount."

"What are they doing sending YOU texts about MY card? How do they even know about you?" A pause. "How do they even know we're here together?"

Those were all good questions. Especially the last one. What sort of computer system doesn't send a message to the person with the card, but to someone else who, in a worrying Big Brother way, it knows just happens to be in the same Post Office in Japan and can pass the message on?

"I have absolutely no idea. But, thanks to not having read the message properly, I did at least tell them it was OK."

There was another text on my phone.

"And that says they've unblocked your card, and you should be able to use it again in another fifteen minutes. That's nice of them."

By now, however, we'd walked further down the street, and had taken refuge in a welcoming coffee shop, all shiny wood and pottery inside, and had started to warm up. The gloves and the down jackets were making a real difference.

"I'll try the card again later. Now, do you feel up to the walk through the cemetery?"

The cemetery is one of the main things to see in Kōyasan. It is huge, with its entrance at the western edge of the town, and about two kilometres from the entrance is the Kōbō Daishi mausoleum, where he rests in eternal meditation. This is one of the most holy places in

Japan, and - I now discovered - is the reason we started our Kōbō Daishi pilgrimage here in Kōyasan.

We walked to the end of the village, over the Ichi-no-hashi Bridge, and into the cemetery. The path through the cemetery ran between towering conifers, but this was clearly not an ordinary forest. It looked as if every spare patch of ground between the trees was filled with a huge variety of moss-covered gravestones, tilting at various angles. And throughout the cemetery there were small carved stone figures, maybe twenty centimetres high, with bright red caps on their heads and their bodies covered in red or white bibs.

These, we had read, are Jizō statues. Jizō is the protector of travellers and children, and is found at the boundary of life and death. Particularly in the case of children who die young, Jizō helps them cross the river into the spirit world. Dressing Jizō helps you acquire merit, which explains the bibs. The statues are everywhere; and it's hard to decide whether to see them as cheerful or sombre.

An unusual, even-handed, memorial we saw was to both the Japanese and Australian dead in North Borneo during World War II, and there was another much older memorial to the dead of both sides in the Japanese invasion of Korea, 1592-1598. These both had English translations below much older signs in Japanese.

"Have you noticed almost everyone here is Japanese?" asked Elaine.

"You're right. It's as if Westerners can't cross the entrance into the cemetery, and the locals don't go into the town."

Two kilometres into the cemetery, we reached the main Okuno-in temple. This was a hive of activity. An office building was manned by a number of people writing on books presented to them by visitors.

"This is where you can come to get your pilgrimage book stamped. We don't have ours yet; we'll get it at the first temple."

"And then we come back here eighty-eight temples later? That's not going to be this year."

"No, but one year..."

Across from the office, there was a queue of people who seemed to be waiting to stick their arms into to a small opening in a wooden construction about the size of a phone box. (Of course, nobody knows how big a phone box is anymore; think of it as the size of Doctor Who's Tardis.)

"It looks as if there's a big stone in there. You reach in and try to lift it. I think it's a measure of your spiritual fitness." Elaine joined the queue. I hung back. Perhaps I was unsure I wanted to measure either my arm's strength or my spiritual fitness, and wasn't sure how they were connected. Perhaps I remembered the unfortunate time I tried to crawl through a small opening in the Nara temple called the 'Buddha's nostril', nearly got stuck, and found my whole side bruised black the next night.

Some of us are more prepared to put themselves to the test. Elaine reached in, grunted, and there was the sound of a heavy weight being dropped back onto a shelf.

"That was much, much, heavier than I thought it would be."

"I saw a sign round the side. Apparently the stone matches the weight of your sins. I'd probably find it quite light."

But I wasn't going to try. Some things you really don't want to put to the test.

Just before the entrance to the main mausoleum, there was a long row of statues of various sizes, with flowers and water troughs in front of them, each with a number of ladles. People were filling the ladles and throwing the water over the statue in front of them. The significance was unclear, but it seemed to be what you did, so we tentatively did the same. Then we bowed, as you should, and crossed the Gobyonobashi Bridge over to the great hall of the mausoleum, past signs forbidding photography in this holy site. I put away my camera.

At various points around the mausoleum people were chanting sutras. We watched one person maintain a long and impressive recitation, the cadences of the sutra rising and falling regularly and formally, while his companions stood silently by. Then he stopped, laughed, went over to his friends, and the whole group went off in a chatter of friendly chuckling. The contrast between the impassive chant and the friendly banter that followed was quite striking. Although its sacred aspects were clearly taken seriously, this didn't feel a sombre place; possibly because Kōbō Daishi isn't really gone, but has merely been meditating for over a thousand years.

In the basement of the hall we passed a display of huge numbers of identical small statues, and another of rather bigger lanterns. The significance of these was unclear, and - as is often the case - we felt we were seeing something we did not understand.

Back outside the office there was a flurry of activity as a trio of orange-clad monks marched rapidly past carrying what might have been a small table. Elaine pointed them out to me.

"That's Kōbō Daishi's lunch."

"It's what?"

"Kōbō Daishi's lunch. Because he's only meditating, he gets meals brought to him. Then anything he doesn't eat is taken away. This looks like the take-away part."

And presumably they've been doing this for over 1000 years.

By the time we got back through the cemetery and to the centre of Kōyasan and were able to look for somewhere for lunch, my hands were feeling decidedly odd. Even with gloves they were cold to the point they didn't feel they were working properly anymore. Just trying to flex my fingers felt awkward. We found ourselves a small place that had an English menu and sat down. Elaine was surprised just how cold my hands were. Maybe I just have poor circulation; that would probably explain why I feel the cold so much. Still, sitting in the warm with my hands around a steaming bowl of udon worked wonders, and I was finally ready to look around Kōyasan and its central temples.

The main street at Kōyasan.

At least it was warm inside the coffee shop.

Red-bibbed Jizō in the cemetery.

A kettle on a grave in the cemetery.

The stamp office at Okuno-in.

"I think that might be Kōbō Daishi's lunch"

Elaine had another attempt to negotiate with the unhelpful ATM at the Post Office. This time, it proved a reformed character, anxious to please, and gave her what she asked for.

"Even so, it's not supposed to work that way. And what if I'd been somewhere on my own? You'd have got that text and probably wouldn't have told them it was OK. I'll call them up when we get back to the room and into the warm."

Kongōbu-ji is the main Shingon temple in Kōyasan. The main buildings are all single storey, connected, traditional wooden structures with covered verandas that you can walk around (having changed into the supplied slippers, of course) and look into the rooms, many of which have perfectly charming screen paintings. Surrounding the buildings is an equally traditional Japanese rock garden, with large granite stones in a bed of carefully raked coarse sand. Unexpectedly, there is also a large hall with a floor covered in red carpet where you are given a cup of tea and can sit and listen to a monk giving a talk on - something. We had no idea exactly what the 'something' was, and I suspect that was true of most of the people there, but the tea was pleasant, the atmosphere was relaxing, and the room acceptably warm.

As we left the temple, I felt something slip from my shoulder and crash to the ground. I'd forgotten how slippery the rain jacket I was wearing was, and there was my camera lying on the ground. Cameras are not made to be dropped; its case was still on my shoulder, but I'd had the camera itself carelessly out of the case and slung over just one shoulder. Take my tip: this is a bad idea. The camera itself, which was reasonably tough, appeared OK, but the small, compact zoom lens I had on it - chosen for being small and compact, but not for its toughness, these things being somewhat incompatible - was in a bad way. It didn't zoom any more, but that didn't matter, since it wasn't producing focussed images either. Now that was a bit of a blow, given the effort I'd put into picking a nice light camera and lens combination.

Elaine insisted, against any logic that I could see, that this was her fault, because she should have told me to carry the camera properly. She does tend to see anything that goes wrong as her fault, which is actually quite touching, but also rather frustrating. In this case I really wanted to indulge my annoyance at having a broken lens, but instead ended up having to tell her it wasn't her fault and in any case could probably be fixed and/or replaced. (The fixing and replacing part might be true, but certainly not in Kōyasan.)

I took my spare small, non-zoom, lens from my bag and fitted it. We carried on to the Kondo hall and the towering red and white Konpon Daito pagoda near it. The Kondo hall, a large wooden hall where major ceremonies are held, was begun by Kōbō Daishi in the late 800s. Lightning storms and fire-based ceremonies are, generally speaking, the natural enemies of the wooden building, and the Kondo Hall had burnt down five times over the intervening years. That sounded a lot, but really, only burning down every two hundred years or so was probably beating the odds. The current version of the pagoda dated back as far as 1937, but it did look in splendid condition. We would have stayed longer, but we were looking forward to getting out of the cold, and the prospect of the onsen back at Souji-in temple was enticing, even for me.

. . .

This time I decided to do the onsen properly. I would not only wash myself at the shower, I would enter the bath itself. I thought I knew the etiquette now. Strip off in the outer room, leave your clothes in a rack there, take a towel, and enter the main bathroom. Once again, it was deserted, which helped. I washed thoroughly, sitting on a small stool by one of the several shower fittings, then headed over to the big grey bath.

At this point, the instructions from Elaine failed to address one question: what do you do with the towel when you enter the bath? There wasn't anywhere obvious to put it down, so all I could think of was to leave it on the floor a bit back from the bath. I stepped into the bath, and while it was hotter than I'd have run it myself, I could handle that.

Walking around Kongobu-ji.

The tea room at Kongobu-ji.

Monks working at Kongobu-ji.

The pagoda at Danjo Garan, Kōyasan.

I lay down in the bath and let the water flow over me. Not just over me, but also over the side of the bath and all over the towel. Clearly I got that wrong. Elaine had said something about some people putting them on their heads in the bath, but it would have been too big for that. At that point I remembered that I was supposed to bring the small towel, *not* the big one. It was just as well there was nobody else there.

Still, there was nothing I could do about the towel, so I lay back in the not-too-uncomfortable warmth of the bath, and started to contemplate the eternal verities. Such as: if you move around in the onsen, you get lots of little bubbles in the water, and some last much longer than others. Why? Was this some sort of metaphor for life? Or did I just not rinse off the soap properly before getting in? Eventually, I got out, wrung out the towel, found another one, dried myself and headed back to our room.

"How was the bath?"

"Oh, fine. I wasn't sure what to do with the towel, so I left it on the floor and it got soaked when I got into the bath and all the water overflowed."

"I told you some people put them on their heads."

"I know, but I'd taken in the big towel."

"But you knew you weren't supposed to do that.."

I've always had an unfortunate tendency to confess my mistakes instead of just shutting up about them. It isn't always the best policy.

While I'd been getting self and towel thoroughly wet, Elaine had called the Commonwealth Bank. The results hadn't been entirely satisfactory, and it still wasn't clear why they had my mobile number instead of hers.

"But, apparently my mistake was to tell my branch I was going to be away in Japan. They, the branch, made a mess of setting that up, but now they have done it instead, and they say it should be OK."

"They being the phone support people."

"Yes, 'they' the people on the phone."

"Wouldn't bet on it."

Regrettably, I turned out to be right.

Another excellent supper, and then, because one visit to a cemetery can never be enough, Elaine had signed us up for a guided night tour. We walked back along the dark and cold street most of the way to the cemetery entrance, then turned into a large courtyard area where a number of obvious tourists were collecting. There was a lot of milling around, people rubbing gloved hands together, waiting, until someone started to take a roll-call. It seemed most people who'd booked had managed to find the place, and hadn't had second thoughts about cemeteries and dark, cold nights. Rather jolly round yellow lanterns, swinging from sticks, were handed out, and we all set off behind a cheery young fellow who spoke good English and turned out, not unsurprisingly, to be a monk.

Lanterns swinging, our repeat of the morning's trek through the cemetery by night wasn't at all the macabre, haunted event it might have been. Our guide filled us in on some of the background to Shingon Buddhism in general and Kōbō Daishi in particular, along the way mentioning "Full moon" meditation, and the symbolism of the lotus flower, which grows in murky waters and yet blooms into something pure and beautiful. I could follow the imagery of the lotus, but the full moon seemed rather to be something one meditated on, and its symbolism wasn't so clear to me. In fact, much of esoteric Buddhism wasn't clear to me, but that's what you expect when you call something 'esoteric'. I probably don't have the soul of a Buddhist, but I am aware of the power of meditation as a way of achieving relaxation, if nothing else.

The Japanese in general seem to take a cherry-picking approach to religion, and even our cheery monk was happy to describe this. He said Shinto provides rituals for events in life, such as birth, significant birthdays, reaching adulthood, and people will turn to Shinto on such occasions. Buddhism is more concerned with spirits and death and transition and most Japanese have Buddhist funerals. And in the middle, people seem to rather like the Christian way of celebrating marriage, and may well have Christian weddings.

Fortunately, we didn't have to walk all the way back to our temple, which apparently closed its gate at 9pm. Even so, in the car park near the mausoleum, as we waited on the bus provided by the cemetery tour, we could see the minutes ticking away. Finally, we were dropped off close to the Souji-in temple and raced up the road to it, slipping in through the small side gate with only minutes to spare.

We felt we understood a little more about the world of Kōbō Daishi. Tomorrow, we'd be off to Tokushima, and would finally be on the pilgrim island of Shikoku.

Waiting for the cemetery night tour.

Touring the cemetery at night.

8

THIRD DAY - RESTAURANT OF THE SPIRITS TO TEMPLE 11 (WEDNESDAY APRIL 11)

Today, our third on the road, should be an easy day. Temple 10 to temple 11 is slightly less than 10 kilometres, and we've already done some of that getting to our somewhat unexpected 'business hotel' with accompanying udon restaurant. So, a nice simple stroll today, in preparation for the serious slog up from temple 11 to temple 12 tomorrow.

We pack up and go out to see if the cool light of morning will illuminate just exactly what happened last night.

It doesn't.

The udon restaurant appears a perfectly normal, albeit closed, udon restaurant, and the anonymous open doorway we went through last night is now an anonymous closed doorway that we can't go through. We decide we aren't going to learn anything more, take a few photos to show to Tomoe-san when we get back, and head down the road to the konbini to see what it can offer us for breakfast.

This turns out to be some small sandwiches and croissants, and coffee. I can see I'm just going to have to get used to drinking real coffee, although it does appear that it's generally weak enough not to be a problem for me.

And a woman comes up to us and gives us a bag with two bottles of green tea, and two things I thought were socks but turn out to be bottle holders. How lovely - our second Henro gift!

There in the corner is an ATM that claims to accept international cards. Elaine makes the mistake of trying to get money out using her card. Now there's a surprise: just as in Kōyasan a few days ago, her card is rejected and my phone - *my* phone - gets a text telling me - not her - the card is blocked. Somehow, this doesn't come as a complete surprise. We thought this nonsense with the bank had been sorted out, but Commonwealth Bank stuff-ups clearly have a natural resilience - fix them, and they just bounce back again, happy to be causing trouble once more.

"I think the bank's computer system is malevolent. I've upset it by asking for money. Still, we've got enough for the moment, and your card is working. I'll call them again. Later."

We head off down the rather boring main highway, and then turn off to the side and spend a while zig-zagging down small roads that take us past a mixture of fields - many with rows of plants under plastic coverings - houses, and small allotment-sized planted areas. We're trying to follow the Henro path, but there don't seem to be many red arrows, so maybe we've wandered off course. We can see from Elaine's phone that we're going in the right direction, and occasionally we see one of the vertical red arrow signs we've seen before, usually on a pole just below one of those convex mirrors that are everywhere in this area of sudden corners and hidden driveways. These give us some confidence, but it would be nice to be sure they really are Henro signs.

Finally, we come out into the open. There's a long road crossing our path, and just ahead are steps leading up to a high artificial bank. We've left the built-up area, and from the top of the bank we can see a long flat stretch between us and the hills on the other side. Those are the hills we're heading for, and they look bigger now, but not scarily big. According to the map, there's a river running through here, although we can't see it yet, and we have to walk quite a long way over to the East, apparently along this raised bank, before we reach a bridge that leads into Yoshinogawa city.

We see another Henro sitting down on the bank, his backpack off, his back to us, drinking from a water bottle. He doesn't seem to notice us, and we head off along the bank.

As we go, we realise that this bank is a levee, raised to protect the built-up area we've just left from what presumably are the floodwaters of the river. This wasn't immediately obvious, since we couldn't actually see the river at first, but as we walk we slowly realise that it dominates the area. We start to see the river itself, small at first, and we see abandoned boats lying at an implausible distance from the water that's trickling along the river bed. At one point, the levee takes a dog-leg turn, and we pass a very substantial-looking pair of sluice gates mounted in a concrete structure that looks designed to control serious levels of flooding.

There is a road along the top of the levee, and the occasional car passes us. Someone walking in the opposite direction stops as we reach them, and hands us ¥500. This tradition of giving to Henro just seems to be something people do, quite naturally.

As we walk along, the river is getting wider and by the time we reach the bridge it's become a decent sized body of water. The bridge spans all the way from the levee we've just walked along to another that we can see in the distance, running parallel to ours on the other side of the river. If the river were to fill all the area between the levees, it would certainly reach the abandoned boats we saw earlier, and presumably there are times when it does.

"Once we get to the city, on the other side of the river," says Elaine, "there's a Lawson shown on the map. I thought we'd get something for lunch there."

Looking back from the levee.

Henro sitting on the top of the levee.

Don't dump rubbish here!

Elaine walks past the sluice gates.

Looking over the river from the bridge.

There are two main chains of convenience stores, Lawson and 7/11. They both sell more or less the same sort of 'convenient' items, stationery, magazines, food, drink, chemist's supplies such as Band-Aids (particularly convenient for the pilgrim with blistered feet), household items, and so on. Both are good places to buy snacks for lunch: rolls, croissants, cheese, and the peculiarly Japanese triangles of rice wrapped in seaweed with various fillings. There are two tricks to these triangles. The first is working out what they contain, because the makers feel no obligation to spell this out in English, although there are some general conventions about the use of colour on the complicated plastic outer wrapping, so salmon-pink may turn out to indicate salmon, but doesn't always. The second is working out how to remove said complicated plastic outer wrapping without breaking the fragile seaweed layer into flaky bits. You pull down where it says '1' and this tears the plastic wrapper, so when you then pull on '2' and then '3' the two halves of the plastic come away leaving the seaweed more or less intact. Japanese people have years of practice at this; visitors end up with a lot of broken seaweed.

The main difference between Lawson and 7/11, as far as we can tell, is that a 7/11 almost always has a small place where you can sit inside to drink your coffee and unwrap your seaweed triangles, but not all Lawsons do.

The Lawson in Yoshinogawa city doesn't have anywhere to eat, so we take our lunch out into the street and walk around until we find a deserted plot of land with a wall we can sit on.

As we eat, I dig out my phone and look at the photo of the puzzling possibly-a-Henro sign with its red arrow and two kanji, and decide to try out the kanji translation features of my dictionary app.

It's not impossible to decode kanji, but it isn't easy, and I'm new to this. But I hate to feel I can't understand something, and I'm fascinated by how things work, and I want to understand kanji. There are thousands of kanji, and Japanese children spend a lot of time learning the 1900-odd basic ones by heart. And sometimes they're used in combination, in the way English would combine 'stair' and 'case' to get a word whose meaning you might not guess from just knowing the component parts. You can try to work out the number of strokes needed to write the character, then you can try to classify its structure - some have clear left and right hand sides, others have up and down parts, and you can count the strokes in each and narrow down the search that way. Sometimes you can find the actual character reasonably quickly. In this case, after a few minutes I have an exact match to the second character, but not for the first.

The first looks a bit like a number of characters to do with water, possibly 'flow' or 'pouring'. The second character has a list of meanings like 'idea, mind, heart, taste, thought'. It occurs to me that this stuff is not easy. Maybe 'flow of mind' is something to do with pilgrimage? Or maybe not. Elaine looks sceptical. This hasn't been the most satisfactory exercise, and it certainly hasn't got me the answer I was hoping for, but I now have a lot of sympathy for Japanese children learning to read.

Carrying on, we head out of town, turning to walk directly towards the foothills. They don't look terribly steep, and the varied greens of the trees even makes them look welcoming. At least, tomorrow's walk should be shady. On the other hand, the vertical distance we're going to have to cover is quite significant, and we found out yesterday how hard it is to walk up a hill with full backpacks.

"Back in Tokushima, David told us about some old chap who did the section from 11 to 12. How long did he take?"

Elaine can always remember names. "Jacques. He did it in 7 hours. And he was 76."

"Well, we should be able to do better than that."

"Anyway, over there looks like the way to temple 11, but where we're staying is really close now, so we can go there first and leave our bags."

Elaine leads us around a final corner, and there is our accommodation, just where she expected it to be, and there's a cheerful chap inside who seems to be expecting us. Which makes a pleasant change from yesterday. Rather like the place we stayed on the first night, it's a fairly ordinary, reasonably large, Japanese house. It takes a bit of back and forth to get across that we want to go to temple 11 now and then come back ("sorekara kaerimasu" - knowing the odd word does help, now and again), but we manage it.

Now a challenge. We want him to book us in to where we want to stay tomorrow night. This is the first time we've had to do this particular negotiation, and this is what we spent one whole lesson with Tomoe-san practicing. We've learned the phrases for "tomorrow night, two people, one night, reservation", etc., and this is where it will all be worthwhile. At any rate, this is where we find out.

We needn't have bothered. As soon as Elaine opens the White Book to point to the name of the place we want to stay, he immediately realises what we want; he says "reservation", which is evidently one English word he knows, and he heads to the phone. There's a rattle of Japanese, including the word "Elaine", which clearly means us, and he puts down the phone and smiles and says "OK".

When you think about it, the one thing almost all foreigners want on the Henro trail is to get their accommodation booked ahead. It's what all the books say you need to get done for you, so it's something anyone running Henro accommodation is asked to do all the time. We needn't have spent all that time practising the necessary Japanese, because all you have to do is point at somewhere in the White Book. Communication becomes tricky only when you want to do something unusual, such as explaining that you haven't been to the nearby temple yet but would like to go there now and could we please leave our bags here while we do?

. . .

It's a relief to be walking without packs again, as we stroll over to temple 11, Fujii-dera. It's a pleasant place; I feel it looks older than some of the other temples, but obviously all are old - a thousand years old - and the 'old' aspect is more that it looks a little weather-beaten and hasn't had a recent lick of paint or whatever one does to brighten up a Buddhist temple. And it nestles comfortably at the bottom of the hills, blending in nicely with the woods around. Famously, it has a 'mini-88' tour of the 88 temples - 88 small stone shrines, each representing one of the temples on the pilgrimage, laid out along a wandering track through the woods. The canopy of leaves illuminated by the sun is a glorious luminous green, and we can tell how welcome the shade will be tomorrow. The mini-88 track gives a hint of what we'll have to tackle, as it winds up into the hills before turning and returning to the temple, but over this distance it's an easy enough stroll. It is, literally, a walk in the woods. The mini-shrines themselves are clearly taken seriously; we see someone quietly reciting sutras in front of one of them.

When we get back to the temple, it's crowded. About two busloads of Henro are clustered around the main hall, and we sit on a bench eating one of our car-Henro choc-bar snacks while they queue to have their books stamped. When their hubbub recedes, we get our books stamped and head back to our accommodation.

Our room is small but perfectly fine; you don't need a big room when you have a pile of futons in the corner instead of western beds. There's Wi-Fi, and we locate the toilets and two small bathrooms, each with the usual shower stool and a hot bath just large enough for one person. There seems to be a sign outside each bathroom that you turn to indicate it's occupied. Since it's not clear what the characters on either side mean, I have to assume that right now it says 'vacant' and if turned it will say 'occupied'. It's this sort of uncertainty that makes travelling fun. As it happens, the bath is rather too hot for me, and I don't stay long. In the drying area, there's a ridiculously hi-tech Japanese weighing scale, whose controls are a complete mystery. I try it, and it indicates 55, which I think is my pulse, and another number flickers between 1.68 and 1.70, which I suspect is my height in metres (how does it know that?) but I fail completely to get this weighing machine to tell me my weight.

Supper, downstairs in an almost full dining room, fortunately with conventional tables and chairs, is excellent and substantial. There's a TV on by the wall, almost none of which we can follow, although there is a weather map at one point that suggests tomorrow will be quite sunny. We'll need the shade of the trees.

Back in the room, I log on to the Wi-Fi, and it occurs to me to try the character recognition in Google Translate on our mysterious sign. I use my iPad to scan the photo of the sign I have on my phone - this is surely using an over-abundance of tech to solve a simple problem - and, rather embarrassingly, it comes up with the answer.

The characters represent the word "chūi", which is Japanese for 'caution'.

"Ahem, Elaine. I've translated that sign we've been following."

"So, is it a Henro sign?"

"No. It says 'caution'. That's why we always see them just under those convex mirrors that let you look around corners. The red arrow points up to the mirror. It's not pointing along the road at all."

"That's a bit embarrassing. We've been navigating across Japan following signs that tell you to look in a mirror to see what's coming."

Clearly, we still haven't got Japan worked out.

And tomorrow, it will be the "Henro fall down" stretch of the walk.

Two of the 'mini-88' temples above temple 11, Fujii-dera.

Returning to Fujii-dera, from the 'mini-88' walk.

Busloads of Henro filling temple 11, Fujii-dera.

Henro at the main hall, temple 11, Fujii-dera.

9

KŌYASAN TO TOKUSHIMA (SUNDAY APRIL 8)

Although we'd been out late the night before, touring the cemetery by lantern-light, our alarm managed to wake us at 5:15 and we made it down to the Meditation Hall for the morning's ceremony. It felt the right thing to do,

The set of monks that filed in was almost the same as the day before, although the Lady monk was missing, and this time the young monk sat over to the left, in Accountant monk's place, and he led the chanting. Sumo monk, in the same place over to our right, still had his cold, but today he seemed to be sitting more comfortably on his heels, not constantly moving the weight from his feet. The audience was much bigger than the day before, and looked to be about half Japanese and half Western. By now we were used to the ceremony, and weren't surprised to be asked to file up to the front and sprinkle powder onto the flame in the tray. And this time I found I wasn't worried about snuffing out the flame with the powder, since it seemed to be out already, nothing more than a wisp of smoke rising from the embers.

At the end of the ceremony, just as before, the Abbot rose to face the audience, but this time, presumably seeing there were enough people there who could understand him, he didn't just smile and leave. Instead, he sat down in a chair and gave a long talk I understood precisely nothing of. However, he smiled occasionally, pausing to let the audience smile as well, so clearly some of what he said was, if not actually laugh out loud funny, at least knowingly amusing. When someone does that, you find yourself smiling too, even though you have absolutely no idea why. When he finished, he handed out sheets of paper to anyone who looked Western. These weren't an actual translation of what he'd said - I looked in vain for the jokes - but were described at the top as a summary of the sort of thing he tended to say, which was mostly on the lines of "you don't know what's going to happen, but make the most of it and be nice to people" which seems pretty good advice, really.

As we passed the main entrance on the way to the breakfast room, we looked out and the whole courtyard was full of small white flecks drifting slowly down, settling briefly on the ground only to disappear, while more appeared from the sky to replace them. Snow! It was the sort of scene that you see through the windows of a country pub in England in winter, comfortable in the blaze of an open fire. Here, to be honest, the open entrance, the shivering cold, and the realisation that we'd soon have to go out in this completely unequipped for snow, did take the edge off the beauty of the experience. It did remind us of how much we'd misjudged the Kōyasan weather, though.

Breakfast was as elegant and splendid as before, but then it was time to go back to the room and pack.

The bathroom was equipped with a proper Japanese techno-toilet, and I wanted one for home. The Japanese only seem to have two extremes of toilet: a squat toilet, little more than a glorified porcelain hole in the ground, and the full-blown techno-toilet, essentially a Western sitting toilet with a control panel on one side right out of a science-fiction movie. With the traditional squat toilet, the only question for foreigners is: which way round do I use this? To which one answer is: facing the small hood at one end, but a better answer is: don't bother, go and find a Western-style toilet instead. With the techno-toilet, there are more questions, all of them variations on: what does this button do? To which one answer is: try it and see, but the most important thing is to know the symbol for 'stop'. Remember this:

止.

This is fairly important, since pressing any of the other buttons can have interesting effects. Some merely control the heated seat, which is a convenient thing for a convenience to have, but press either of the buttons with pictures of jets of water and you'll discover that what you're sitting on is strictly a 'washlet' - a combination toilet and electronic bidet, proud product of the Toto toilet company. There's the sound of a nozzle moving into place, and a warm spray of water into the nether regions. If you find this too hot or too powerful, you will appreciate knowing which button means 'stop'.

I'm personally rather fond of the products of Toto, Prince of Toilets, but there was a limit to how long one could spend with them, since we needed to be off. We needed to start the journey across the mainland that would take us to the port of Wakayama, where we'd take the ferry over to Shikoku and the city of Tokushima.

Kōyasan turned out to have a gleaming set of red fire engines and white ambulances, all garaged over from the bus stop where we waited to be taken back to the 'cable car' for the journey down to the train. The bus came and we all piled on. I noticed that Elaine had a ticket. I didn't.

"Where did you get the ticket?"

"From the machine as you get on the bus. Didn't you get one?"

"No. I didn't realise that was how it worked."

For the journey to Kōyasan we'd bought tickets before getting on the bus. Still, no problem, and I went to get a ticket from the machine. I saw the silver box mounted by the door, but there was no sign of a ticket to take, and no sign of a slot to put money in. In fact, it wasn't clear how you got a ticket out of this thing.

"The machine isn't giving out tickets. I can't see a slot for money either."

"You pay at the end. The ticket just shows where you got on. You know that."

Elaine is often surprised by what I don't know. She's occasionally surprised by some of the things I do know, but only rarely impressed;

most of the odd things I do know tend not to be particularly useful. (Although this is clearly evidence of a wide-ranging and enquiring mind.)

"I don't think I did know that."

The bus stopped again and I went back to the machine. There was a ticket poking out of it, and I took it. A lady half-way on to the bus looked at me oddly, and I wondered if that was supposed to be her ticket. But no, the machine fed out another ticket and she took that. I headed back to Elaine with a ticket and a wide-ranging and enquiring mind that was starting to wonder how the ticketing system works. Does the machine put out one ticket for each person who gets on at each stop? If so, how does it know how many people are getting on? If it just keeps feeding a new ticket out as each one gets taken, why isn't there one left hanging out after each stop that forgetful people (me) could come back and take? But this weighty problem would have to wait.

We took the cable car down to the bottom of the hill, which was like being in a railway carriage someone had tilted at 45 degrees and then propped up the seats so they formed staggered rows like those at a steeply inclined cinema or theatre. From the back, you got a clear view of your fellow passengers as they struggled with their luggage and checked their tickets.

At the bottom, I paused to take a photo of the cable car, and Elaine said something about a reservation for the train. I found I'd lost track of her, but I could see a queue of people waiting to get on to the platform. Maybe she'd already gone through. I got to the front and showed my ticket, but they wouldn't let me past; it was a limited stop train - the local version of an express - and evidently you needed a reservation. Which Elaine had been getting for us, suddenly appearing from behind me with the necessary pieces of paper. No doubt I'd have worked out the system if I'd had to do this by myself, but isn't it nice to travel with someone who's done the research beforehand?

The trip back to Hashimoto, through the green valleys and past small stations, where the 'limited' doesn't stop, but where uniformed staff still appear on the platforms and bow as it passes, was pleasantly relaxing. I passed the time experimenting with my rather scuffed camera, making sure it was still working. Still, in Tokushima I would have to see if there was any chance of buying a replacement for that damaged lens.

This time, we'd decided to head directly to Wakayama from Hashimoto using the local Nankai line, rather than take the JR route up and then down again, taking one side of a triangle instead of the other two. It wasn't entirely clear at first if our tickets were good for that, and when we tried to use them we discovered they weren't, which meant doing battle with a totally inscrutable ticket machine which made no concessions at all to the non-Japanese speaker. A helpful lady explained the process to us, but at full speed and all in Japanese, leaving us baffled. I found I'd forgotten the Japanese for 'slowly please'. Still, eventually she pressed the buttons for us and we put in money when directed, and out came what turned out to be two tickets that got us to Wakayama.

Wakayama had a boringly modern train station and we found a faux-Italian fairly-quick-service eatery that served a faux-Italian mushroom pizza, which was perfectly OK, and a glass of Kirin beer, which was welcome. We took a bus to the ferry terminal, and got onto the Tokushima ferry.

Snow at Kōyasan.

Our room, cleared for departure.

Going down to Gokurakubashi.

At the station at Gokurakubashi.

I'd imagined a small vessel a bit like a Sydney harbour ferry, but this was a huge boat that was basically a car ferry. What we hadn't expected was the layout of the passenger deck. Next to a door on one of the upper decks was a life-size drawing that reminded me of the Sailor Moon anime character - a Japanese schoolgirl who is also a cosmic heroine, usually shown in a short-skirted schoolgirl costume, and this character was to turn up in other parts of the ship as well. Through the door was a huge open cabin, the main section of which consisted of raised platforms covered in carpet tiles, rather like tatami mats. You took off your shoes and sat - or lay - on these, rather than on chairs. It felt such an obviously Japanese way to organise a ferry. As usual, I wasn't at my most comfortable having to sit cross-legged on a floor, and most people were stretched out, heads resting on cushions or backpacks. The biggest problem for us was having to put on or take off our heavy over-laced hiking boots every time we moved on or off the matted area.

There wasn't a lot to see on the upper decks, which were cold and blustery and almost deserted. One room had a sign on the door with one line in English that said "Nap room for truck drivers only", which sounded thoughtful.

When we disembarked at Tokushima it was very clear we'd arrived somewhere that didn't feel the need for English translations. Even the bus signs didn't have destinations in western characters. Fortunately, we'd booked into the Japan Railways hotel at the station, and the sign for 'station' ('eki') was one we knew:

駅

Japan Railways (JR) cleverly chose initials that bear some resemblance to the kanji for 'station' - at least the 'R' at the end is a giveaway. A bus bearing such a sign dropped us at the station, and we walked into the lobby of the JR Hotel Clement, Tokushima.

There's a school of thought that might see this as cheating, a cop-out from the self-flagellating, penitent, life of a pilgrim. The JR Clement was a Western-style grand hotel such as any Western railway might have at its stations to make life easy for its weary travellers. The staff at the front desk spoke excellent English.

"The thing is," Elaine said, "traditionally, this pilgrimage isn't an act of contrition. You don't do it to mortify your soul to atone for sins."

"Not like a Christian pilgrimage. Not that I have sins anyway."

"Exactly. It's an act of celebration. Buddha's happy that people do the pilgrimage any way they like. You can be a walking Henro, a bus Henro, a car Henro, …"

"A helicopter Henro." You can too. You hover over each temple in turn and pray and recite the sutras. Seriously. I'd have thought that might tax even Buddha's patience, but it seems to be OK.

"Right. So, it's perfectly OK to start off as JR Hotel Henro, at least for the first night. After that we can do it a slightly more authentic way."

I'm no great fan of bland, usually American, chain hotels that could be anywhere in the world, and Elaine usually manages to pick smaller places with some character. As a result, we've stayed in some fairly eccentric places, including convents and monasteries, and while the JR Clement had Western-style rooms, it was clearly a Japanese hotel. You could tell from the number of buttons on the toilet.

"Now, get ready, because we're having supper with David."

From the train, Gokurakubashi to Hashimoto.

Leaving Wakayama on the ferry.

On the ferry's passenger deck.

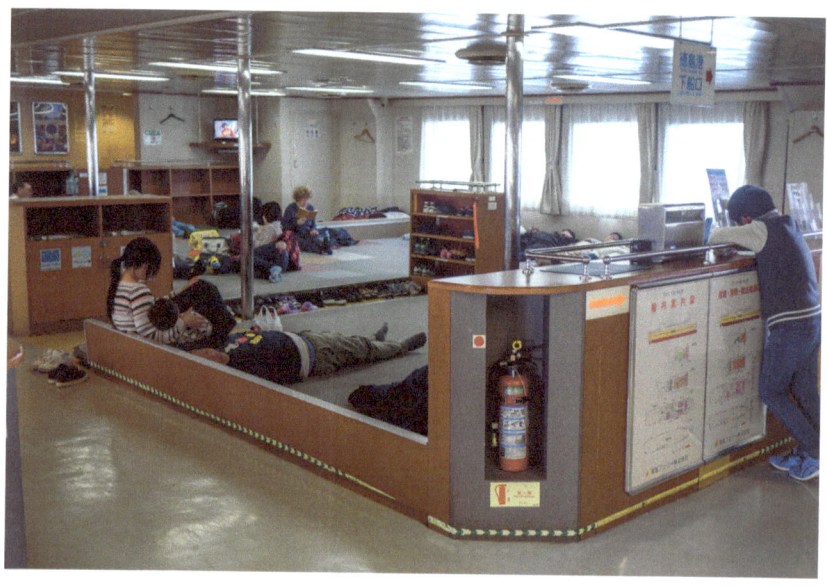

The carpet-tiled area of the passenger deck.

David Moreton is listed on the inside back page of the White Book as 'project coordinator and translator'. He's a Canadian who has lived in Japan for years and has made a particular study of the Shikoku pilgrimage, particularly the history of Westerners and the pilgrimage, and the tradition of giving gifts to pilgrims. He can be seen with Joanna Lumley ('charming') on the section of her TV show about Japan that deals with the pilgrimage. Elaine had made contact with him as part of her preparations for our trip, and he'd been particularly helpful and she'd arranged for us to meet him for supper.

We met at a small udon restaurant in the station complex just next to the hotel, which was convenient. David handled the ordering, and we chatted generally about the pilgrimage, and living in Japan - he now works at the University of Tokushima, and told us Japanese universities don't have long holidays, which made it hard even for a pilgrimage researcher to do the complete pilgrimage himself. It's sad, he said, that many temples no longer offered accommodation, and this was because people had greater expectations - they didn't want shared rooms any more - and building regulations had become more onerous and temples couldn't afford the changes that would be needed to comply with them.

Seeing outsiders, like us, doing the pilgrimage was good, but the attitude of some was terrible: there had been cases of graffiti on walls, with the moss ripped away to form words - "France" he said, in one case but, more worryingly, even some cases of writing in Japanese, which suggested this had spread to the locals as well. And most surprisingly, when someone complained about this on the Henro Facebook page, they were abused - "the concrete wall that was covered in moss shouldn't have been there in the first place". Ah, social media, we said, in the way that when two or three are gathered together they always find something to deplore about the way the world is going.

We talked about the dreaded section between temples 11 and 12, where the track climbs up steeply and seemingly forever, only to drop away again so you can climb back up again, and does that repeatedly.

It's tractable, said David. He knew a 76-year-old, Jacques, who did this part in seven hours, so we should have no real trouble. That was encouraging.

It made for an interesting evening. And tomorrow we would set off in earnest.

Sunset over Tokushima.

10

HENRO FALL DOWN - TEMPLE 11 TO TEMPLE 12 (THURSDAY APRIL 12)

Getting up with the lark is all very well, but this is 5:15 in the morning, and any sensible lark is still snoring in his nest and dreaming of worms or whatever it is larks dream about. However, breakfast is 6am, and we need to be off early, because this is the day we tackle the climb from temple 11 to temple 12. Even I realise we need to be up and doing.

Breakfast, downstairs, is substantial and probably needs to be. We're given an additional pack of something that could be balls of rice and is evidently intended for lunch, which is extremely thoughtful. The cheerful chap running the place ushers Elaine and I outside and takes our photo, in front of the building, all decked out in our Henro whites and conical hats, holding our staffs as if we can hardly wait to tackle 'Henro-korogashi'. After all, surely most Henro don't fall down there?

As we go back inside to collect our backpacks, one of the other guests looks at our hats in a rather disapproving way and indicates that we shouldn't have the rain covers on them. 'Only rain' he says. Well, we knew that was what they were for, and it isn't raining, but having the plastic covers fitted is a convenient way of carrying them, and nobody else had seemed to object. Still, often in Japan you find you've been doing something horribly wrong but nobody wants to offend you by telling you about it, so maybe we should be grateful. I find I don't feel enormously grateful, but we thank him, take the covers off, and find room for them in the backpacks.

Now we're ready for the big challenge.

We follow the road back to temple 11 and, as we near the entrance, a minivan stops in the car park, a middle-aged Henro gets out, and the driver strides over to us with some determination and says, 'Wait!'.

Maybe he's going to give us something? No, he isn't. He looks at my messenger bag, with the same disapproving look we just got for having rain covers on our hats when it wasn't raining. What does he think is wrong with my messenger bag?

I think he wants to adjust the straps. To be honest, it has been banging about rather awkwardly, and yesterday I discovered that as it did so it caught on my belt strap and kept releasing the buckle. I'd fixed that by moving it to the other shoulder, but maybe this chap knows the proper way to carry these things?

He certainly thinks he does. He pulls the straps of the messenger bag, making them incredibly tight so that the bag rides up most of the way to my chest, totally rigid and horribly constricting. Then, before I can do anything, he also tightens all the straps of my backpack as far as they'll go. He nods, looking satisfied, says something about being from a hotel, dropping off a German guest, and heads back to the van.

I cannot move my arms, which are fixed rigid out at about 90 degrees from my body, and I can't breathe properly. I manage a strangled 'aargh!'.

"I ... can't... breathe..."

"Come on, around the corner where he can't see us and we'll take it all off..."

We head around to the main part of the temple, me with my arms bent out horizontally, struggling to move. Once out of sight of this misguided lunatic, we release every fastening on the backpack and pull the messenger bag over my head. Breath makes its way back into my lungs.

I don't know what he thought he was doing, but he clearly had no idea how these backpacks are supposed to be adjusted. Actually, nor do I, which is why I'd had mine set up to fit me in the shop back in Sydney. There are a lot of straps, and getting them right had been tricky. And now every one of them is back to being seriously *not* right.

"This might take a bit of sorting out. He's set every single adjustment to full strangulation mode. He was a complete looney."

After a great deal of trial and error I get things almost back as they were, or at least close enough to carry on, although some bits are still clearly not as they should be. We move off.

The trail for temple 12 branches off from the route around the 88 mini-temples, so we know from yesterday where to find it.

It's steep, it's narrow, and it has steps. The steps are made from logs, laid across the path and held in place by smaller vertical wooden supports pushed down into the earth. It's not like going up a staircase, because the separation is irregular and doesn't fit well with our step length, but they do mean you can get up a slope that would be too steep to walk up comfortably without them. The staffs are getting almost constant use, and I'm leaning on mine a lot.

The earth is covered with leaves, and when you look up the sky is covered with branches, but it is shady, and the colours are lovely. There are small flowers in places by the side of the track, and occasional patches of red among the irregular greens of the trees.

But it *is* unrelentingly up.

And worse is the realisation that eventually it will start to go down, and then a lot of that effort will have to repeated to get back to the same level before you can get even higher, and then it will go down again...

Still, David had said 76 year-old Jacques was able to do it. I think I find that comforting.

"How are you doing?" asks Elaine.

"I'm managing. But it's a lot of up."

"There are supposed to be three proper rest places along the way. But we can stop anywhere we want, obviously."

Just as well. We pause frequently. The track varies, with steps only at the steepest points, but it does keep going on up. And up. Others are clearly faster than we are, and we're overtaken by quite a few of them, all Japanese. We pass one girl sitting by the side of the path talking on her mobile phone, but later she passes us again, now chatting with an older Henro, who she will probably eventually pass and leave in the distance.

After about two hours walking, all unrelentingly uphill, and looking for somewhere to pause for a while, we come upon the first of the three nominal rest places. It's nothing much: a shelter, and somewhere to sit, but both are welcome, and there is a splendid view over the countryside. We can see down to the plain, with the river and the bridge we crossed yesterday. It's something to think that we've walked that distance, and climbed as far as we have.

As we sit, a group of three other Henro appear. One looks Japanese, one is American - we hear his accent immediately, asking if there's any water at the rest point. There isn't, but the third Henro, a bearded fellow who answers him in English with a European accent, offers him some that he's carrying. The bearded European, we discover, is German, from Stuttgart, somewhere we visited only last year. Small world. Steve, the American, is from Arizona. It's not clear how they formed this group; they don't seem to be travelling together, and we assume they just found themselves walking at the same time and at about the same pace.

We move off first, but it isn't long before the disparate three pass us, making rather better time than we are. The track has flattened out slightly, and appears to be following some distinct ridge lines, although it still climbs in places. We're managing OK, even if we aren't the fastest walkers on the track. Rather incongruously, we pass a large electricity pylon, with wires leading out over the hill into the distance. And then we start going down. Going down after all that effort to go up, we'd been told, is discouraging, but actually it makes a nice change, so long as you don't think of it as giving back all the height you'd struggled to gain.

You have to be careful going down, so you don't get carried away and slip, but just over an hour since we left the first rest point we see the tiled roof of a slightly abandoned-looking hut. As we look at it, wondering if this is the second rest point, we see a group of buildings among the trees a little further down. When we reach them, we find a small flat area with temple buildings, somewhere to sit, and beautiful cherry blossom on a tree in the middle of the clearing. This will be Ryūsui-an, if we're where we think we are on the White Book map. There is a toilet, but its condition leaves something to be desired. Actually, quite a lot of somethings. We rest for a while, then move on.

About ten minutes later, still moving down, we come across another small wooden hut, this time in much better condition, on a patch of grass by the side of an unpaved road, and sitting on the porch are two of the three lads we met at the first rest point. The missing one, American Steve, is lying down inside, and it looks as if getting him moving again might not be easy. The hillside drops down to a valley below, with a blaze of colour from a red flowering tree by the size of the road. It's a setting that wouldn't be out of place in Switzerland, and we pause for some lunch, grateful for the rice balls we were given in the morning.

We move on, leaving the other two to decide when they should rouse the sleeping Steve, and follow the trail down to where it crosses a small river and then starts to climb again. This climb is tough, and we're starting to get tired. It's a steep, narrow path that zigs and zags up the side of the hill. There are erratic steps, mostly made out of roots across the path, but with a few stone steps in places. We're pushing down firmly on the staffs with each step.

Another Henro working his way up the path.

A break at Ryūsui-an.

In the morning, ready for the climb to Temple 12.

Light through the trees, just above temple 11.

Looking out from the first rest point.

The chalet just down from Ryūsui-an.

Blossoms near the chalet, close to the cliff edge.

The view from the first rest point.

It takes us about an hour of steady, slow, climbing to reach the top, and just before we get there we hear the group of three coming up behind us. They're faster than us, but making heavy weather of it all the same, with Steve limping slightly. He seems to have some sort of leg strain, perhaps a pulled muscle. You realise how awful that can be in these conditions.

At the top is Jōren-an, a small temple dominated by a statue of Kōbō Daishi. This is the highest point of the track between temples 11 and 12. We all sit down and rest. Elaine used to live in Arizona, some time ago, and we ask Steve which part he comes from. He turns out to be from Phoenix, but he used to live in Japan - he talks to his Japanese companion in a mixture of Japanese and English - and had wanted to come back and do the Shikoku pilgrimage. He's trying to do it on the cheap, staying in huts and other free places, and we notice he has a sleeping bag hanging from his backpack, making for what looks an awkward load. The Japanese is telling him he needs to rest up in a town somewhere to let his leg recover.

Almost from nowhere, the two Taiwanese lads appear, nod a brief hello to us, and move on. We'd thought they'd be well ahead of us by now, but they obviously have their own schedule.

There is one more drop of about 320 metres to go, followed by a final climb of about 280 metres up to temple 12. The drop down is tough, and we have to use the staffs to keep our balance at every step. And then it starts to climb again. This is real "Henro fall down" territory; it's a hard, muscle-strainingly steep climb, and we're definitely feeling worn. We've not exactly made the sort of progress we'd expected. The White Book says the walk temples 11 and 12 takes four to six hours but it's clearly been written by Olympic athletes in their prime. We're now coming up to seven hours, and we aren't there yet.

"I don't know how 76-year old Jacques did 11 to 12 in seven hours," says Elaine.

"I think 76-year old Jacques was lying in his teeth."

"Maybe he was just an incredibly fit 76-year old."

Finally, about seven and a quarter hours after leaving temple 11, we come out of the woods, and there is the car park for temple 12, Shōsan-ji. Realising there's a car park makes one question all the effort we've put in to doing this by foot.

Realising that this is *only* the car park, and there's still a long uphill walk to the temple itself, doesn't help much either.

There is an impressive marble balustrade along the side of the road to the temple, and an equally impressive view down into the valley. It is a spectacular setting for a temple, with huge trees towering over the area by the stamp office, fish in a stone pond outside the main hall, an interesting variegated tree with a mixture of red and white flowers that doesn't look completely natural, and a rather welcome pair of vending machines that have water, coffee cans, coke bottles, but regrettably no Pocari Sweat.

The pity is that, having put all this effort into getting here, to such a spectacular place, we really need to be moving on, because we have to get quite a long way down to our accommodation. We'd been told temple 12 didn't do accommodation anymore, so we're booked into a place down in the valley at Nabeiwa, just over three kilometres away.

We notice the two Taiwanese lads are still going around the temple, and, just as we leave, the disparate three finally arrive, looking rather grateful to be there. We head down the road.

Taking a rest at Jōren-an.

Another pause along the route.

Temple 12, Shōsan-ji, at last.

It feels good to put the packs down.

Main Hall, temple 12, Shōsan-ji

Going down is surprisingly hard. The route is mostly paved, but is slippery with leaves and twigs, and it would be easy to slip. The staffs prove vital, once again. My 'down' muscles are feeling worn and were obviously anticipating a rest. Finally, we come out onto a road, with a few houses over to our left. Elaine checks her map.

"There should be a bend in the road, and then this should be Nabeiwa village, and where we're staying - 'Nabeiwa-so' should be just on the right."

Except that it isn't. There is one house around the bend over to the right, but it's a house. It's a small house, and it's deserted.

"It must be. There's the bend in the road, this is Nabeiwa, this ought to be where we're staying."

We go back to the road. There are the few houses we saw originally, and a couple more in a group down the hill to the left. If there's anyone around, I can't see them. Elaine normally manages everything amazingly well, but has a tendency to imagine the worst when things start to go wrong.

"What if we can't find where we're supposed to stay? What if it doesn't exist?"

"It must exist. We're booked in. I'll see if I can find someone in these houses."

While Elaine minds the packs, and contemplates a night in the open and certain death from pneumonia, I head down the path to the nearest house. There's a shiny white car with the rear door open, so there surely must be someone here. I wander through the back yard, and can see someone tending his vegetable garden.

The exchange that follows only just qualifies as communication, being conducted in Japanese on his side and something miles away from being Japanese on mine. He doesn't know 'Nabeiwa-so', but he does know Nabeiwa. And this isn't it.

"Nabeiwa. Tōi desu-ka? Is it far? Nan kiro? How many kilometres?"

He holds up three fingers, thinks again and holds up four. He points down the road.

I report back. Elaine has to consider whether to trust more to her own map-reading or to my seriously dodgy command of Japanese. That's a tough call, as even I recognise.

"But the map shows we're in Nabeiwa."

"I'm pretty sure he says we aren't. He ought to know. He lives here."

"Are you sure that's what you asked him? Can you show him the map and ask where we are?"

I take the White Book and find him again. He's helpful, but he finds the map puzzling. It's to a confusingly large scale, and it doesn't help that it gives prominence to the Henro trail, rather than highlighting the roads. But eventually he makes a mark on the map, and it does look maybe three kilometres from Nabeiwa, and much closer to the temple.

I report back, and some understandable scepticism is expressed. I think it sounds consistent, but it would be nice to get a second opinion.

"I'm sure I can see someone outside those houses down there off the road. Let me try them."

The other houses are a more modern group, with no sign of anyone except for a little old lady watering her garden. She's clearly surprised to see me, appearing out of nowhere, but she's helpful, if prone to gush in rapid and impossible-to-follow Japanese. But she does know 'Nabeiwa-so'.

"Ryokan," she says, and makes a sleeping gesture, with her hands together over to one side and her head resting on them. She points down a track, which I now see is marked with Henro signs, leading past her house, away from the road, finally disappearing into some woods. "Nabeiwa-so", she says. "Ni kiro," and holds up two fingers. Two kilometres.

I report back.

Both stories I've been told are sort of consistent, if you assume she knows that following the Henro track is a short cut to Nabeiwa. And since it went past her house she could point me that way, while the first chap could really only tell me to follow the main road.

More to the point, it's trust her or spend the night out here by the side of the road. Elaine reluctantly agrees. We head off down the Henro track, past the old lady, who carefully watches us, making sure we head off the way she told us to, then disappears into her house.

I have the uncomfortable realisation that we're heading into these unknown woods purely on the strength of my conversational Japanese, and it's getting darker and colder. Elaine suggests I try to call Nabeiwa-so. She has the number, and I try, but the person who answers has no English and I'd not worked out anything in advance to say in Japanese, and it isn't clear that it would help anyway, given I can't ask for directions from here because the basic problem is that we don't know where 'here' is.

Elaine's phone is running out of battery, so I try to run up Google maps on my iPad. The result is interesting, mainly because there's almost nothing there. We really are out in the back of beyond. There's no 'here' here. The map shows a dot where we are, and there may be a road somewhere near. But there are no places marked at all. Certainly, Google doesn't know about Nabeiwa.

Our dot on the iPad is definitely approaching a road, and the road does have a distinctive loop back, not unlike what the White Book shows near Nabeiwa. Elaine finally concedes the remote possibility that this might get us to the right place, although it doesn't explain where we've been.

The path comes out onto the road, and we follow the road along for a while. We come to a village. There's someone by the side of the road, and we call out, hopefully, "Nabeiwa-so?". She points further down the road. Our hopes rise.

Finally, there it is!

Just off the road, as expected, just two kilometres down that wooded path from where we thought it should be.

We are so, so glad to have arrived.

Nabeiwa-so is a big place, by the standards of Henro accomodation, and our room is huge, up on the first floor, and the two futons already laid out take up only a quarter of the available space. Elaine heads for the bath, and I make tea. Then I take myself off to the bath, looking forward to a good hot soak after all we've been through.

For the first time, I'm in a communal bathroom and there's someone else there already, an older Japanese sitting by the side of the bath scooping water from the bath and tipping it over himself. I look at the showers by the side, noticing there are towels on the floor that would get wet if I used the shower, and he indicates I should do the same as him, showering by bath scoop. The bath is a decent size, plenty of room for two or even three, so we both get in.

It's a reasonable temperature, hot but not really excessive, and pleasantly relaxing. I feel I should say something.

"Atsui desu-ne?", I venture. "Hot, isn't it?" He nods, and we attempt some sort of conversation, as two of his pals come in. They move the towels and do the showering properly, with lots of suds that they carefully wash away. I get across that we've just done 11 to 12. "Aruite - walking."

Evidently, being a walking Henro gets you some brownie points in Shikoku. This group seem to be bike Henro. My companion in the bath has some English, and mimics cycling, pedalling his hands in front of him. It's communication, after a fashion. I get out to let his pals get in and head back to the room.

There's a bang on the door just after 6pm, which must be how they announce supper, and we go down the stairs to a big high dining room with a long row of tables over by the windows. At one end we see the two Taiwanese lads, which somehow isn't a surprise, chatting away in Chinese.

We find a space next to a couple of Japanese, a young lady who might have been the girl we passed at the start of the day talking on her phone, and a lad who tells us his name is Kenichi. He works for Mazda in Hiroshima and speaks pretty good English. The girl, Tomiko, doesn't appear to have any English, but Kenichi is happy to translate for her. It seems Kenichi is a bike Henro, but not part of the group I encountered in the bath earlier. He's doing the pilgrimage in the opposite direction, but Tomiko is walking in the same direction as we are, and suggests we stay in the same place as her tomorrow, just past temple 13. It's about 21km to temple 13, and we aren't sure we can manage all that in one day, so we say we'll decide in the morning.

The group of three cyclists from the bath appear and sit next to us. One of them has a mobile phone and, to our surprise, shows us pictures of Australia. I think he's saying that his daughter married an Australian in Cairns, but Elaine thinks she was just married in Cairns, presumably to another Japanese. Anyway, it's all extremely jolly, and when they all order beers - one large bottle each - Elaine and I order one to share. By the time we're finished and leave for our room, the three jolly cyclists have moved on to sake and look as if they could be there for a while.

It's been a long and exhausting day. But we've done the really hard day's walk that we'd been worried about (just a bit) and we managed to find Nabeiwa-so (if only just), and we feel pretty pleased.

Tomorrow should be much easier.

11

THE DAY AFTER THE WALK BEFORE - ON TO TEMPLE 13 (FRIDAY APRIL 13)

Today I'm expecting a longish, but fairly easy walk, mostly on the level. A nice change from yesterday's mostly vertical trek between temples 11 and 12, and the less said about the search for the lost village of Nabeiwa the better.

The question is, how far do we try to get today?

"It's 22.4 kilometres from temple 12 to temple13". Elaine has the White Book with its charts and maps. "But we've already gone on a bit from temple 12, so it's really more like 18 kilometres".

"That's still a decent walk after what we did yesterday. But I am feeling OK. Surprisingly so."

"Well, we're limited by what accommodation is available, and there's not many options. We could go about eight kilometres today and stay at a place by the river in the valley, and go on to 13 tomorrow, or we can go all the way to 13 today and stay at the same place as Tomiko, which would be nice."

Somehow, eight kilometres and a place by the river sounds rather attractive, but it also feels like the wimpy option, and we end up agreeing to go for temple 13 and staying at the place Tomiko has suggested. Of course, that makes the actual booking easier, because she's said she'd do it, so maybe this is the wimpy option after all.

We have breakfast downstairs, tell Kenichi and, through him,

Tomiko, what we've decided, take a group photo in front of the cherry blossom outside, and go up to pack. By the time we get down, everyone else has already moved off, and we set off to continue our trek. A little bit back along the way we came, and then we pick up the Henro track again, where it heads off into the hills.

It seems to be going up. It seems to be going up quite steeply. The narrow track is going up through the woods, in a series of bends that snake up the side of the hill. There aren't any actual steps, but it's steep enough that I'd welcome steps if they were here. What happened to the "it's mostly downhill from here" that I was expecting?

Just up ahead of us we hear the faint sound of Chinese music. A little further up, and there, sitting down at a point in the track as it bends back on itself in an attempt to keep the slope merely seriously challenging as opposed to impossibly steep, are the two Taiwanese lads. They're playing what I assume they find inspiring music through a mobile phone. We say hello, sit down with them, and I take a look at the White Book.

Looking at the useful 'elevation and distance' map at the front, we can see that today's route may indeed be mostly downhill, but it starts with a seriously steep uphill section. This very section, which we now realise is only just starting. Neither Elaine nor I had really appreciated this. The Taiwanese lads move off, and we eventually follow them, decidedly more slowly. One of us might even be grumbling, quietly.

I'm slowly becoming aware that the small toes on each foot are hurting. Maybe they're rubbing against the inside of my boots. My left foot is clearly unhappy and wants me to share its misery. And this climb, although no worse than we did yesterday, is taking it out of us much more. Partly it's because we're worn from yesterday, partly it's sore feet (at least for one of us), but mostly it's that we hadn't expected to have to do this climb, and that makes it so much worse. It wasn't part of the deal, and we feel cheated and resentful.

Finally, after just over an hour's hard slog, we reach the top of this particular challenge. There's a Henro hut there, and we pause for a while. The hut is nicely set out, comfy inside with a decent floor and a shrine, although there's no sign of running water in the nearby toilet.

I take off my boots and look at my toes. Both the small toes are looking unpleasantly red, although I don't see any blisters, which is almost disappointing, given the discomfort.

Over the years I've had a lot of trouble with painfully sore heels (plantar fasciitis, or jogger's heel, which is most unfair, since I don't jog), to the point that I occasionally find I can't put any weight on whichever heel is playing up at the time. I wear orthotic inserts in my shoes, which make a big difference. It had never occurred to me that there was a wrong way to walk, but a few years ago I started seeing a podiatrist, Mark, who cheerfully told me that I'd been doing this walking stuff wrong all my life - taking too long strides, too fast, and digging my heel into the ground at each step. With newly-tweaked orthotic inserts, and a newly-practised more relaxed walking style, I've been fine for a while now, but the possibility my heels might let me down has been one of my major worries about this pilgrimage.

As a result, I'd worried about my heels. I hadn't considered anything as mundane as blisters or sore toes. Fortunately, Elaine had, and is carrying a supply of some seriously high-tech blister bandages, as well as old-fashioned adhesive tape and Band-Aids. We put some cream and a bandage on the sore left foot toe. The right foot doesn't feel too bad.

We set off again. I'm still aware of my small toes, but now the one on the right foot is the more noticeable. This means the left is clearly improved, so I reckon I can carry on.

The path has now joined a road, and is dropping slowly down, moving out from the woods into the open. Down below us we see right across the countryside, down into a valley with a small river running through, and across from us are several ranges of hills. There are scattered red roofs, merging to form a village down in the valley. Some almost conical hills rise up on their own, others form into slightly jagged ridges, all covered in a mixture of dark and light greens lit by the sun into strong deep colours in the close hills that fade slowly until the most distant high hills are almost misty. You could call these 'the green rolling hills of East Shikoku'. I suspect the

Japanese don't go in for country music, but looking at this view you could forgive them if they did.

We stop to look at a small cluster of houses by the roadside that have a well-cared for verge covered in small flowers of varying pinks and whites, with trees on the hill above in a glorious variety of colours, from cherry blossom to oranges and reds that should only be out in fall, all amongst the usual mixture of shades of green.

At this point, we're caught up by two familiar faces: the Japanese and the bearded German from yesterday's group of three. We ask about American Steve, with his aching leg. They say they stayed last night at temple 12 (which we had thought you couldn't do), which means they've been going quickly to reach here by now. Apparently, a nice Japanese lady had taken pity on Steve and had booked him in to where she was staying and was taking him to temple 13 by what the German calls 'the easy way'. We assume this means car or bus, but don't get to find out more details, because now they're powering off down the road at a pace we aren't going to try to match.

We reach the floor of the valley, and follow the road along. Just outside a reasonably sized village, about an hour after we last saw them, we catch up with our two Henro again. They're looking at two figures in a field. These are nearly life-size dolls, held up like scarecrows, dressed in green and red robes, with large padded heads that have markings for eyes, nose and mouth sewn in black.

The Japanese Henro points out that the markings on the face are actually Japanese kana characters.

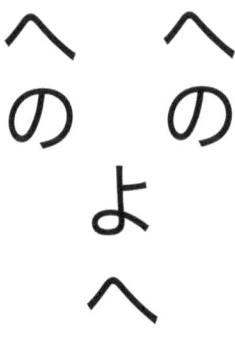

"We made faces like this at school," he says. "You use a 'no' character for the eye, and a 'mo' for the nose, and 'he' for the mouth."

It's an interesting effect, and we assume these are just elaborate scarecrows. Our two energetic companions head off, apparently preferring to walk quickly and then take longer rests. We stroll on into the village, and we see more of these figures. There are two sitting at a bench outside a shop, in a slightly different style, an old couple, a man and a woman, in ordinary clothes and with walking sticks.

What we don't see in the village, we suddenly realise, are people.

We go through the main part of the village, and cross a river to where there are more houses and some fields. In one field, there are a whole group of these figures, apparently set up as if they're working the field. One has a check shirt and is using a hoe. A figure sits by the edge of the field with a basket, either planting or weeding, and there are others in the background.

But no people.

This village is inhabited only by life-size dolls.

Then we do see one real person, in the distance, by one of the houses. But she's too far away, and in any case, we don't have the Japanese to be able to ask, "Excuse me, why are you the only person in a village full of dolls?" And we'd not understand the answer anyway.

The really strange feeling is that we may end up never finding out exactly what's going on here. Japan is often so unlike what we're used to, and even if we could find someone to ask, we probably couldn't get over the fact that we know so little of the language. Presumably - presumably - this isn't actually some ghost village, but what is going on?

The green rolling hills of East Shikoku.

Group outside Nabeiwa-so. Kenichi, us, Tomiko.

Foot check at the Henro hut.

Dolls with characters for faces.

Dolls working in the fields.

I realise I'm now quite conscious of my right foot, where the small toe is feeling decidedly sore as it pushes against the boot. The same is happening with the left foot, but it's the right that's making itself felt more. Elaine's back is twinging a bit, and she's constantly niggled by a tapping noise from her backpack. We can't see what's causing it, but tightening one of the straps seems to help. A bit. This was supposed to be the easy day after yesterday's triumphant conquest of the 'Henro fall down' section (even if we've conveniently forgotten we took longer than 76-year old Jacques). But it isn't easy.

We pick up something to eat at a shop in another village, and then see that we've caught up with our German and Japanese pair again. It's funny how we rarely find out the names of people - Henro often ask each other where they come from, but names are somehow irrelevant when you're just passing on the walk. They're sitting down by a bridge over the river, and next to what they helpfully point out to us is a public toilet.

The Japanese tells us he thinks the dolls we saw in the village are something to do with a problem the village has and the villagers think the dolls might be lucky, but it isn't clear where he got that story from.

This village we're in now has a Post Office. More in hope than genuine expectation, Elaine makes one more attempt to get money from its international ATM. To the huge surprise of neither of us, the transaction is declined. But, in the interests of variety, this time neither of us gets a text message. I suppose it had already told me two days ago it had blocked her card, and obviously doesn't think I need to be told again. And it clearly never had any intention of telling her.

"Well, whatever it is that's gone wrong with my account and the Commonwealth Bank, it's still not fixed. I'll call them this evening. But this is getting annoying."

A couple of hours later, the Henro path is now following the rather boring main road, route 21, along the other side of the river. The valley is pleasant, and the river is flowing in a slow, relaxed way, but the road is out in the sun, my feet and Elaine's back are all unhappy with the state of things, and we haven't seen a coffee shop or anything similar for a long time now. Although we've passed through a few small villages, none have had anything to offer except the ubiquitous soft drink vends.

We come to a new village. This one has a big billboard that says, in English, "Henro" and "Coffee" and "30m ->", and appears to be pointing off to the right, down a side street. My feet have spent a while now making sure I really appreciate the meaning of the word 'footsore', and we're most reluctant to add a thirty-metre detour to what we're asking of them, but for coffee it should be a worthwhile investment.

It isn't. We find the place. It looks as if it would have been just the thing. Comfortable, somewhere restful to sit, a menu with pictures that we could point to. Everything one could possibly ask for. But it would have helped if it were open.

"I don't mind it being closed," says Elaine, "but it could have been closed nearer to the main road. As it is, that's 60 metres of unnecessary walking."

Just to rub it in, we pass another Post Office that, in a show of auto-teller solidarity, also rejects Elaine's card. We weary our way onwards down the main road.

I'm walking on autopilot, just about keeping up with Elaine. I find myself repeating, mantra-like: "Each step you take is a step closer to not having to take any more steps today". Both feet feel sore, but the small toe on the right foot has become the focal point of each step; not crippling, but noticeably painful. The weight of the backpacks is becoming more obvious, kilometre by kilometre, and at every step I'm pushing down more on the staff, even on the level.

At last, somewhere we can get coffee! A most welcome 7/11 by the side of the road, with a car park in front of it and continuing around the side. We get two coffees, but there's nowhere inside to sit down and drink them. Outside, people are sitting in their parked cars, drinking and eating. Since we don't have a car, we sit down as best we can on some concrete barriers at the edge of the car park. A youngish chap in a white van puts out his cigarette and chats to us through his open window, in pretty good English. He asks the usual question: where are we from?

"Australia."

"Why are you doing the Henro?"

We'd not been asked that before, but right now it feels like a particularly relevant question.

"We like Japan," we say, "and walking, and the culture..."

"It is not for religion?" he asks. I'm not sure what he'd like the answer to be, but actually, no, it isn't for religion. We're interested in the temples, and we respect them, but this is not a religious thing. He sounds happy with that.

"I surf," he tells us. Yes, that would fit with the white van. He tells us he'd like to come to Australia one day. We tell him he'd like the surf. It seems he learnt his English in Canada. Come to think of it, so did Kenichi; do a lot of Japanese go to Canada, or have we come across an unrepresentative sample of two?

He drives away, we finish our coffee, and carry on.

Slowly.

A mere 650 metres, and counting every step ("closer to not having to take any more steps today.."), and we're finally at temple thirteen, Dainichi-ji. One of us (me) can hardly move by now, but we give most sincere thanks to Kōbō Daishi for having got us here. The temple is, as they all are in different ways, charming, but it's a little hard to appreciate it properly. Opposite it, on the other side of the road, is a Shinto temple, and we have a quick look in there as well.

Fortunately, where we're staying is only a couple of streets away.

Walking down to a bridge over a stream.

Finally, at temple 13, Dainichi-ji.

Jizō at temple 13, Dainichi-ji.

The grounds of the Shinto temple opposite Dainichi-ji.

We hobble in through a deserted reception area, swopping our boots for house slippers, and find an old lady in what appears to be a main room, doing a jigsaw puzzle. She seems to have trouble moving, but she gives us keys, appears to be indicating which room is the bathroom, and points us at a tiny lift at the end of the hall. We go back to reception for our bags, just as a small car drives up. We see Tomiko get out, followed by the driver, who turns out to run the place. We show her that we've arrived, and say several 'arigatō's for booking us in, but our Japanese doesn't get us much further than that. Still, it's nice to see a familiar face.

Up in our cosy little room, I collapse down on the cushions near the table, groan, get up and try to see if the pile of rolled up futons is more comfortable. I really am not designed for sitting in Japanese rooms.

"Back in Sydney," I say, "not only did we not really practice going up and down hills, we also didn't practice doing it two days in a row." This is only just beginning to become clear.

"True," concedes Elaine. "Are you able to stand up? You don't look it. Poor you."

I realise I'm crawling around the room on hands and knees. Standing up is not something that I particularly want to do right now.

"You'll feel better after a good hot bath." The thought of the bathroom, if I can only get there, is enticing to a weary body.

Elaine goes first, while I try to lie down somewhere. When she comes back, she explains that there are two bathrooms; she used the one on the left. It's a one-person bathroom, you can lock the door, and it's one with a sign on the door you have to turn around, but the two sides just have different coloured kanji, and the significance isn't obvious.

I go down. Of the two doors that I can see, one leads to just what she described, a single-person bathroom. The other leads to a yard that seems to function mainly as somewhere to store brooms. A lot of brooms. On the other side of the yard is something that might be another door, which might even be another bathroom, but I don't feel like investigating. I use the room Elaine used. I have no idea what to do with the sign, but I leave my house slippers outside and lock the door. I don't stay long - the shower turns out to be warmer than the tub, and I see no reason to linger.

Back in our room, both of us now feeling rather better, Elaine makes another call to the Commonwealth Bank in Australia. Telephone support explain that the problem was originally caused by her branch, and express surprise that it wasn't fixed as a result of the previous call. It was, it just didn't stay fixed. Would Elaine mind being put on hold and transferred to the security section? Elaine explains that this is now her second international phone call to fix what should never have been a problem, but doesn't have much choice. It takes security, whoever they are, about twenty minutes to answer, and when they do they don't act surprised either that a branch would mess something up or that ordinary phone support would fail to put it right.

"But now," says Elaine, putting the phone down, "now security have fixed it, and now it should stay fixed. So they say."

"They would say that, wouldn't they?"

"We'll see. Anyway, by now it must be time for supper."

Just after 6pm, there's a public-address announcement preceded by an attention-grabbing squawk. I recognise almost exactly none of the words, but it ends 'dinner time desu'. We go down and find Tomiko sitting at the table next to us. A little later an older Japanese lady comes in and is sat down opposite her. We see if we can manage a bit of conversation, grabbing words from either language as best we can. Tomiko says, I think, that she's already been to temple 14, Jōraku-ji, so clearly she made much better time than we did, which is hardly surprising; a dead snail could have overtaken me on the last couple of kilometres. She must have been picked up from Jōraku-ji by the chap running the accommodation. We'd heard that was fairly common, but you obviously need to be able to call up and ask them to come and get you, something we would find tricky.

Communication improves somewhat when Tomiko pulls out her phone and fires up Google Translate, and starts using it to show us roughly what she's trying to say. Elaine does the same with her phone, and a rather slow high-tech conversation ensues. I have mixed feelings about this; having tried hard to learn some of the language, even if fairly unsuccessfully, this feels like cheating to me. And it's cheating that produces better results than I can manage, which is rather irritating. But it is effective.

The supper is the usual enticing spread of things in front of us, including a candle-heated dish of mushrooms and 'other things'. We can't identify all the 'other things', although some might be chicken, but everything tastes splendid. We're starting to feel rather better.

To bed. At least tomorrow genuinely isn't going to be a long walk. Some rain is forecast, but only late in the afternoon. We should be happily housed in Kuramoto by then, blissfully relaxing and resting our feet.

12

MORNING OF THE FIRST DAY (MONDAY APRIL 9)

Monday morning at the JR Clement. The day we started our pilgrimage, in a meaningful, feet striding out along the road, sort of way. Even if we did start by train.

Elaine had a swollen eye, which looked more than a little uncomfortable.

"I wonder if it's from the ferry trip. It's possible. I've got some antihistamines; I'll see if they help."

The JR Clement did a fine breakfast, positioned culturally at an intersection between Japan and the West, and physically just off from the lobby on the ground floor. They had a simple system where they gave you a small tag as you went in, you selected a table, and left your tag on the table to flag it as taken while you milled around the buffet, trying to work out what everything was. They had ordinary plates, but most people - well, everyone but us - looked to be Japanese, and were collecting small items in plastic trays with small compartments. As usual, there were some interesting offerings that I couldn't identify - even after I'd eaten them. A small bamboo tube with some sort of fish wrapped around it was apparently a local speciality. I thought it acceptable, but cold and unexceptional. Clearly mine are not locally grown taste buds. There were croissants, but you had to be quick to beat the crowds to them and we weren't.

Back in the room, Elaine's eye seemed to be a little better. We didn't have a tight schedule for the first day; the temples around Tokushima at the start of the route are relatively close together and Elaine had planned to start around midday and reach only the first four or five in the afternoon.

"I'd thought we'd start late," she said, "because I'd thought it might be hard to get you out of bed, but in the end it's my eye that isn't quite right."

We packed our backpacks and realised that we should try to lighten them as much as possible. Elaine didn't think she needed her Kōyasan down jacket any more, and the scarf and gloves were deemed equally surplus, so she proposed to pack them up and post them back to Australia. With my sensitivity to cold and suspicion of optimistic weather forecasts, I was reluctant to part with my nice warm jacket just yet. In any case, I saw it as replacing the jumper unintentionally donated to Qantas on the flight out.

So we had a few things to do. First, the Post Office, which was only a few streets away. There, a conversation that involved two people each speaking their own language to someone else who didn't understand it nonetheless managed to end up with a packed box being posted off to Australia, to the satisfaction of all concerned. I kept out of the discussion, mainly because it took me so long to think of any relevant Japanese words that things had moved on by the time I had anything to contribute, and Elaine was doing fine in a fluent mixture of gestures and English. Technically unsatisfactory, but effective in practice.

"On the way back, we can call in at the tourist office at the station. They should be able to make our bookings for the next few nights."

The tourist office was at the top of the building that rose above the station. We were greeted by a pleasant lady with almost fluent English, who was a huge help. Elaine had already made our booking for that first night, but the tourist office lady was able to get us in to where we wanted for the next couple of nights as well. For the second night, she booked us in where we wanted, but had to tell us that, unlike most places, they didn't do food.

"You have booking. You go there 5pm. They say no food there. But they say there is udon restaurant just next door. Is OK?"

Yes, that sounded fine. There was no reply from the only place near to temple 12, which was potentially a problem, but we could get someone else to make the booking for us later. She helpfully wrote a note asking someone to do just that, which we could show at one of the other places we stayed. Learning how to book rooms for ourselves had been part of our somewhat sketchy Japanese language preparation, but we felt it would be much safer not to have to rely on that.

We had a little time to spare, so I said I was going to try to find a camera shop in the next block that I'd looked up on Google. I might be able to I replace my broken lens. Camera shopping is not how Elaine likes to pass the time, so I headed off on my own.

The block by the station that Google claimed housed the shop called 'Camera-no kitamura' looked more like a multi-storey car park than anywhere containing shops. In fact, it *was* a multi-storey car park. The building next door looked only marginally more promising, but I could see an alleyway running through it that had some shops, so I went in.

The alleyway was small, and erratically lit. Most of the shops looked fairly nondescript. They were all relatively tiny, and while some sold food of various sorts, it really wasn't obvious what sort of business some of the others did. I didn't see anything that resembled the sort of sparkling, high-tech, modern camera shop I was going to need.

Then, on the second pass back through the alleyway, I looked more closely into one of the smaller shops, and saw that it had shelves on which were a fairly antique line of cameras; old Nikons and the like. I went in. It was a fairly deep, narrow shop, with a scrappy wooden desk opposite the shelf of cameras and an older lady sitting behind it. Looking further into the shop, at the far end there was a fiftyish-looking chap sitting at a bench and not obviously doing anything very much.

"Camera-no kitamura desu-ka?" I ventured. (Is this 'camera-no kitamura'?)

Blank looks. This was going to be something of a struggle. I tried to construct something coherent, out of my minimal vocabulary.

"Olympus camera no lensu-wa burōkun desu" (I wasn't quite sure about 'burōkun', but that sentence at least contained the words 'Olympus', 'camera', 'lens' and maybe 'broken'). I mimicked something falling to the ground.

Sympathetic looks. Progress.

"Lensu-wa doko kaimasu-ka?" (Lens, where buy?)

"Yamada denki". That didn't mean anything. Maybe it was the name of a shop. Or a place. Or the Japanese for 'oh, no chance, not around here'.

"Doko desu-ka? Tōi desu-ka?" At last, some phrases from the Pimsleur Japanese course came back to me. (Where is it? Is it far?)

"Takushi" she said. Oh, 'Taxi'! Clearly not in the next block.

"Nan kiro?" (How many kilometres?)

The chap at the back of the shop suddenly sat up and took an interest.

"Go kiro," he said, with absolute certainty. (Five kilometres.)

"Takushi," she repeated helpfully.

And at that point the phone rang, with Elaine pointing out we were nearly at check-out time and needed to be moving.

I couldn't decide if that counted as a success or not. I didn't have a new lens, but that had always been a long shot. I hadn't found the shop I was looking for, but that was Google's fault (surely) and I did have what might be the name of a shop that might sell cameras. And I'd managed to stretch my embarrassingly limited Japanese to the point where I'd had what might generously be described as a conversation.

I headed quickly back to the room, thanking the two in the whatever-sort-of-shop-it-actually-was, and we took our backpacks down to the station next door and bought tickets to Bando, which was where we would find the first temple.

We were really on our way now.

At Tokushima station, waiting for the Bando train.

13

THE SHORT BUT UNCOMFORTABLE WALK TO KURAMOTO. TEMPLES 13 - 17. (SATURDAY APRIL 14)

The first thing I do when I wake, around 6am, is look at my toes. They're red, and look uncomfortable, but there's no sign of any actual blisters, which surprises me. I feel there ought to be blisters. My feet feel as if there ought to be blisters. I put an inadequate-feeling Band-Aid on the left small toe. Maybe it will help.

At 6:30 the PA system fires up again. "Ohayo," it says, Good morning. This is followed by nothing else I recognise, but we assume this must be breakfast time.

Downstairs, and breakfast is enjoyable and satisfying, as expected, although there's a lot of egg, both once-fried-now-cold and raw (both of us leave the raw, although the idea is to mix it with the hot rice and let it cook in that). Between them, Tomiko and Google Translate tell us that she's leaving at 7:30, and we expect we'll be off at about the same time.

We pack - it's not as if packing takes a long time, given how little we're travelling with - and head downstairs. As we leave, we see Tomiko getting into the small car we saw yesterday, about to be driven back to temple 14.

"So it's OK to be driven around, so long as you start walking again from where you left off the day before." It's always as well to be clear about the rules of the game.

"That way, you *have* walked the whole Henro route. Just not continuously. Not that there are rules," says Elaine, "Kōbō Daishi is happy with any way you do the pilgrimage."

I like Elaine's view of Kōbō Daishi. I like my religions on the tolerant side.

We set off down the road, and it's obvious my feet are still sore, which is hardly surprising. Still, today's section is supposed to be relatively easy. All the temples we've been to so far, since we left Tokushima on Monday, have been on a looping route that is now going to take us back into the suburbs of Tokushima. Temples 14,15,16, and 17 are all close together, and it's not far from temple 17 to the Tokushima suburb of Kuramoto, where Elaine has booked us in for a couple of nights in what she describes as "really quite a nice traditional ryokan".

Resting up for a couple of nights somewhere nice would be a reasonable reward for having completed what's really the first, separate, part of the Henro path, before it heads down south into the more remote areas. That had been Elaine's idea, and right now it sounds splendid.

We just have to walk to Kuramoto.

The route winds through a mixture of houses and paddy fields, and we find it fairly slow going. It takes us just under an hour to cover the two and a half kilometres to temple 14, Jōraku-ji, which sits just past a lake in a well-wooded setting, and whose dark wooden buildings merge in well. Outside the office is a life-size doll, made in just the style we saw in the almost-deserted village yesterday, this time in full Henro kit but with dayglow-pink rain jacket and trousers under a white Henro waistcoat. It looks as if it might have walked here by itself from the village. But we have no easy way of asking about it.

Bright red bibs and headscarves on the statues give a needed touch of colour, and there is an area under canvas with substantial wooden tables and elaborately carved wooden seats. A cat darts across the courtyard. A number of temples seem to have cats.

"I think I'll pause and bandage my right foot at the next temple," I say as we move off.

"You could do it now. Of course, the accepted thing is to bandage toes *before* they give you trouble. At least, at the first sign of a problem. But you knew that?"

"Actually, no." I honestly don't know anything about bandaging feet. The only thing I've worried about, foot-wise, was not triggering my misnamed jogger's heel problem, and I feel I may have managed that thanks to the proper foot stretches. I've never had a problem with sore toes before. This is new territory; just like rural Shikoku, really. "Anyway, we're moving now, and it isn't far to temple 15."

Temple 15, Kokubun-ji, is only another kilometre down the road. When we get there, it looks completely encased in scaffolding. A large and rather permanent-looking sign explains in both Japanese and English that the temple was erected in 741 (and that date alone is something to consider - I realise I expect dates to have four digits, especially when they're to do with buildings), and recent excavations show it to have been much larger when first built.

As we stand reading this, an older Henro comes up and asks us, in somewhat minimal English, where we're from. We tell him, and he gives us one of his name slips before moving off and getting into the back of a small van. It's extraordinarily fancy, and Elaine almost gasps when she sees it.

"It's a brocade slip! You only get these if you've done the Henro trail more than 100 times."

And on the slip is the number 115. We are 15 temples into our first time on the Henro path, and this fellow has done all 88 of them 115 times! Obviously, not always walking - we watch the van drive off - but we try to calculate what fraction of a lifetime this must represent. Even a motorised circuit takes a couple of weeks, and he must have done this multiple times every year. And he gave us one of his slips. It's humbling.

A lady laying out an assortment of items on a wall calls us over and she gives us each a pair of chopsticks, a boiled sweet, and some highly flavoured dried plums. We still aren't really used to being given these gifts, but it's lovely. David Moreton had emphasised that you have to accept all gifts; that's important to the giver.

After we get our book stamped, I sit down and look at my right foot. And now, it's clear why it's hurting so much. There is one enormous blister there now. I'm surprised it's come up so suddenly, but it does explain a lot. That toe is not going to feel at home in a hiking boot, and it's going to make its feelings known.

In the past, I've occasionally had blisters, but they've never been much of a problem. I usually live with them for a day or so, and if they persist I puncture them with a sterilised needle. It may not be what a doctor would recommend, but it works for me. However, right now that isn't an option, so we bandage it carefully, putting on some of Elaine's cream, then wrapping it in tissue held on with adhesive tape.

We move off. Achingly slowly. It isn't just me who's feeling uncomfortable. Elaine's back twinge has improved a bit, but she continues to be bothered by a constant tapping from her backpack. Yesterday's strap-tightening fix isn't working today, and we end up carrying out a scientific process of trial and error as we go; take out the water bottle, walk a bit, no, it wasn't that, put the bottle back, tighten this, walk a bit, no, not that either. It takes my mind off my foot, as we slog onwards, left foot, right foot, ouch, left foot, right foot, ouch…

The area we're walking through has lots of small plots of land, maybe 50 metres square, nestled alongside houses modern, not so modern, and occasionally tumbledown. We pass a field with water pouring in from a pipe in the corner. It looks as if irrigation here is a serious matter.

It's two kilometres to temple 16, Kannon-ji, and it takes us about forty minutes. At first the temple looks quiet and unassuming, just off a street and with a fairly small, pebbled courtyard. But then it grows on us, possibly because a number of other Henro arrive, including a Japanese couple with two young kids, both in junior Henro outfits, and we watch them lining up and bowing in front of the rather small main hall. Above them is a white cloth with the reversed swastika that always makes me feel uncomfortable, but which in Japan is merely an ancient symbol for a temple.

We chat to a lady from Hilversum, in Holland, who seems to be walking this stretch of the Henro path in reverse. She's off to temple 15 next, and says she's going to meet up there with people she left at temple 11 rather than tackle the 'Henro fall down' section between 11 and 12. She explains about her dodgy back, so you can't blame her for skipping that section; still, it reminds us of how hard it was, and we do feel a little chuffed that we managed it.

Of course, we might be in better shape if we too had skipped that section. Or if I'd known more about basic toe maintenance. We struggle onwards. We stop, gratefully, at a FamilyMart for coffee and confectionary (a carefully chosen word, as we aren't sure what we've bought, but they turn out to be custard-filled buns). The FamilyMarts are another chain of convenience stores, and they generally have a small corner where you can sit down and drink your coffee.

Elaine tries the ATM in the corner, resigned to it not working for her, but it does! That at least is a good sign. We don't know how long her card will stay fixed, but right now, she has access to money, and in a Japan's cash-based society, that matters.

This FamilyMart has two groups outside, and they may or may not be connected. One consists of people in green uniforms trying to interest anyone coming in or out in what could be credit cards; a leaflet says 'FamilyMart T-points' in the interesting way Japanese advertising often comes with a few words of English. They aren't having much success.

The other group is much more eye-catching. In a corner of the parking area outside the FamilyMart, a small group of children are sitting down on folded tarpaulins watching a carefully choreographed battle between the forces of what I assume are good and evil. The two doing most of the fighting are either supposed to be in armour or supposed to be robots. It's hard to tell. They have helmets that cover their heads, and coloured panels, red in one case, gold in the other, in various strategic places. They clash from time to time like characters in an anime movie - which I imagine they are - while a disparate set of four other characters in brightly coloured jump suits strike a variety of dramatic poses in the background and occasionally wander in closer to the main action. A cameraman is rather idly filming all this, and I see a girl apparently working as some sort of compere come up to the red character during a pause in the action to discuss something or other.

On the window of the FamilyMart we notice a poster. It has a picture of the red character, a lot of Kanji with exclamation marks, and the single English phrase: "Child Care Person Hero Break". We aren't much wiser.

Now we need to carry on to temple 17, Ido-ji.

Checking out in the morning.

Henro doll at temple 14, Jōraku-ji.

Rice fields between temples 14 and 15.

Young Henro at temple 16, Kannon-ji.

Good and evil face off in the Family Mart car park.

With our FamilyMart break, and somewhat slowed pace, it takes us about an hour and a half to cover the three kilometres between temples 16 and 17. This is an area of spread-out houses, with fields in between, looking rather like large vegetable gardens, but there's no sign of irrigation. In one more densely clustered area we pause by an imposingly tall sign, with four large green kanji and something below them that we think indicates a range of times. We wonder if something important happens here, but since we have no idea what, we take a photo for Tomoe-san and carry on. (Back in Sydney, she will tell us it's a dentist's sign, and those are the surgery hours. Which is a bit disappointing.)

Ido-ji, when we finally get there, is a larger temple with open grounds, carp in a pool, and, unusually, a car parked outside one of the temple buildings, something that feels a bit out of place. A large group of Henro are going around, and by the time we leave they're sitting down by the washing place tucking into their packed lunches.

Remembering the forecast for rain later in the afternoon, we move on as quickly as we can. It's another three and a half kilometres to Kuramoto, but this is the last lap. For this week, at least.

I notice that, as we move off, she does so much faster than I do. I just can't accelerate any more. Elaine clearly thinks this is something I'll recover from quickly.

"Most people," she says encouragingly, "don't seem to have foot problems by the second week." She's been reading the postings on the O-Henro Facebook page.

"It's natural selection. People who still have bad feet in the second week give up". It's hard to accept encouragement when you have sore feet.

Finally - finally! - the buildings get closer together, the fields disappear, the roads get busier, and we're in Kuramoto, only a couple of streets from Taishō-rō, the ryokan Elaine has booked us into.

"We're back in civilisation! There are lines of shops. I can see a coffee shop."

"I can see an Italian restaurant. It's shut, but it's a very good sign."

Interestingly, most of the villages we've passed through recently have had no sign of any sort of coffee shop, café, or anything similar, but every one has had a beauty parlour. I'm sure this tells us something about Japanese culture; Japan provides endless scope for speculation about such trivia, especially when all you're doing is walking and trying to take your mind off your feet.

Still, Kuramoto looks like a good place to have reached. We turn down a side street, and there is the entrance to Taishō-rō. Now this *is* a traditional, elegant, old-fashioned ryokan. Apparently, it's 110 years old, all tasteful polished wood inside, restrained lighting, and the usual line of house slippers on a raised floor as you go in.

A helpful chap with more than acceptable English meets us and lets us check in, although we've arrived rather early. He leads us down a charmingly elegant passage, neat and almost modern but with a traditional feel that's helped by the light coming in through paper-lined glass panes all down one side, down another passage decorated with fairly minimalist ornaments, and to our room.

We have an extremely pleasant room, large enough that the two sizeable futons take up only a fraction of the space. We unpack and have a look at our home for the next two nights. Elaine has done us splendidly. The room has a window out onto a small garden, and on the wide window ledge, next to a phone, is a splendidly ornate clock in a glass dome with its mechanisms shining in the sunlight. What's more, the room looks as if it caters to people who feel the cold, and that's me. The futons have electric blankets, and the small low table at one end of the room has something I'd not seen before. It's low and covered in what looks like a thick duvet, draped over it and hanging down over all four sides.

"It's a kotatsu," she says, "it's got an electric heater underneath it, you sit with your feet under it and they get all toasty warm."

"*That* is my kind of table."

Glorious. I trace the wires to see where it plugs in, switch it on, sit down by the table and push my feet underneath. It doesn't take long for them to reach the advertised toasty warmness. They still hurt, but warm and hurting is much better than cold and hurting. I want a kotatsu for home, to go with the Japanese techno-toilet. I feel it may be a fire hazard (I see what may be burn marks by the plug), but that is a chance I'm prepared to take.

"That's lovely," I say with feeling. "The only downside is that you have to sit on the floor with your legs under it, and my body still doesn't really bend readily into that sort of shape. I think you have to be born Japanese to sit like this."

Time to get a light lunch. We head out and see what Kuramoto can offer us in the way of coffee shops and the like. We find a nice modern little place that serves us tea with ham, cheese, and tomato sandwiches. There's no English menu, but the waitress knows the English words for the various sandwich options. There are two locals sitting chatting a couple of tables away, one smoking, friends passing a nice relaxed Saturday afternoon. It's quiet, pleasant, and relaxing.

We discuss our options, based on a number of indisputable facts:

1) We've already done 17 temples out of 88, and that's not bad.

2) It's really nice here.

3) Elaine's back is continuing to twinge uncomfortably, especially with her backpack, and I'm hobbling around slowly on my blistered foot.

4) The next leg, to temple 18, heading south, away from Tokushima, is a long one (nearly 19 kilometres) and from 18 to 19 is another 4 kilometres, although both walks are flat. We had assumed we could do that walk as far as 19 on Monday, and already have a (non-refundable) booking near temple 19 for Monday.

Can we make that 23km walk on Monday? Clearly, not as we stand - or sit - right now.

But, tomorrow is a rest day. We'd always intended to stay here in Kuramoto for two nights, making the Sunday tomorrow a break from walking. Over Sunday, Elaine's back may recover, and I reckon if I pierce my blister, which I plan to do tomorrow if it hasn't gone down, my past experience is that I'll feel much better. So it's wait and see, really.

"Of course," adds Elaine, "some Henro base themselves in Tokushima and come back there after each stage they walk. So long as you start walking where you left off the day before, that's fine."

"Which is what Tomiko was doing this morning, getting a lift back to the temple she was picked up from yesterday."

"It's an option," says Elaine, "just in case we still aren't up to it on Monday. Mostly it means we don't have to carry the backpacks."

I feel that if this had been suggested a week ago, I might have used words not unrelated to 'cheating'. But now, I can see it's no more than a common-sense solution to a problem. And, of course, there's one more point:

5) This is meant to be a holiday, not an ordeal.

We agree we'll review our position after our day of rest.

At the entrance to temple 17, Ido-ji.

Henro at temple 17, Ido-ji.

Our large and comfortable room in Kuramoto, with the kotatsu in the foreground.

Back at the ryokan, we confirm that they do breakfast in the morning, but not an evening meal. We ought to get an early dinner, and then an early night. We've been given a map that shows a few local recommended restaurants, but we decide we'll head into central Tokushima instead. We'll be wanting to go into the centre tomorrow, so this will get us familiar with the local trains, and there's probably a bit more dining choice in the centre.

Kuramoto has a suburban rail station on a line that connects to central Tokushima, and after a bit of a struggle with the posted timetable, it looks as if there's a 'limited' express going to Tokushima at 5:39 from, well, *a* platform. What's less clear is which platform. The station's layout will turn out to be a common one in Shikoku. There's only one line, but there are two platforms, and the line splits into two for the length of the platforms, which allows trains going in opposite directions to arrive at the same time but at different platforms, and then carry on. The station is both a station and the only passing place, which must make for interesting scheduling problems. Indeed, there is a train leaving in the opposite direction, also at 5:39, which makes sense, but makes it even harder to be sure you're on the right train.

We try to ask a local about platforms, pointing at the timetable and outside to the two platforms we can see. The reply comes gushing in a flow of Japanese that leaves us bewildered, but he does appear to be pointing to platform 2. We buy our tickets - you can work out the price from a diagram on the wall, and it looks like ¥320 each. There's a ticket machine that takes money from you and flashes up the possible tickets this will let you buy, so that's easy enough. We're starting to feel we understand how this works. We head for platform 2.

Two trains pull up, one on each platform, coming from different directions. Ours seems to be 30 seconds late - Shikoku isn't mainland Japan, after all - but we get on and make ourselves comfortable. Both trains pull out at the same time. It's neat. A conductor checks our tickets, which turns out to be a mixture of good news and bad news. We're going the right way, which is good. On the flip side, we've not paid the supplement for the 'limited' and have to hand over another ¥210 each. But he's nice about it.

We get out and find ourselves, as we'd expected, in the familiar surroundings of Tokushima station, with the JR Clement, Hotel of pleasant memory, just next door.

Both of us fancy eating Italian. We both enjoy Japanese food, but it can be something of a salt overdose, and we'd appreciate a change. The internet recommends a place - Fontana - near the station, and we manage to find it without too much trouble, on a street with a number of other restaurants of varying genres. In we go, and it looks completely empty, but the chap at the desk says, in clear English, "full". Well, it's a Saturday evening, maybe they've got a big booking. We won't take it personally, but it is a pity.

A bit further down the road there's somewhere with an Italian flag outside, and we have a look inside. It seems to be a small wine bar, but there is a mention of 'pizza' on a sign by the door. We'd really been thinking more of pasta than pizza. There was an Italian place upstairs in the station building, and we go back to have a look at it. It isn't far to the station, and we find the Italian there, up on the second floor, but it's almost empty and looks cheap but uninspiring - somewhere for something quick at lunchtime, not an evening meal. We head back to the wine bar. Without the backpack, I'm not walking too badly, but we're now in heavy drizzle, and the wine bar is a welcome sight.

We enjoy the Uoroman wine bar. It's small, and only has a couple of proper tables, both occupied, but they find us a space at the bar counter. We look in some dismay at the completely Japanese menu, but the waitress finds us a couple of English menus, or at least menus with English translations below the Japanese text. We order two pizzas, a seafood one (the 'Uoroman special', described in the menu as a 'seafood parade') and a Margherita.

Words I had made a point of remembering were the Japanese for 'wine', 'red' (for me) and 'white' (Elaine).

"Winu, kudasai. Aka, ichi, shiro, ichi." Wine please, red, one, white, one. Not many marks for grammar, but I thought that spelled out what we wanted.

Not in a wine bar, it doesn't.

She shows me the full wine menu. Which has not a single word of English anywhere. Tomoe-san had told us to ask what they recommended, and I'm trying to remember the right words.

"Susu.... Recommend..." The correct phrase is "o-susume-wa, nan desu-ka?" but she gets the idea. She points to some options, and gets across that this one is Japanese, this one is Chilean, this one Italian. I get the Italian red, Elaine a Chilean white. She leaves the wine menu on the counter, and after a bit of work with the katakana script I work out that the one I'm drinking is Chianti. Now, if only I could do that in a second or two instead of a couple of minutes, I could order wine fluently.

The pizzas are excellent, thin and authentic, and the atmosphere is warm and cosy.

Finally, we hobble out into the street, back to the station and on to Kuramoto and the comfort of our room. This traditional, elegant, ryokan with its toasty-warm kotatsu will do nicely as a place to recover from our first week of walking.

14

RECOVERING IN KURAMOTO (SUNDAY APRIL 15)

I wake in our comfortable room, lying on my futon, wrapped cosily in my duvet, wondering what condition I'm in, and how fit I'll be feeling tomorrow. Will we be able to do that long walk to temple 19, or will we have to rethink our plans? For today I have in mind just one short test walk, and it's connected with my broken camera lens.

Back almost a week ago, in Tokushima, the lady in the not-actually-a-camera-shop-as-far-as-I-could-tell had told me I could probably get another lens at Yamada Denki. Since then, I've looked them up; 'denki' just means 'electronics' and 'Yamada Denki' appears to be a sort of high-tech superstore, and it's within walking distance of where we are in Kuramoto. Well, it would have been an easy walk a week ago; today it may be more of a test, and that's what I have in mind. Taking aim at two birds (getting a replacement lens, seeing how well I'm walking) with one stone. According to Google, Patron Saint of navigators, it's a 43-minute walk away, or 20 minutes' walk from Sako, which is the intermediate station between Kuramoto and Tokushima itself.

As we get up, I have a look at my bandaged right small toe. My plan is to borrow a needle from Elaine's sewing kit, boil some water in the tea maker in the corridor outside our room, use that to sterilise the needle, and puncture the blister. Nothing complicated (although I've carefully not explained the details to Elaine), and it's what I usually do with blisters that won't fade away of their own free will.

That isn't what happens here.

I have a look at the toe. Still one huge blister, under the bandage. As I unwrap the tissue that's been protecting the toe under the tape, the blister bursts, splattering in an explosion of slightly bloody liquid, which forms an unsightly puddle on the sheet covering the futon, and slowly starts to seep in.

"My blister has just burst spectacularly."

"You haven't got it all over the tatami mat, have you?" Such concern for my well-being.

"No, but there's now an embarrassing looking wet patch on the sheet over the futon."

Now that she knows we've not committed the unforgivable act of staining a tatami mat, Elaine sympathetically helps apply ointment and a fresh bandage to my rather unhappy-looking toe. On the plus side, it now feels rather more comfortable, although it's still awkwardly tender. We'll see how it handles a walk to Yamada Denki.

But first, to breakfast. Which is upstairs, which means negotiating not just the corridors but an awkwardly steep staircase in house slippers. Which are well-named devices that slip off at every opportunity, particularly when you lift your feet as you climb stairs.

"Do you suppose Japanese burglars have to change into house slippers before they burgle anywhere?" I'm speculating here.

"Japan doesn't have burglars. It doesn't have that sort of crime."

"I reckon it's because of the slippers. That's why Ninja go up the outside of houses. So they don't need to go up stairs in slippers."

There's a large upstairs room with a TV showing breakfast programs that that are the same as breakfast TV the world over, but we go past it through to a smaller room with a table laid out for two. The same chap who met us yesterday is there, and he lays out the usual breakfast fare, small dishes with a lot of pickled things, rice, eggs, and mackerel.

On the table is a helpful note listing all the items, in English, although you have to guess which one is which. He shows us how to manage the sheets of nori - seaweed - that often accompany breakfast, and which up until now we've tended to ignore, or just flake into the rice. He shows us how to dip them lightly in soy sauce, which softens them just enough that you can wrap rice in them. That's useful, and we try it. The breakfast is a delight, and the mackerel is excellent although, with its bones, it's another of those dishes that I find a challenge with chopsticks.

Electronics superstores and camera shopping aren't Elaine's idea of a fun morning, but she says she'll come along to see how well we manage the walk. Taking the train to Sako and walking from there would be an option, but we'll try for the long, 43-minute walk all the way. Elaine's back is still playing up, and my toe is still sore against the boots, although not as much as it was by the end of yesterday. There's a long main road that leads from Kuramoto to Sako, and we manage that reasonably well, but it really helps not to have the backpacks. At Sako station, Elaine pauses.

"I think I might give you a clear run from here to your camera shop."

I don't blame her. Even I don't really care for electronics superstores, and I'm aware that a long discussion about the relative merits of different camera lenses is going to test her technology-I'm-not-really-very-interested-in tolerance level. So, she'll head back to Kuramoto, and I'll carry on.

Google directs me down a long wide open street, bending away a little from the centre of Tokushima, full of large warehouse-type buildings with large parking lots in front of them and neon signs that I can't read. An electronics superstore would fit in nicely here. I'm reminded a little of Speedway, in Tucson, which sticks in my mind because the caption for a photo of it in my copy of Alastair Cooke's 'America' said that Tucson's mayor considered it the ugliest street in the world. Which I think is harsh on Speedway, and this street here is in fact fairly unremarkable - and doesn't have Speedway's used car yards - but they do both have that large-scale billboard-heavy feel.

As I'd hoped it might, Yamada has its name written clearly in

Western characters on the side of the building: three storeys full of brightly lit displays of almost anything that you can plug into the mains or slip a battery into. It isn't a camera specialist, as I'd worked out by now, and the camera section up on the third floor is a bit limited, but I do find one lens on display that will do as a replacement for the one I've broken. It's not ideal; mine was a compact, light, lens that worked well for travel, while this is a larger, higher quality more professional one that will do the same job rather better, but which is noticeably heavier, not to mention more expensive. But taking photos of new places is one of the things I travel for, so I don't have much choice. I'm happy that I've found something that will do the job.

I beckon over a helpful someone in a blue Yamada top. At least I don't need a lot of Japanese. It's the same as pointing at a photo of food at a restaurant. "Kore-wa, kudasai", this, please, and he nods.

He doesn't have a lot of English, but he knows some of the essential words for his line of work.

"Warranty, one year, only Japan." Then he says, "price" and writes it down, and "tax" and writes another number. I suspect trying to get out of the tax is a lost cause, but I try anyway:

"Australia-jin desu. Tax?" He doesn't look hopeful. He goes away and comes back with the box for the lens, and says, regretfully, "Tax, yes." I can't say I'm disappointed. By Australian standards it's a reasonably good price anyway. As he packs everything up, I get across that I had a lens, but 'jiko' - accident - 'burōkun'. He sympathises, and takes me to the checkout, which is happy to accept my credit card.

I've found that managing even a simple transaction in Japan gives me a pleasing sense of accomplishment, although in all honesty all I did was point at something on a shelf and hold out a credit card.

It feels a long walk back, retracing my steps most of the way, although I reject the main road in favour of some slightly more interesting side streets. As I go, however, I realise that although my rightmost toe is still uncomfortable, it isn't as bad as the odd pulling feeling I'm now getting from somewhere around my left buttock. Not as low as sciatica, not as high as back pain, but possibly kin to both. I suspect I've been walking asymmetrically, favouring my left foot, and this has now turned up as a result. By the time I get back to the ryokan, I'm seriously grateful to be able to stop walking.

Elaine is pleased I've sorted out my camera problem, and while I've been away she's been sitting with her twinging back and has been thinking about our various options.

"I have a proposal for what we do next," she says.

"Yes." I say, in full agreement.

"You haven't heard it!"

"No, but I'm in favour. I can guess what it is, more or less."

Actually, all I've guessed is that it doesn't involve trying to walk 23 kilometres to temple 19 tomorrow, and I know I'm in favour of that. As she explains the details, I'm even more in favour.

"It's this. We base ourselves here in Tokushima for the next few days. We'll go back to the JR Clement, which is close to the station, we'll have our own bath and a Western chair you can sit comfortably on."

I'm embarrassed by that, but she's right, a chair that suits my body would be a big plus. I'm OK with Japanese baths by now, although it would be nice to control the temperature myself, but I still struggle to sit comfortably on a tatami mat or one of the low, legless seats they have here.

"Then," she continues, "we can do the next few stages of the pilgrimage from our Tokushima base, including the next 'Henro fall down' section between 20 and 21. And we should take tomorrow off. A bit more recovery time, we'll have to move hotel anyway, and we can have a proper look at Tokushima."

There is absolutely nothing not to like about this plan. I hadn't realised there was another 'Henro fall down' section still to come, because I tend not to read ahead even in guide books, but that makes doing it this way sound even better. We'll have a base camp in the JR Clement, next to the buses and trains, we can do a day's walk - without backpacks! - get a train or bus back to base camp, and the next day we return to where we left off and continue walking. This is just what Elaine had described yesterday.

"That really isn't cheating, is it?"

"No," she says. "I'm sure Kōbō Daishi doesn't expect Henro to suffer unnecessarily on the pilgrimage. And it's only for a few days, as we get back into shape."

So that's settled, then.

We have lunch in the same Kuramoto cafe as yesterday, just down the road. This time, we're looking for something more substantial than sandwiches, but we end up staring at the lunch menu in some puzzlement. Everything is described in katakana, the characters used for imported words like 'spaghetti'. I used to be able to decipher these, very slowly, but I'm clearly out of practice. The fellow in charge comes over and rattles through the whole menu in great detail, all of which goes over our heads. The 'omelette' I order turns out to be a rice omelette, which is tasty but large and filling and way more than I need, while Elaine gets 'Italian spaghetti' with a tomato and mushroom sauce. The star turn, however, is the orange juice, served up with slices of real orange on the rim of each glass.

A fairly gentle lunch, then, that sets us up for a gentle afternoon, spent mostly in the cosy room, letting our various aches fade a little. I manage to get my diary up to date. I notice that even in a diary my writing style has always had something of a tendency to verge somewhat towards the verbose, with sentences that run unnecessarily on and on. If I ever write a book, I should probably try to get that under some sort of control…

I become increasingly fond of the Kotatsu, never entirely comfortable sitting with my legs stretched out under it, but putting up with that for that feeling of toasty warmness.

The ryokan has rather elegant corridors.

Walking along, looking for an electronics superstore.

So many overhead wires...

"Are you OK with eating locally tonight?", asks Elaine. "We've got the map we didn't use last night with the local restaurants. We could try one of those."

We're going to be moving to the centre of Tokushima tomorrow - Elaine and the internet have now booked us in to the JR Clement - so tonight it makes sense to see what Kuramoto has to offer.

Zenya is one of the local restaurants we were recommended, although we can't remember anything we were told about it. We find it easily enough and walk past, trying to see what sort of place it is, what it might serve.

"Does it have chairs?" Never mind the food, I don't think I can do cross-legged on the floor, not today. Elaine peers in.

"Yes, I can see stools at the bar."

"Fine by me."

They seem pleased to see us. We're led, not to the bar, but to a small room with an ominously low table.

"You're OK, it's one of those fake low tables with a pit underneath for your legs."

Those seating arrangements are fine, and we manage to order wine, one red, one white, as usual. Then the waitress hands us the menu, points to a bell on the table, and leaves. Most menus we've had up until now have had a smattering of English, or pictures, or something we can work with. I think this is the first menu we've seen that is entirely incomprehensible. It looks to be all hand-written, mostly in small and intricate kanji. The two English words, "Menu" in the middle, and, helpfully, "Sweets" in one corner, look completely out of place. I look desperately for a word written in kana, something I just might be able to look up, but most of what I see is kanji and you just have to know those and I don't.

Then, as we're struggling, the waitress comes back with the wine, and a high-tech food ordering device. It's an iPad-type tablet, that displays the menu, all in Japanese, but with photos you can scroll through and presumably you can click on them. We've not seen one of these before, but it looks like something we can work with. It might take a while, though.

"Chotto matte, kudasai." I learned this several trips back. 'A bit longer, please." She leaves us with our new toy.

Even with the photos, it isn't always clear what's on the menu, and what really isn't clear is the size of each portion. Are these small dishes we order a lot of, or is one a meal in itself? The price is a bit of a guide, but haven't got this place calibrated as far as value for money goes. Tentatively, we select some tempura and some fried fish.

"If they turn out to be small, we can always order more. What do we do now?"

"I suppose we press the bell."

We press the bell, and two lads dressed in black appear, ninja-like, out of the darkness. One looks at the tablet, scrolls through to see what we've picked, and clicks on what we suppose anyone else would have known was the 'order this now' button. Then this dynamic duo leap back to where they came from.

A short delay, and the food arrives. It's a decent size, two tempura prawns with vegetables, and calamari fried in onion and what is probably butter, and it all tastes glorious. We realise we didn't order any rice, and press the button again.

Enter one lad in black, stage right.

"Gohan, chiisai, kudasai", we manage to ask. He takes the tablet, gives it a quick professional swish over to the rice menu, selects something, and presses the 'order' menu. He smiles as if we ought to have known that, but he's happy to show us, and vanishes again. A few minutes later, the rice appears.

All in all, an excellent meal, considerably enlivened by the ordering experience. We head back to the ryokan, the bath, the now traditional taping of the slowly improving small right toe, and bed.

And tomorrow will be another quiet day.

The menu makes few concessions to those that don't read Japanese...

...but the tablet helps a little.

15

A QUIET DAY IN TOKUSHIMA (MONDAY APRIL 16)

This will be another easy day, setting ourselves up to head back onto the Henro trail tomorrow. We're sorry to be leaving this wonderfully pleasant Ryokan, and indeed, Kuramoto itself, which provided a haven just when we needed one. I never thought it would seem important, and I feel guilty about this, but I'm looking forward to being back in a room with a chair with legs I can sit on. Even if only for a few days. A room with our own bath and toilet, where we don't need to be constantly changing into house slippers, doesn't sound too bad either.

What we're losing, I feel, is some authenticity. What we've had so far has been a pretty authentic Henro experience, walking the whole of the route unbroken, just as Kōbō Daishi would have done, staying in Japanese-style accommodation every night.

Of course, we only have to look at a statue of Kōbō Daishi, and there's one at every temple, to realise there are levels of authenticity. Each statue shows him wearing fairly basic robes, a small bag around his neck, a staff in one hand and prayer beads in the other. At first glance, his feet look bare, but a second look shows he's wearing thin sandals that cover only the soles of his feet; his toes are open to the elements.

I, on the other hand, am carrying a modern framed backpack that distributes the weight properly between my hips and my shoulders, I have waterproof hiking boots with substantial uppers that support my ankles to stop me twisting them, I have hiking clothes that dry fairly quickly and thin rainproof outer clothing made of modern materials. I'm carrying a staff in one hand and a digital camera in the other, and for navigation we have mobile phones with GPS receivers that work by measuring the relative velocities of satellites orbiting the earth. Put like that, staying in a room with a chair so I don't have to sit on the floor is hardly adding a substantial amount of inauthenticity.

None of the statues seem to show blisters on his feet. But maybe that's artistic licence.

We pack, have breakfast, and set off.

"Now, of course," says Elaine, "the Henro route goes more or less through central Tokushima, so we'll be following it at first. But we walked the part from Kuramoto to Sako yesterday, so we can take the train to Sako, and then we're picking up the trail where we left off yesterday, and all we have to do is walk Sako to Tokushima."

She's getting no argument from me.

It's only a short walk to Kuramoto station, but with full backpacks it shows we're not back to full strength yet. Definitely not. We get tickets to Sako, get off there, and walk the remaining kilometre or so along the Henro path to the point where we have to turn left to get to the centre of the city.

"And this is the place we come back to tomorrow to pick up the Henro path again. Now for the JR Clement!"

Just walking this little stretch has convinced us we're doing the right thing, and authenticity be blowed. I'm clearly limping, and Elaine's back is not getting along well with her backpack. It's a relief to walk in through the doors of the JR Clement and arrange to leave our packs there until we can check in properly.

. . .

When I'm somewhere new, I like to get to somewhere high up, somewhere I can look out and see as far as possible. As it happens, the obvious place to do that in Tokushima, Mount Bizan, is close to the centre, and is also high on most lists of things to see in Tokushima. We can manage the walk over to its base, and to get to the top there's a 'ropeway' which turns out to be what *I* call a cable car (as in something that swings from a cable and takes you up a mountain, something I don't really feel comfortable in, but will happily tolerate today).

As we head away from the JR Clement, we pass a small shop that has a long queue outside it. Curious, we come closer. The shop has a machine in the window that fills a moving line of containers with some sort of dough mixture, then adds some sort of filling, then cooks them in some way. Then the staff put them in boxes and sell them to the queue of people. It isn't clear what these delights are, but they're obviously popular on a Sunday morning in Tokushima.

"We should try those, sometime."

The cable cars going up Mount Bizan take about eight people each, and have a curious arrangement where they go up in pairs, one pair leaving every fifteen minutes or so. That's not a lot of people an hour, but there don't appear to be many people wanting to go up, which seems a shame, because it's a beautiful sunny day and Mount Bizan provides a scene-setting panorama of Tokushima, looking right over the city and the river running through it, over to the port and the Inland Sea.

Mount Bizan also provides a view - in the opposite direction - of those rolling hills of East Shikoku, lots of flowers and cherry blossom, warning signs about snakes and wild boar, a lot of radio masts, and a coffee shop that isn't open.

We spend a while walking around, taking photos of ourselves with Tokushima in the background, not seeing any snakes or wild boar, and finally take the cable car back down.

As we get closer to the JR Clement, we start looking for somewhere for lunch, and spot a small place calling itself 'Fontana Deli'. Given the large outline of Italy painted on its windows, we can at least guess what sort of food this has, and we go in.

Communication turns out to be easy, mainly because as soon as the Japanese staff realise the extent to which we don't speak Japanese they call for the owner, who turns out to be an Italian who speaks fluent English. He tells us he comes from around Florence, married a Japanese girl, and is now running this place in Tokushima. And Fontana Deli provides a lovely light lunch for us; it's a change to have a serious salad, with a bit of lasagne and some other pasta. And a glass of wine, of course.

Once we've checked in at the Clement, we collapse into our small but familiar room, and I try out the chair and the bath, both of which perform as expected. We both feel tired, which may possibly be connected with having caught the sun a little on the top of Mount Bizan, and I manage to fall asleep in the bath - not that that's dangerous; in this bath, you couldn't contort your body to get your head under water no matter how hard you tried.

This is all satisfyingly recuperative, but by evening we need supper, so we have another try at the Italian place a couple of streets away that had been full on Saturday evening. Lunch seems to have triggered a taste for Italian food. This time it's as empty as before, but apparently not booked out, and we're sitting in our little booth wondering if it's a coincidence that both this restaurant and lunchtime's little snack bar were both called 'Fontana', when in comes the snack bar owner himself, who evidently runs both. Tokushima really is something of a small town. And that solves this evening's language problem. Not that it was a big problem; there's an English menu and an English drinks menu - although, for some reason, not an English wine menu.

Elaine has a penne arrabbiata (described as 'hot tomato sauce' on the English menu) which is excellent - startlingly chilli-hot at first bite, but cooked so the heat doesn't overwhelm the sauce. I wish I could cook like that. And my pizza capricciosa is almost as good.

The corridor leading to our room in Kuramoto.

Passers-by looking at the shop's production line.

The Mount Bizan cable cars.

On the way up Mount Bizan.

Blossom at the top of Mount Bizan.

It seems there are wild boar on Mount Bizan. We didn't see any.

View of Tokushima from Mount Bizan.

Well-fed, and fairly well-rested, we head back to the hotel. We'll see what condition we'll be in in the morning. Will we make it to temple 19? Will we make it anywhere?

16

BACK ON THE ROAD - TEMPLES 18 & 19 (TUESDAY APRIL 17)

Come the morning, we take stock. Elaine's back is still twinging, but only slightly, and while I can still feel the ache in my right small toe (it had been less of a problem last night, when I wore the light loafers I packed as spares instead of the hiking boots) I can convince myself it's improved a bit. We bandage both small toes, lightly, with the less bulky Band-Aids instead of tissue & tape.

"How are the feet feeling now?"

"Not perfect, but I think we can get somewhere. After all, we'll be travelling fairly light."

"OK. We'll see how far we get."

The breakfast buffet is crowded, and today, unlike last week when everyone seemed to be local, there seem to be a lot of Europeans all milling around. I hear someone ask "where is bread?", and the container labelled 'croissants' is empty. We have a decent breakfast, although I go for a selection that's light on pickled items; I feel I've had a lot of salt recently.

We prepare for the day's walk, aiming to travel as lightly as possible. I have my camera bag, and the white messenger bag loaded with a few snacks and a serious amount of tape and Band-Aids, along with the name slips and our stamp book. There's a possibility of rain, so we need our rain jackets - Elaine's will squeeze into the messenger bag; mine won't, but it rolls into its small pack and clips onto my camera bag where it dangles there like a spare sporran. Then we collect the staffs, put on the white vests and the conical hats, and feel as if we're Henro again for the first time in a few days. Ready for the open road.

In the hotel lobby a large fellow, who turns out to be German, comes over to us and asks about the Henro trail. It seems he's planning to walk it. He's done the Santiago de Compostela pilgrimage, so he should be fit enough, but his entire preparation appears to consist of simply having arrived in Tokushima. We show him the White Book, which he'd not seen before, tell him the trail starts at Bando and he can get there by train, and suggest he talk to the tourist information office next door about bookings and all the other many things he's going to need to know.

He looks at us, and notices how little we're carrying.

"You are walking the Henro, and you have just this small bag? No rucksack?"

That involves a little more explanation, which we hadn't really intended to go into.

Finally, we hit the road.

The overall plan is quite neat and quite flexible. The first seventeen temples lie on a loop that heads out west from Tokushima and then comes back, and we've done that. From here, the Henro path heads south, just a little bit in from the coast, taking in temples 18 and 19, before heading west a little to 20, 21 and 22, and then works its way south-east, meeting the coast again a little past temple 23. From there it follows the coast south until it reaches the southernmost point of this side of the island, at Cape Muroto. It then follows the coast all around the rest of the island, but we're not thinking that far ahead.

For today, all that matters is that the railway line heads south from Tokushima, keeping close to the coast. This means that for most of the way to 19, the Henro route stays reasonably close to the railway line. This means that Henro with questionable feet and backs and a room waiting for them back in Tokushima, could, should they wish, bail out at a number of points along the way and take a train back to room 1506 at their comfortable base camp. Tokushima to temple 18 is about eleven kilometres, and it's another four or so to temple 19.

"I think, under the circumstances," I say, "doing ten kilometres or so would be very good going, and frankly, anything over five would be fine."

"And tomorrow, we go back to wherever we left off today."

It's not a detailed plan, but it has a lot of contingency in it. We like it.

We head back to precisely where we last left the Henro trail, on the way from Sako. We're determined to have walked the whole distance, even if not in one continuous, foot-destroying epic march. It's just like Tomiko getting a lift from temple 14 to the ryokan and back to 14 the next morning. Well, it's a little like that.

The route takes us along suburban streets and out of central Tokushima. We stop to watch a bright orange mechanical digger, implausibly perched on the third storey of a building being demolished, apparently in the process of slowly digging away the floor it's standing on. We're not at all sure how this trick proceeds. As we watch, a medium-sized crane drives up and tries to install itself in the alleyway by the side of the building - this is tricky, because the alleyway is already occupied by a lorry collecting the concrete being ripped out of the building. The crane inches back and forth, trying to get off the footpath, and puts out its stabilisers for no obvious reason, as it doesn't lower them - maybe it's using them as feelers to check width of the gap - and inches forward. The concrete lorry shudders, as you might if banged into by a seriously substantial crane. This is fascinating, but it looks as if it will go on for a while, and we have temples to reach.

The route winds out of suburban Tokushima, taking us past a small Shinto temple, and finally out onto a main road that just goes on and on and on - a four-lane divided highway, sparsely but continuously populated with the sort of sales outlets that need space - car yards, big equipment, Hi-Fi and computer warehouses. A number of these seem to deal in mechanical diggers; perhaps ones that demolish the buildings beneath them tend to need replacing fairly often. There are paddy fields on either side in the gaps between buildings. Apart from the paddy fields and Japanese signs, this part of Tokushima reminds me a little of suburban Los Angeles.

One yard seems to be a mega-supplier for temples. On display outside are all sorts of carved stone items, marbled seats, small Buddhas, even a skeleton dinosaur with a laughing Buddha next to it, and a pair of Kongō-rikeishi (figures that guard temple gates, Un-gyō on the left, A-gyō on the right) in brightly painted colours and incongruous pink skirts. Now that might have looked out of place in LA. And it takes a lot to look out of place in LA.

We stop by a ramen shop to look at a set of concrete constructions that appear to be the supports for a planned-but-unbuilt elevated roadway. And not far from them, there's an incomplete concrete bridge that doesn't exactly line up with those unused supports. The combination gives the impression of a project that's been started a couple of times but never completed. As we stand there, a chap on a small motor bike stops and silently gives us two packs of raisin bread and two containers of what we eventually decide must be soup. This giving of gifts really is a wonderful and often surprising custom.

A little further on we're stopped by a smartly dressed man, walking in the other direction, who asks where we're from and then reaches under his jacket to give us something. This gift turns out to be a Jehovah's Witness pamphlet, in English, which is also surprising, if not necessarily as wonderful. And why carry them in English?

We are doing OK. Surprisingly so. I can still feel my right foot - the little toe is sore, no question, but it's no longer actually making me limp. Elaine's back isn't right either, still twinging, but not slowing her down now that she's without her pack, and our legs are managing OK.

Digger in a precarious position, on the way out of Tokushima.

On the outskirts of Tokushima.

The temple goods emporium...

...and some of its offerings.

A well-furnished Henro hut.

We are doing better than others who've passed this way. We stop at a remarkably well-furnished Henro hut with a marble table that could have come from the temple emporium down the road. It also has seats, and a sign and photo showing it was set up by the local Rotary president, born on 31/3/1915, and with a recent sign dated, inconsistently, 2018/3/31 - his 103rd birthday! Sitting thankfully on the seats he provided, we hope he's still doing well. There's a visitors' book which makes interesting reading - Jack from New Zealand slept here, and there's 'Edwina from Lithuania': 'My foots are bleeding, limping for last 15km, but if I can make it so can you.' I'm wondering what Edwina would think about my sore toe and the way we've fallen back on the JR hotel in Tokushima.

Only a little further on, the Henro route parts company with the railway line, and heads off inland to temple 18. We have to decide whether to follow it, or to bail out at this point and head for the nearest station. If we go to 18, we're committed to doing the extra four kilometres to 19 as well, because the only sensible route to a station from 18 will take us past 19 anyway.

"So, we've made it this far. Do we go on to 18 and 19?"

"I don't think we could look Edwina from Lithuania in the eye if we quit now."

So, we turn off towards temple 18, Onzan-ji. We're now off along secondary roads, heading deeper into the country. We pass another nicely appointed Henro hut. It too has a visitors' book, and we flip through it to see if Edwina from Lithuania made it this far, but if she did she didn't write anything. Going from the entries, a significant number of people have slept the night here over the last year.

The road takes us through a small village, and at this point we're overtaken by a Henro striding along in full whites, who tells us he's from 'somewhere near Paris', before hastening off into the distance. We may not be moving at his speed, but we feel we're doing OK.

The Henro route heads towards the foothills, and we're now off the road entirely and walking along a woodland track. We're climbing up to temple 18, Onzan-ji. Not a steep climb, but we can definitely feel it in our legs, which had been hoping to avoid this sort of thing. We come out into a temple so deep in the woods that it almost seems to be overgrown by them. The buildings are arranged on a number of levels, and a discouragingly imposing flight of stone steps rises up to one of the main halls. All the temples on the Henro trail are old, but this feels it. The White Book says this has an interesting history; originally off-limits to women, until Kōbō Daishi's mother came to visit her son, who was training here. She was not allowed onto the grounds, so Kōbō Daishi performed an esoteric rite for 17 days, finally succeeding in getting the restriction lifted, so allowing her past the temple gate.

"Does it say what sort of esoteric rite it was?"

"No," answers Elaine. "I think they mean a rite of Esoteric Buddhism, not just any esoteric rite."

"Seventeen days, though. You'd think she'd get a bit fed up waiting."

"Imagine. 'Seventeen days, you've been at this rite. You'd think a mother could just visit her boy at his temple without all this...' Still, he did get her in, in the end."

We can see the Henro from 'somewhere near Paris' who passed us earlier. He's reciting the sutras outside the halls, and when we take our book in to be stamped, we see him unrolling the scroll he has for his stamps. We're impressed, mostly by the feeling that this is someone to whom the pilgrimage has real meaning, in a more profound way than it does to us. We are doing the walk, and we are Henro, but we're not Henro at that level.

Going down from temple 18 is hard on the toes, which slide to the end of the boot and take all the weight, but it doesn't take too long. The path crosses a small valley and starts to climb again, but now through completely different scenery. We're in a bamboo forest. Tall, bare, bamboo rises up on both sides of the path, and dead bamboo litter the ground. It all appears remarkably uncontrolled. Is this farmed in any way? It doesn't look like it. Occasionally there are signs of some attempts to control it, because some of the growth has been cut back, probably with a chainsaw, but mostly it's been left to decay, go brown, split and splinter. At least the path is wide enough and fairly clear.

We stop by a small shrine, with a few red-bibbed Jizō and bunches of fresh flowers arranged on a scattering of stones and concrete blocks, and the bamboo towering up above us.

Eventually we emerge from the bamboo. The track levels out and takes us past a number of groves of citrus trees - we can't see any fruit, so we're not sure what sort they are. We cross a red-railinged bridge over a river and into a village where we find temple 19, Tatsue-ji.

Tatsue-ji has a jolly feel, mostly because of all the brightly coloured flowers in the grounds. I thought they were roses, Elaine said they were camellias, and she's probably right. In any case, we've made it all the way, and we feel quite pleased.

As we walk the final kilometre or so to Tatsue station, the sky is ominously grey, but it hasn't rained yet. Tatsue station is the smallest station I've ever seen. What looks more like a bus shelter has a sign that says 'Tatsue stn'. There is a timetable mounted on a board, along with a list of fares to various destinations, all in kanji, but no ticket machine. Two machines outside only sell soft drinks. We go through the bus shelter and over the tracks and there's the platform with the single track splitting into two to pass either side. There are rice paddies on the other side of the track.

"I can't see anywhere to buy tickets," I say.

"Maybe they sell them on board."

A train - going the wrong way - arrives and a guard gets off, but stays on the platform after it leaves. We try to ask him if we get tickets on the train: "kippu - densha?". He nods. And indeed, when the train arrives, it has a conductor who sells us tickets.

What the train also has are half the schoolchildren in Tokushima province. We've obviously hit the end of the school day. Throughout the carriage there are uniformed boys and girls chatting and congregating as school kids do everywhere. The uniforms are very formal, mostly with ties, even for some of the girls. Some of the boys are in uniforms with a distinctly military-college look, with brass buttons all the way up the neck and a stand-up collar. It looks remarkably

Western, apart perhaps from the brass buttons and stand-up collars, which also look Western, but from a West that no longer exists.

Steps at Temple 18, Onzan-ji.

Henro at Temple 18, Onzan-ji.

Washing place with dragon spout, Onzan-ji.

Bamboo between temples 18 and 19.

Jizō among the bamboo.

Back in Tokushima and room 1506 at the JR Clement, our equivalent of a Henro hut for the night, we decide we've done well. Walking without backpacks certainly helps a lot. It's not yet clear that we're ready to resume the conventional approach of simply walking to somewhere to stay, staying there, and then walking on the next day. And pretty soon, perhaps even tomorrow, we're going to have to tackle the 'Henro fall down' section between temples 20 and 21. We'd not paid much attention to this earlier, thinking that it was nothing compared to the slog from 11 to 12, but that was when it wasn't such an immediate prospect. But that's for tomorrow, and right now we need supper.

We decide we'd liked the Italian wine bar from a couple of nights ago, and head back over there. This time it's almost empty, a couple of Japanese girls in their twenties at one of the two tables, and us at the other. We look for two dishes we could share, to get a bit of variety.

"How about the mushroom risotto, and maybe a pizza?" asks Elaine. "Do you have a preference for any particular pizza?"

"Not really. Well, probably not the Rotus Root." The menu really does list this as 'Rotus root', but presumably we'd have written 'Lotus root'. Either way, it's not a pizza topping I fancy. "I'm fond of octopus," I add, pointing to the entry on the menu just above the Rotus Root.

When the waitress comes, we point to the mushroom risotto and the octopus pizza on the menu. Just to make sure, I say "Octopus" fairly clearly.

When it arrives, I take a look at it and say:

"Well, that is a) interesting, and b) not octopus."

"I would say that's Rotus Root. Do you want to try to change it?"

But trying to negotiate an exchange is going to take time and will probably be tricky. And in any case, one should be open to trying new things. Actually, it's not unacceptable. 'Interesting', even. It wouldn't be high on my list of preferred pizzas, but now at least I know how it tastes.

"I wonder if she thought I was pointing to the Rotus Root when I was actually pointing to the item above," I ponder. "And I said 'octopus' without thinking, which may even sound like 'rotus'." On reflection, I should have remembered the Japanese for 'octopus' is 'tako', but these things slip your mind.

I'll remember next time. On balance, I would rather not have another Rotus Root pizza if I can help it.

And so to JR, and to bed.

Statue of Kōbō Daishi at temple 19, Tatsue-ji.

Temple 19, Tatsue-ji.

The railway tracks at Tatsue station.

Inside Uoroman wine bar.

Rotus root pizza.

17

HENRO FALL DOWN AGAIN - TEMPLE 20 (WEDNESDAY 18 APRIL)

In the morning, we agree that we feel about the same as we did yesterday morning. Not completely recovered, but obviously capable of covering a useful distance, at least if unencumbered by backpacks.

"We've a few options for how far we try to get today," says Elaine, "but basically it's 11 kilometres from where we finished yesterday at Tatsue to a village called Ikuna at the base of the hill leading to temple 20."

"I think I should be able to do that OK. How about you?"

"My back's not too bad. After that, we can get a bus back from there, or we can carry on. We'll see how we feel when we get there. And there are plenty of places we can bail-out earlier and come back by bus if we have to."

This is how we do it right now. We're doing the pilgrimage, but in bits, retreating to Tokushima every night, and with contingency plans in case we need to bail-out and return early. But this shouldn't last much longer.

On that basis, we go down to breakfast, and then head next door to the conveniently located Tokushima station and the train to Tatsue. (Handy, the way Japan Rail run both the hotel and the station and put them next to one another.) The sun is shining brightly today, which is great for the look of the countryside but will make it hotter for walking. This time we've put the messenger bag and my camera and anything else we might need (raincoats, spare socks, Band-Aids etc.) into my otherwise empty backpack. It feels surprisingly heavy, although really it must be about the same weight as I was carrying yesterday. Maybe there's something psychological about wearing the backpack, or maybe it's just that the backpack itself does add a noticeable amount of weight, high-tech device though it may be.

We get off the train at Tatsue, walk quickly back to temple 19 to use the toilets there, and notice how the flowers shine in the sun. And there's nothing like sunshine for showing off the red railings on the bridge over the river for the benefit of the camera. Then off again, walking past paddy fields and through small villages. Finally, the track meets up with a long main road, but it's a road that's passing truly lovely foothills with their variety of different greens glowing in the sun. It's an enjoyable walk, the sun is on my back but not on my head thanks to the pilgrim hat, and my foot is, well, my foot is behaving. It's not getting worse. Elaine notices this.

"You're doing better than you were yesterday. You're not complaining so much about your feet."

"It's the sunshine. I never complain so much when it's sunny."

"You don't?"

We reach a big T-junction where our road runs into another main road running along a river valley. There's a Lawson with a big sign outside.

"Look, that Lawson sign says it has a seating area."

"I think that's a sign, don't you?"

"I think it's a sign too. Someone wants us to have coffee."

We go in and it not only has seats, it has black tea, something I don't think I've seen since leaving Australia. We sit down by the big windows and look across the valley, and consider our options.

We've walked about 7 of the 11 kilometres between Tatsue station and Ikuna village, where we'll find the bus stop that could take us back to Tokushima. At this rate, we'll be in Ikuna, in reasonable shape, by about midday. And then it would seem a bit of a cop-out to head straight back to Tokushima.

"The thing is," Elaine spells out, "it's only about 3 kilometres up from the Ikuna bus stop to temple 20, but it has a Henro-fall-down section, so it isn't an easy climb. But the real problem is, what we do next. The obvious thing is to go on, down the other side of the hill, and on to 21. But once you've gone down after going to 20, you then have another climb up to 21, with yet another death-to-Henro section. And then you're at the top of that hill, and have to go down the other side of that before you can get a bus back to base."

"Doing both 20 and 21 sounds like a big ask, given we'd have walked 11km before we even start up the hill to 20."

"I don't think it's as bad as the 11 to 12 section. Most people do the both in one day, but they probably start early in the morning and come down from 21 late in the afternoon. Which is what we could do tomorrow, if we came back early on the bus to Ikuna."

The real problem is that there's no obvious way to bail-out anywhere between 20 and 21. If you do the one, you pretty much have to go straight on to do the other.

We don't really want to quit for today at the Ikuna bus-stop, and come back tomorrow and do 20 and 21. But we can't see how we can get to Ikuna today and reach 20 and then reach 21 and then come down from 21 to reach the bus-stop on the other side.

"There is a cable car that goes down from 21 and drops you near a bus stop," says Elaine, looking at the White Book. "If we got to 21 today we could take that down, come back tomorrow, take it up, and then go down by the normal walking path." That would at least eliminate the walk down from 21, which is about 5 kilometres all by itself. But getting even to the top of 21 today sounds like a pipe dream, and getting there by 5pm, which is when the last cable car leaves, looks out of the question.

It's hard to see an option that gets us to 20 today that doesn't leave us stranded between 20 and 21.

. . .

Then Elaine comes up with a bit of lateral thinking, prompted by a close look at the map in the White Book.

There's a road from Ikuna that skirts the hill on which temple 20 stands, running around it, more or less on the level, crossing the Henro path on the slope between 20 and 21 and carrying on to meet up with other roads to, well, somewhere else. The point is that it crosses the Henro path.

"We could walk to Ikuna, go up to 20 and then come down again from 20 *back the way we went up*, back to Ikuna. We take the bus back to Tokushima, and in the morning, we take the bus back to Ikuna, start walking where we left off today, but we walk along the road around the hill, on the level, meet up with the Henro track and then take that on up to 21 and down to the bus on the other side of 21."

"Brilliant! So, that lets us do 20 today, and 21 tomorrow."

There follows a brief philosophical discussion about the continuity of the Henro trail. If we do this, I say, we haven't actually followed the Henro trail as intended. If we do this, says Elaine, we've still walked continuously from Ikuna to 20, down to Ikuna, along the road to the intersection point with the usual trail, and then followed the usual trail from there. We've walked a continuous route that takes in both temples, and we've even walked further than we would had we followed the traditional trail.

"In any case, the trail is just a guideline. There are lots of alternative versions of the trail shown in the White book. People often visit other temples along the way and detour for that. Kōbō Daishi won't mind."

What's more, this sounds like something we can manage, unlike the other options. I'm convinced.

Shadow on the path to temple 20, Kakurin-ji.

The bridge over the river at Tatsue.

Looking down to the valley, from the track up to temple 20.

Hut by the track up to temple 20.

Part of the track up to temple 20.

We leave this highly satisfactory Lawson and carry on along the valley to Ikuna. We pass some roadworks, towered over by a big new-looking 'Mitsubishi' sign. This doesn't look an obvious place to find a car dealership, and in fact there doesn't seem to be one. The buildings are falling down and rusted and don't look like they've ever displayed a car in their lives. So are they building a new car dealership, and they've started with the sign? Just another of Japan's little mysteries.

Finally, the little village of Ikuna. There's the bus stop, and we see a path leading off in the general direction of up. We spend a while trying and failing to make sense of the bus stop's timetable, which is unsurprising since everything bar the number of the route appears to be in kanji. An attempt to use Google Translate on an image of the timetable produces a smattering of words that have only entertainment value, none of them anything to do with buses. We also notice that this is the only bus stop, and it's on the wrong side of the road - where do we catch the bus going the way we want? But these questions are for later. We pick up some rice triangles for lunch from the Ikuna FamilyMart, just down the road. This involves some debate as to what each one might contain, based on uncertain memories about the colour codes used on the labels.

"I think orange is salmon. I seem to remember it was last time."

"I'm sure I've had the pink one before and it was OK, but I can't remember what it was."

And so, uncertainly provisioned, we set off on the 'up' path.

There's no question that this path goes up. It starts off paved, or at least concreted, quite unlike the forest path we took when we set off from temple 12 about a week ago. It's easier to walk up this maintained, artificial, surface. But it is steep. It looks to me as if it's around a 1 in 3 slope. I don't think it can be that bad, as it's going to take about three kilometres to go up 500 metres, so I'm probably just a poor judge of slopes. All I can say is that it feels like hard work. The path starts off in the open, winding its way around the side of the hill, with views down into the valley, where we can see the river reaching into the distance. We come across a collection of staffs in a tall wooden box, like umbrellas left at a restaurant entrance on a rainy day. It looks as if they're intended to be borrowed by anyone who might need one, which is a thoughtful arrangement. It also suggests this is a path where staffs are seriously useful. I even wonder about borrowing one, so I'd have two, one for each hand, but decide against it.

We get deeper into the woods, and the path isn't paved any more, but it is well maintained, and seems to be taking a straight line, with remarkably few zigs and zags, right up the hill. The steeper sections, of which there are far too many, are set with steps made from logs held in place at what always seems to be the wrong spacing, about one and a half paces apart. I'd not want to be doing this without the staffs.

At one point, a booming PA announcement echoes from way down in the valley. If it can be heard up there, how loud can it be down there? More to the point, what is it about? Is this what a nuclear warning sounds like? Has North Korea done something rash? But it doesn't sound frantic, just loud, like a town crier's "Five o'clock and all's well", except that it goes on for several minutes. Since there wasn't a word we could make out, all we can do is ignore it, trust to the good sense of North Korea, and carry on.

My foot and back are managing OK, but I'm feeling the effort of the climb in my legs. Elaine's legs are doing well enough, but she's having to take deep breaths as she goes, and we find ourselves pausing constantly. This must the Henro-korogashi section of the climb. We've not actually fallen down, but we are leaning on our staffs most of the time.

Through a gap in the trees we can see down to the valley, which looks a long way away now, with the blue-green river emerging between smooth green hills in the distant haze, bending back on itself and running on past a scattering of tiny buildings and out of sight.

There are markers by the path with numbers that get smaller as we go, and we realise these are showing the distance in metres to the temple. Five hundred, pause, four hundred, rest, three hundred, sit, two hundred, pause, one hundred…

And we're at the temple. Well, almost. We're at the foot of a set of stone steps, with nice shining new handrails, that lead us slowly and achingly up to the main temple. Once there, however, it's delightful. I love the way this old wooden temple nestles comfortably into the green leaves of the enveloping woods. This is Kakurin-ji, temple 20, the temple with the cranes. Its crane statues, their long necks stretching out, honour the story that when Kōbō Daishi visited here, he found two cranes protecting a statue of Jizō Bosatsu, and carved a larger statue in which he placed the smaller one. What the cranes thought of this isn't recorded, but they're regarded as lucky in Japan, and Kakurin-ji is said to be the only temple out of the 88 never to have been burnt down, which probably explains some of its well-worn, aged, charm.

We sit down and eat our triangles. I'd been right about the orange label and the salmon. Elaine's pink-labelled lunch turned out to contain strongly-flavoured plum, which was a surprise, but a pleasant one. I'm even remembering to drink lots of water.

Now we have to retrace our steps, back down the way we came. I'm hobbling rather, and leaning on my stick like some old codger looking for a young whippersnapper they can tell how much better things were years ago.

"If we get down at a decent pace," says Elaine pointedly, "we can catch the 4:15 bus back to Tokushima. The one after that is 5:30."

"Did you manage to work that out from the timetable?"

"That's what it shows on the transport app on my phone."

Whippersnapper! We didn't have transport apps in my day. But it occurs to me that I'm pandering unnecessarily to my foot, so I stop limping, and realise that makes things easier and I can manage a decent pace on the way down. It still takes a bit of care - it's all too easy to get carried away and trip when going down these paths - but it takes us just over an hour to get down, and we're standing at the bus stop at around 3:45, happily pleased with ourselves.

But where do we wait for the bus? By the bus stop that's on the wrong side of the road? On the other side? What's the convention here? We cross the road and walk a little way down, to what could be the sort of space a bus might possibly be prepared stop at if someone waved at it, but we don't feel convinced. Then we see a little old lady walking along the road. We try to ask her. 'Ask' implies a bit more coherence than we actually manage.

"Sumimasen - ah - busu-wa - ah - Tokushima? Doko desu-ka?"

She looks at us as if baffled, and then suddenly scurries over to the bus stop so fast I have difficulty keeping up. There's then a confused conversation with a lot of pointing at the timetable. She says "Tokushima eki" - Tokushima station - and points excitedly at one column. Now that she's pointed it out, I can recognise the 'eki' kanji with its distinctive right hand side that resembles an 'R'. It was in terribly small printing. Anyone could have missed it.

But the timetable shows no sign of a 16:15 bus. In fact, the row starting with 16 o'clock - and it's nearly that now - is completely empty. I realise she's pointing furiously at the row above, for 15 o'clock, and that shows the numbers 1 and 51. But if she's talking about a 15:51, then that must have gone by now. I try to remember how to say, "but it's nearly 4pm, too late" but can't get anywhere near the right words, so I pull back my sleeve to show her my watch. She looks at it and nods, pleased. I realise it is actually only 15:50. Still, if there really is a 15:51 it must almost be here.

"Doko?" - where?

She points across the road and looks pleased that I've got the idea. By now Elaine has come over, having waited with the bags further down the road, and I drag her over to where the old lady is pointing. There's an element of scepticism.

"But the bus is at 4:15."

"Well, she showed me the line in the timetable, and it's got a 3:51, but nothing for the next hour."

"It's 3:51 now."

"OK. I don't see a bus. That is a bit of a flaw in the argument."

And then, around the corner, at 3:52 (transport in Shikoku seems to operate with about a minute's leeway; it is a fairly rural part of Japan) the bus comes around the corner, with a sign on the front saying - in writing we can read - "82 Tokushima". We wave our Henro staffs in the air and it pulls over and stops for us. This time, I remember to take my 'I got on at this stop number' ticket from the machine by the door.

Thinking back, what surprises me most is that that old lady seemed to know that we needed to rush, as if as soon as we mentioned Tokushima she knew that there was a 3:51 and it was only 3:50 so there was still time for us to catch it. Did she know the time that accurately as well as knowing the timetable by heart?

Now that we're on board, it's obvious that once again, we've hit going home from school time. The bus is full of school kids, there's only one pair of seats left, and they turn out to be the bench seat with the bump over the rear wheels. I get the seat by the window where the bump intrudes the most, and sit with my knees up and my backpack wedged between me and the seat in front. Elaine, who always hopes to minimise her discomfort when travelling, keeps looking around on the off-chance of spotting a better seat. She thinks she may have seen a spare one, and works her way down to the front of the bus for a reconnaissance, but is soon back.

"It was the seat with the bump over the *front* wheels."

It's a slightly bumpy and crowded ride, and it takes an hour and a half. We pass the implausible Mitsubishi dealership, all rusted corrugated iron and spanking new Mitsubishi sign, and more and more kids get on at each stop, all now crushed into the aisle between the seats. We appear to be the only Western Henro on the bus. We're the only Henro on the bus. We're the only Westerners.

We pass the time by feeling cramped, the rest of the bus passes the time by chattering furiously. I suspect not many are discussing their schoolwork. The bus stops at a train station, and we consider getting off and carrying on by train, but we don't know the train times, and we can't see that there's much to be gained.

And, as the bus works its way closer to Tokushima, more and more of its chattering passengers get off. It looks as if not many actually live in the city itself, and we wonder how the catchment area for the school must work. Seats are now coming free, and Elaine moves to one further back, which gives us both more space. Finally, the bus stops at Tokushima Eki, right outside the good old JR Clement, and we head inside. It's been interesting to experience a Japanese school bus, but it feels wonderful to be able to stretch out a little.

"What do we do tomorrow?" asks Elaine. "Today was quite a climb, and up to temple 21 looks just about the same. Do you think we can manage that?"

"Possibly. When would we have to get the bus back to Ikuna?"

"I've been looking. The only sensible one leaves here at 7:25. You might find that a bit early."

"I might just possibly find that a bit early." I've never been good at mornings.

"I thought so. What we could do is give ourselves a rest day tomorrow, and then we could be up bright and early the next day, 7:25 to Ikuna, and we could probably manage both temple 22 and on to temple 23, which is easier to get back from, because it would be a train rather than a bus."

We both find that remarkably convincing. Today was a long walk, first to Ikuna, and then up to 20 and back. I think we've agreed tomorrow will be a rest day.

Almost at temple 20, Kakurin-ji, looking down to the valley.

Kakurin-ji is the temple of the Cranes.

Armed statue in the grounds at Kakurin-ji, temple 20.

Kakurin-ji, temple 20.

On the way to supper, we look around the bus station, just outside. It's a big place with a number of stands, and it takes us a little while to find stand 5, where we can catch the number 82 to Ikuna. But now we know where to go, and we've checked the time for the morning, so we've left open the option of going tomorrow, at least in theory.

We walk up and down a bit, looking at the menus outside the various restaurants, and finally settle on what claims to be a French bistro. We aren't entirely surprised to see there's no menu in English, and we'd not seriously expected one in French. We then waste a serious amount of time trying to understand the Japanese menu. In some cases, things on it are in hiragana or katakana, which I can decipher but only character by character, and even then I have to try to look up the resulting word, so this is frustratingly slow. We try taking a photo of it and seeing what Google Translate can make of it. Nothing useful, I fear. It picks out a few words, but nothing that gives a coherent picture of what's on offer.

Elaine thinks Google Translate is potentially useful; I find it annoying, and claim that the time spent with it gets in the way of me plodding through the kana characters. I suspect that what I find most annoying, though, is the fact that it's still doing better than I am after all the effort I've put into trying to learn to read the kana.

Fortunately, the waiter who comes over has a smattering of English, and we end up with a): an order for a green salad, fried octopus, two glasses of wine and a vegetarian spaghetti with onions, and b): an agreement not to waste time with Google Translate's photo option in future, which panders to my irritation at being bettered by a computer, no matter how marginally.

The octopus is tender, the mixed green salad is more mixed than green but still crunchily tasty, and the vegetarian spaghetti with onions has bits reminiscent of onion bhaji, which I like, and pieces of what we think are bacon - 'vegetarian' seems to refer to the dominant ingredients, rather than a guarantee there isn't anything else.

We return to our temporary base camp at the JR Clement, and I for one am looking forward to our rest day tomorrow.

通過予定時刻表 生名

徳島バス株式会社
平成30年4月1日改正

	平日				土・日・祝日			
行先	徳島駅前	中田八幡社	横瀬西	黄粟上	行先	徳島駅前	中田八幡社	横瀬西	黄粟上
経由	日赤・津田	日赤		横瀬西	経由	日赤・津田	日赤		横瀬西
5					5				
6	03,	徳島 47,			6	03,			
7	06,	徳島 50,			7	03,	徳島 52,		
8			28,	10,	8		26,		
9		徳島 01,			9		徳島 01,		
10		徳島 26,		43,	10		徳島 26,		43,
11					11				
12	01,		03,		12	01,		03,	
13		徳島 26,		08,	13		徳島 26,		08,
14			33,		14	46,		33,	
15	01, 51,				15				
16				08,	16	21,			08,
17	16,		23,		17			23,	
18			03,		18	41,		03,	
19	01,			18,	19				33,
20			36,		20		56,		
21			26,		21				
22					22				

備考: 徳島 = 徳島駅前行きに接続

※徳島駅前行き・中田八幡社前行きをご利用のお客様は、停留所の道向かいの安全な場所でお待ちください！

土曜、日曜、祝日、阿波踊り期間中 (8月12日～15日)、年末年始 (12月29日～1月3日) は、土日祝ダイヤで運行します。
ノンステップバスは車両の都合により一般車両に変更することがあります。あらかじめご了承ください。
交通状況により遅れる場合がありますが、ご了承ください。　　お問い合わせ先 (088)622-1811

The bus timetable at Ikuna. We found this just a little confusing.

18

HENRO FALL DOWN ONCE MORE - TEMPLES 21 & 22 (THURSDAY 19 APRIL)

I wake up and see that it's only 5:45. Early. And we don't need to be up early, because today is going to be a rest day.

"How are you feeling?", asks Elaine. "Because if we're going to decide to walk today, we'll have to be up and doing for an early breakfast."

I'd thought that was settled. I thought we weren't going to be up and doing early. I thought we were going to have a late breakfast and devote a day to letting our weary bodies recover. I say something to this effect.

"No, no," says Elaine, "The rest day is an option. But if we do want to walk, we have to get moving, because the bus is 7:25 and we need breakfast first."

"I'll see how I'm feeling," I say, feeling strongly that a day off gets my vote.

But I get up to try to judge how I do feel, and am a bit surprised to find I do want to do the walk. My toe doesn't feel any worse than yesterday, we managed temple 20 yesterday, temple 21 should be the same, so it looks as if we can do it. Honestly, though, it's not so much that I want to do the walk, more that I want to *have* done it. This is the last big climb we'll hit this trip, and I don't want to take a rest day and then find we're no better and still have problems. Let's just get this done. I think.

The doors for breakfast open promptly at 6:30. We find ourselves sitting at a table next to an American who tells us he's a poet from San Francisco, and who seems to be here to see a bit more of Japan while searching for inspiration for two poems. I'm surprised he says 'two' poems - it seems an unusually specific objective when you're looking for inspiration - but we have to be off, and we're at bus stand 5 by 7:20, when the number 82 bus pulls up and opens its doors.

Only a few other passengers get on with us, but as the bus rolls along its route, through suburban Tokushima and then out into the country, it fills with dark-uniformed school kids until its aisles are completely jammed. Their uniforms do look seriously uniform, except for the wide variety of backpacks and footwear. Bright coloured trainers are well in evidence; sombre sensible school shoes are not.

"Do you suppose Japanese schools make you change into school slippers for the classrooms?" I wonder. "It would certainly slow down any running in the corridors."

Elaine is non-committal.

We're sitting close to the doors in the centre of the bus, and I point out to her how the ticket machine works.

"When the doors open, it puts out a ticket, and when someone takes that one, it puts out another. But when the doors close, it's left with a ticket poking out, so - and here's the trick - it sucks that back into the mechanism. See? It must have a waste box in it that has one printed ticket it discards after each stop." I'm feeling pleased to have understood this, which had puzzled me ever since I forgot to take that ticket in Kōyasan and couldn't get the machine to give me one in between stops.

"I thought this through, and worked out that must be what it did, and on the ride back yesterday I watched it in action, and I was right." I think this is a triumph of logical deduction confirmed by observational experiment.

"Sometimes," says Elaine, "I'm amazed at the things you will spend your time trying to understand."

After a little more than an hour on the bus, we pass the Mitsubishi garage that isn't, just glimpsing it through the crush of school uniforms standing in the aisle.

"We must be coming up to Ikuna any minute." Elaine hits the 'stop' request button, we push our way through to the front of the bus and pay our fares. Getting off these buses is a slow business. Each passenger in turn has to show the ticket with the number of the stop where they got on, check the screen at the front of the bus that displays each numbered stop so far and the fare from that stop to this, and pay that into a box by the driver. Most people don't have the right coins, so there's a note changing machine at the front that returns what seems to be a carefully calculated assortment of coins that can be combined to pay almost any of the possible fares. It's an interesting mixture of high-tech - the screen that constantly updates to show all the possible fares to the current stop - and low-tech - paying using actual money, supervised by the driver.

For the third time in two days, we're at the Ikuna bus stop. I'm getting fond of Ikuna, which is a small village with a main street, a few shops, including the FamilyMart, and helpful old ladies who appear to have built-in atomic clocks and an encyclopaedic knowledge of bus timetables.

We stock up on lunchtime seaweed triangles and Pocari Sweat at the FamilyMart, and set off to find the road that will take us on a level path around temple 20, avoiding its challenging hill, and which will intersect the path from 20 to 21. At which point, we can head for temple 21 and tackle *its* challenging hill.

We're not following the standard Henro route, so the White Book isn't particularly clear about which road we should take, but eventually we find it, and we're off on our level road around the hill.

Except that it isn't a level road.

It's actually a pretty steep climb, something that hadn't been obvious from the map. In fact, when we look more closely at the map, we realise it should have been obvious, but only if you look awfully carefully at the contours, which show this road climbing up about

200 metres vertically. This isn't the 500 metres up to temple 20, and it is on a decent surface, but it's still a bit of a shock to the legs. Legs that had been promised a rest today.

Almost as soon as we set off, a helpful local in his garden signals to us that we're heading the wrong way. This isn't the usual Henro route, so he assumes we're trying to get to temple 20 and are lost. We have to try to explain.

"Um.. Wakarimasu. Er.. Ni-ju-e ikimasen. Ah.. Ni-ju-san-e ikemasu" (Understand. Not going to 20. Going to 23.)

He seems to get the idea, and waves us on. I realise I told him we were going to 23, not 21, but at least I was wrong in the right direction.

We're hardly around the next bend in the road, which has developed a particularly steep incline at this point, when someone else, driving a small van, stops and asks us where we're going. He has some English, but when we say 'temple 21' he asks us the name of the temple. We don't know, because we've just been going by the numbers. Which, on reflection, feels slightly disrespectful, because we don't like to think that these lovely ancient individual temples are just numbers we're ticking off, but we find the names are hard to remember. It's interesting that at least some of the locals don't know the temple numbers though. He offers us a lift, and is surprised when we turn it down. At the time, I can't remember the phrase for 'we like to walk' and we just fall back on 'no' and 'arigatō'.

The road winds on, up through woods with occasional patches of wild flowers, then finally levels off and we can see across the valley to the hills opposite, bright in the sun and covered with a range of light and dark greens, specked in places with reddish-browns, all looking as if they belong on the box of a high-quality jigsaw. We'd not expected to have to climb up this far, and we're feeling the effort, but this view helps make it worthwhile.

Now the road slopes down, and we're going to have to give back all that height as we drop down to the valley and the mid-point between the hills of the two temples. We reach the point where the Henro trail crosses the road. To our right the path goes up to temple 20 - the section we've cleverly avoided - and to our left it carries on to temple 21. We're now back on the conventional Henro route.

A rather heavily loaded Henro comes down the side of the hill, on his way down from temple 20. He pauses when he reaches the road, and we greet him. He's another Frenchman, again from Paris, and he tells us he needs to do all of 20, 21, and 22 in one day. He'd wanted to book in for the night somewhere just after 21, which would have been sensible, but he couldn't get in there, and has had to book in somewhere much further along, close to temple 22. He's going well, but says he's really a runner, not a hiker, and this isn't what he's used to. We watch him set off into the distance along the downward path, as we plod behind slowly in the same direction.

The path now takes us steadily down through a fairly thick wood, emerging after a while into a clearing with what is probably either a large shrine or small temple. A wooden building with a bell rope stands at the top of stone steps flanked by statues of small dog-sized animals. According to the map in the White Book, this is Jizō-ji. We pause briefly, then carry on, as the woods turn into more open countryside and we start to pass buildings. A sign by the side of the path says:

"トイレ"

Almost every Henro knows this is 'to-i-re', or 'toilet', in this case with a red arrow pointing to the left. This turns out to lead to a deserted school. Apparently, the school has closed, presumably as numbers dwindled, but in a thoughtful way the toilet has been left working and open for passing Henro.

Right at the bottom, in the valley before the track starts to climb again, there's another Henro rest place. This is a large covered area, with a table on which we find various leaflets and a Japanese copy of something by the Dali Lama. It also has an interesting assortment of benches and chairs.

"I can imagine," says Elaine, "people saying 'we don't need these bar stools or these 4-wheeled office chairs, let's donate them to the Henro hut', and here they are."

Wherever they came from, they provide a shaded and fairly comfortable place to have lunch, and we happily take advantage of it. But we have a hill still to climb, and a temple still to visit.

The sign points left, to a working toilet in a deserted school.

More of Shikoku's green rolling hills.

Stopped for a rest. Henro hat and staffs, by the side of the track.

Slightly rusty bridge over the river, with bike.

There is a river running through the valley here, and stretching over it is a long, quite narrow bridge, wide enough for one car, with rather rusted once-cream railings. The bridge is high enough to give an impressive view of the river. We pause in the middle to take in the view, and a small motor bike nips past us with a big red container mounted on the back, looking as if it might be a rural postal delivery. Above the white clouds the sun shines from a blue sky, and and I feel I could happily just stay here. But we can't.

A little further on, as we enter the woods that cover the hill up to temple 21, the track starts to bend upwards, and we know that more effort is going to be called for. The Henro jackets start to feel too warm for this sort of uphill slog, and we put them in my backpack. At the beginning, the track is well maintained concrete, fairly straight, rather like the start of yesterday's track leading up to temple 20, but not as steep, and the woods are rather tranquil. They're quite thick, but occasionally we can see down to a stream that rises up with us in a series of small waterfalls, each about a metre or so.

At one point the track opens up slightly, and just by the side of the path is a blue tarpaulin that looks as if it has a car, or at least something remarkably car-shaped, underneath it. How did someone get a car here, and why did they carefully cover it with a blue tarpaulin and leave it? No doubt the explanation is prosaic and uninteresting, but the opportunity for speculation about such things is irresistible. Especially when all you're doing is putting one foot in front of the other, slowly plodding up an increasingly steep hill, as your mind flitters around.

We've made good progress so far, but a look at the map in the White Book tells us that's because we've not yet reached the 'Henro fall down' section. That's waiting for us up ahead.

And, indeed, progress starts to get slower. We can see steps! The path is now just a continuing set of tree log steps. We've come to really dislike these. You're forced to measure your step size so that it matches that of the steps, which is never just right, and each step requires its own effort, helped only by sticking the staff down and levering yourself up on it. And these steps go on and on.

And on.

But, about an hour and a half after entering the woods, the steps stop. We reach a road running up the hill, and can see an arch that surely is the entrance to the temple. We pause, put on the Henro jackets and, once more dressed as the pilgrims we are, we go through the arch.

We're not at the temple, we're at the temple car park. At least at this point even the car Henro have to get out and walk. The road climbs cheerfully upwards, testing the Henro spirit for another 200 metres, and then we can collapse onto a bench at the lower level of the temple.

We can see our French acquaintance from earlier, and we nod an acknowledgement to him, then force ourselves up to look around the temple. The main buildings are up a flight of about 100 stone steps, and I realise I've really taken against steps. I pull myself up by their glistening new steel handrail, and we finally feel we've arrived.

Tairyū-ji is a lovely temple. They call it 'Western Kōyasan' because it's built in the style of the Kōyasan temples, although I'm not enough of a temple connoisseur to spot that for myself. It has extensive gardens, and it has people scurrying around tending those gardens, with a monk in rather heavy outdoor sandals and a yellow skirt apparently directing things. But after that walk and that climb, we're far too worn to take it in properly.

"It's lovely, but I'm too tired to appreciate it," I say.

"We could always come back one day on the ropeway, and have a proper look at it then," suggests Elaine. Somehow this idea of a later, more relaxed, visit - no matter how implausible - makes us feel better about not giving the temple its full due this time. It does deserve a good look, though. The sun breaks through the trees to light up the red-bibbed Jizō statues, red-leafed trees hang over a stone bridge leading to one of the temple halls, and the whole place sits serene in the wood at the top of its seriously challenging hill.

It's now about half past one in the afternoon. If we set off now, we can probably cover the 11 kilometres or so to temple 22 this afternoon, and then it's only another two kilometres to the station at Aratano and from there back to Tokushima. The Henro route that turned inland to get to temple 20 is now bending back towards the coast and the JR railway line that runs down to the south. The 'level road' around temple 21 had only been 'level' in the highly limited sense of being not actually as steep as going up to temple 21 and down again, and that has worn us out more than we'd expected, but with a bit of wishful thinking we can even start to consider which train we could get from Aratano.

"There's a 4:50 train," says the optimist with the White Book. The White Book is a treasure trove for this sort of detail. "After that, there isn't one until 6:30. So it's 13 kilometres, but it's pretty much all downhill, so I think we could aim for that."

And she heads off in that spirit, setting a lively pace down the narrow asphalt road that carries the Henro path down the other side of the hill towards temple 22, Byōdō-ji.

At temple 21, Tairyū-ji.

Steps on the way up to temple 21, Tairyū-ji.

Tending the gardens at temple 21, Tairyū-ji.

Walking over the bridge at temple 21.

Red-bibbed Jizō at temple 21, Tairyū-ji.

After about an hour, the road has levelled off and we pass through the outskirts of a small village. We notice a distinctive cluster of three contrasting houses; there's a fairly conventional modern two storey house with a plain sloping roof, one next to it adorned with those elaborate faux-Meiji roof-works, and then a slab-sided flat-roofed white concrete construction that could have been at home on a Greek island. It's no more of a clash than can be seen in any Sydney suburb, where wooden-balconied Federation houses rub walls with modern concrete executive apartment blocks, but it's still the sort of thing that jars the eye.

In the middle of the village, sitting down and weary-looking, we meet our Frenchman again. He has, after all, done both the 'Henro-fall-down' hills of 20 and 21 already today, while we feel shattered enough and we bypassed the first of those hills. He explains that he's simply taking it easy, having realised that all he has to do now is reach temple 22 sometime today, given that his accommodation for the night is right next to it. He points to the place in this village where he had originally intended to stay tonight, but hadn't been able to get into, which must be annoying for him. We still have hopes of the 4:50 from Aratano and an early supper in Tokushima, so we leave him there, taking it easy, while we head off along the road.

The path is now rather boring, simply following a main road. It does seem to be going up rather than staying on the level, which we'd not expected, but it's doing so fairly slowly.

"At this rate, we may even have time to visit temple 22 and still get to the station for the 4:50," says Elaine. "But even if we have to skip the temple today, we can go there when we come back to Aratano to carry on."

We cross over a main road, route 195, and now the path takes us off-road, alongside a number of small fields. In one, overgrown by grass, by the side of the path, is an abandoned jet-ski. (How did that get there? Who brings a jet ski so far from the nearest water, just to abandon it in a field?) The path now takes a noticeable turn for the up, and appears to be heading for a respectably sized hill.

"The Welsh, being a sensible people, put their churches in

valleys," I remark, a nod to Elaine's Welsh background and a way of expressing mild discontent at having to head uphill again.

"The mountains are sacred to Buddhists. That's why they put their temples there."

"You could pray to your sacred place. You don't have to pray at it."

And then Elaine says, "Steps!"

She's right.

There are tree-log steps leading up the hill as far as the eye can see. Admittedly, the eye can only see as far as the next bend, but neither of us believe they're going to stop there. Rather too late in the day, we get out the White Book and look more closely at the route's profile. It is true that temple 21 is at the top of a hill, and temple 22 is comfortably close to sea level. It is not true that the path between them just slopes continuously downwards. There is a slow 50 metre rise, which must have been the slope in the road we've just come along, and then there is a discouragingly steep hill, which rises 100 vertical metres and is outlined in blue, which the White Book's profile pages use to highlight the difficult stages of the journey.

After about thirty of the tree steps, I start to count them, my way to stop thinking about how hard the climb is. Staff onto the next step, haul yourself up. A small shuffle to get in position for the next step. Repeat.

As my count hits one hundred and ninety-nine, after a large number of zigs and zags as the path switchbacks up the hill, the tree steps cease and the path levels off. We lean on our staffs and pause. Somehow, that effort was made all the worse by the fact that it was so unexpected, and we are both exhausted.

Then, what goes up - both the path and us - starts to come down. Suddenly, we're passing through a truly spectacular bamboo forest. Huge, thick bamboo rising neatly on either side, meeting to form a canopy. A strong, solid, bamboo forest, this, not one littered with rotting bamboo, and with the late afternoon sun coming in through the light green leaves far above.

"Kōbō Daishi sent us that uphill section because we'd been rushing and not contemplating the journey." Elaine is getting in touch with her inner Buddhist. "But then he sent us this lovely bamboo forest."

She has a point. It is lovely. Although I think I'd have appreciated it just as much if I'd come upon it along a level path.

As we come out of the bamboo we notice someone coming up behind us. Our French Henro has caught us up. He seems happy enough to slow down to our pace, and we carry on together. He tells us he'd wanted to do the Henro trail for years, but only this year had he managed to get enough time off from his work. He tells us he speaks Japanese, and can read a bit of it, although he keeps hitting kanji he doesn't know, at which point written Japanese becomes almost impossible to understand. Imagine having to learn to recognise each English word individually, and you get the idea.

Interestingly, he says that even though he could phone ahead himself to book accommodation, he always gets the people where he stays to do this for him. He worries that places can be reluctant to take bookings from foreigners, so it's a little like having one place vouch for you to another. "So they know you don't behave too badly," he says. We'd come across this bit of advice before, but our Japanese will have to improve out of sight before it's something we have to worry about.

The time taken to struggle up that last hill has completely ruled out the 4:50 train, but we're still hoping we can make temple 22 before it closes at 5. And, of course, we know that temples start to close a bit before that. We're now walking past larger rice paddies than we've seen before, all full of water and all with the shoots of the rice plants already visible above the surface. The paddies come right up to some quite fancy houses, and in the afternoon's light their yellow-orange reflections blend with the rice stalks in the water.

We get to temple 22 at about 4:40. They're already starting to pack up, moving around closing shutters and tidying away. We get our book stamped first, just to be safe, and then go on to the temple halls. Byōdō-ji is a relatively small temple, at the base of a hill, with the main hall a flight of about 50 stone steps up the hill. By the time we get back down, the shutters are up at the smaller hall, but we can still put in our name slip and offer up a coin.

A small, square, almost shed-like building houses a display about Frederick Starr, the American anthropologist from the University of Chicago who was one of the first foreigners to walk the Henro pilgrim route. It has a handwritten sign with American spelling, saying "To the Honor of Kōbō Daishi", signed "Frederick Starr", and dated 10.2.26. I wonder what he'd think of our train-Henro, walk-Henro, bus-Henro, walk-Henro progress of recent days, bouncing back to the relative comfort of Tokushima each night.

We say goodbye to our French companion, whose accommodation is indeed right next to the temple, and set off on the final 2km to the station, our shadows on the road getting longer and longer as the sun sets. We arrive at Aratano at about 5:40, in plenty of time for the 6:30 train, and collapse onto the benches in the waiting room.

Aratano only has one track running through it. The station's waiting room is bigger than the bus shelter that was all Tatsue had to offer, but even Tatsue had tracks that split to go past each side of the platform. Any trains that try to pass each other at Aratano are going to have a spectacular problem. Fortunately, the schedule cleverly avoids that, and at 6:30 we and a small group of schoolgirls get on the rather crowded train that pulls in to the platform. By the time we get back to Tokushima, having changed trains once, it's 7:45 and dark.

Today has been a long day, and much harder work than we'd expected, but we managed, although our muscles are decidedly stiff. Still, we're both glad we decided to knuckle down to the walk today, and we clearly both deserve and need a rest day tomorrow.

For supper, we head back to Fontana, which is somewhere we feel we know by now and, in particular, where we think we know our way around the menu. We order a pizza capricciosa and a pizza marinara. I'm fond of seafood, and a 'marinara' sounds just the thing - it's what I often have in Australian pizza places. The capricciosa is all a capricciosa ought to be. And so is what I get, apart from one thing.

"This is not actually a marinara," I grumble slightly. "There isn't a hint of seafood. Actually, there isn't a hint of much at all. It seems to be mainly tomato."

"Maybe they misheard and brought you a margherita," says Elaine.

"I can't even see any cheese." I cut off another slice. "Look, it tastes nice, and I'm not really complaining, but I had fancied seafood."

Obviously, I need to be more careful when ordering, even somewhere like this. What with the Rotus Root and this, somebody somewhere doesn't want me to eat seafood in Tokushima.

At temple 22, Byōdō-ji.

In the bamboo grove on the way to temple 22.

Rice fields and houses, close to temple 22.

Remembering Frederick Starr; a display at temple 22.

Temple 22, Byōdō-ji

19

TOKUSHIMA CASTLE AND OCTOPUS PIZZA (FRIDAY 20 APRIL)

Today, finally, a rest day. It's pleasant to wake a little later than usual, with no particular sense of urgency, and see how we feel. And we feel sort of OK. Elaine's back muscles are still sore, but it doesn't always seem to be the same muscles, so there's probably nothing fundamentally wrong there. My right small toe is still a bit sore and tender, but seems to have survived yesterday's harder-than-expected walk without actually getting worse. All in all, nothing a rest day won't improve.

We head back up to the tourist office, next door on the sixth floor of the station building, and sort out a few logistical details. It's time to give up our comfortable Tokushima base camp and head back onto the road like real Henro, since the road is now taking us further and further south from Tokushima. Temple 23, just over twenty kilometres on from 22, is on the coast near the small town of Hiwasa. From there the route follows the coast all the way down to the tip of Cape Muroto. Over the weekend, taking things easy, still based in Tokushima, we should be able to reach Hiwasa sometime on Sunday. There's supposed to be a particularly interesting ryokan in Hiwasa, and Elaine is planning on getting the tourist office to book us in there for the Monday and Tuesday nights.

I ask why we don't book in for Sunday, if the idea is take two days getting to Hiwasa and so arrive there on the Sunday.

I've clearly not thought this through properly.

"If we do that, we have to carry our backpacks for the whole of the Sunday section down to Hiwasa," explains Elaine. "This way, we stroll down to Hiwasa on Sunday unencumbered and take the train back for one last night at our cosy JR Clement. On Monday morning, we check out and take the train down to Hiwasa, and we should be able to leave our bags at the ryokan there. We do Monday's walk, and train back to Hiwasa for the evening."

This is back on the road again, heading south down the coast, but we're doing it by moving base camp south to Hiwasa for a couple of nights. My feet and back vote unanimously for this plan. I'm prepared to convince myself Kōbō Daishi would have done it this way if there'd been a train line running between his temples.

Elaine has been doing her research.

"It's a long haul south from Hiwasa to Cape Muroto," she says, "It's about 76 kilometres from temple 23 to temple 24, but I think we can do the Monday and Tuesday legs from Hiwasa the way we've been doing them from Tokushima. The route follows the train line. After that, we're going to have to revert to carrying all our kit. But the real reason to spend two nights in Hiwasa is that it's supposed to be an interesting place to stay, and they speak French at the ryokan. Maybe English as well."

I'll settle for that. A French-speaking ryokan in Hiwasa sounds interesting, and not having to rely on our few words of Japanese just has to make things easier.

It's the same helpful, English-speaking, lady at the travel office, and she has no trouble making our Hiwasa booking for us. As she does so, I look around the office. It's staffed by about eight Japanese ladies, all but one dressed in casual Western outfits. The other is in full kimono, bow at the back, awkward shoes, sitting behind a laptop just like all the others. Is this her choice? Or does the tourist office like to have at least one person in traditional dress? I want to be able to ask, but don't.

. . .

Tokushima castle is close to the centre, and we stroll over to have a look at it. We pause by a restaurant that has a menu in the window, and while I'm struggling to work out the kana for some of the items - a slow process, but I need the practice - Elaine suddenly reads out a couple of them in English. I turn around, and as I'd suspected, she has her phone out and has run a photo of the menu through Google Translate. I'm unreasonably annoyed.

"I thought we'd agreed we wouldn't use Google Translate!"

It isn't rational, but I've put the effort into trying to learn these blasted characters and here I am, beaten by technology. It's a clash of attitudes; is the point to try to get to grips with the culture and the language, or is it to find out as quickly as possible that there's penne with mushrooms on the menu?

"I thought you'd appreciate not having to struggle with that, so we could get to see the castle."

She has a point; she always does. We head on to the castle and I try not to sulk. We do come to most things from completely different directions, but there are surprisingly few cases where we clash; I'll follow her almost blindly on a pilgrimage across Japan, but I want to be allowed to practice translating a menu.

But here's the castle. Actually, here's the very little that's left of the castle. It was pulled down during the Meiji restoration, like many other Japanese castles, and Second World War bombers polished off most of what little was left. There's a bit of moat, and a few adjacent stone walls, but not much more to tell you this was once a castle.

What has survived is a charming Japanese garden with a small lake and a dry pebble garden, both crossed by stone bridges, with a group of cranes in residence standing on rocks, as cranes do, and flying away when you try to get close enough for a photo, as cranes also do. We get a leaflet in English from the ticket booth at the entrance to the garden (admission a bargain at ¥50), which explains that it is a typical garden in the Momoyama style, designed to be both gazed upon from the castle above - back when there was one - and walked around. The bridges are typical of the style and made promenading around the garden more interesting for the castle's lords, the daimyo. One bridge over the dry garden is ten metres long and made from a single rock, while another over a part of the lake is also a single stone, although rather shorter. Since the Momoyama period was notable for wars between the Japanese feudal clans, one can see that the various daimyo might appreciate the tranquillity of such a garden, while beyond the walls the Kurosawa movie that was life back then in Japan went on its violent way.

In fact, this garden could almost define 'tranquil'. The stone garden, with its ridges of raked stones, the lake and the fairly sparse trees give it an open and airy feel, especially on a sunny day like this. We spend a while there, walking around and trying to photograph the blurs that are the flying cranes.

There is a castle museum, although it takes us a few false starts before we find the entrance, which is much closer to the garden that we'd thought from the map. Inside is a room-sized detailed model of the castle as it was - impressively big, with what amounts to a whole village inside the walls. There doesn't seem to be a real central 'keep' and the moat only goes part of the way around, which appears to be a flawed concept, but we have no way of finding out more. An interesting video is playing, and it might have been informative if only we could follow Japanese. There are no concessions to English here, not even a pamphlet. We spend a little while there, then head back towards the centre to look for lunch.

We pass an old railway steam engine on display in the grounds of the park near the castle. I'd not thought of Japan as somewhere that might have steam train enthusiasts, but I imagine it does.

Tokushima has only one department store - SOGO. We look in to see if it has any Hello Kitty-type stuff our daughter might like, and to see what its restaurant floor has to offer for lunch. There's not a lot in the way of Japanese-cute, and many of places on the restaurant floor are closed - firmly shuttered. One feels business may be declining, and remember David Moreton saying something about the decline of the city centre. We try a 'family' restaurant purely on the basis of the plastic version of the shrimp fried rice set in the window. Inside, we discover the menu has this in the 'Chinese food' section, which I suppose is fair enough. As is the food - nothing special, but it goes well with a couple of beers.

Outside in the street, we remember the queues we'd seen outside the shop with the food production line in its window, and manage to find the place, now without queues but still open and happy to take ¥140 from us for two freshly made samples of - whatever it is they're producing. These turn out to be some form of bun, and we take them back to room 1506 and have them with tea. The flavour isn't something I can put a name to, and it doesn't do much for me, but they're filling and nice when fresh and warm like this.

We have a quiet afternoon. Elaine goes out looking for a Japanese equivalent of the sore muscle gel she uses, having found a picture of the box on Google. I go to the Post Office to get some money from their helpful ATM and to post my broken lens back to Australia. I suspect it can't be repaired, so I'm happy to just pack it in an envelope and not struggle with discussions about packaging and insurance options.

Elaine has been thinking ahead, and has realised that the time we're going to be leaving Shikoku is going to coincide with Golden Week, the cluster of four National holidays in seven days, when Japan traditionally takes the week off and everything gets booked up. We're booked to fly out of Takamatsu, up in the North East of Shikoku, and it would be a sensible idea to make sure we can get there by train when we need to. We don't know exactly how far we'll have got by then on foot, but a safe bet is that we'll be within reach of Kochi City, even if we have to get there by bus. So we'll book a couple of nights in Kochi for the end of the trip and reserve train seats from there to Takamatsu.

The railway tracks leading into Tokushima station, seen from the JR Clement.

A rather upmarket Henro hut. The foyer of the JR Clement, Tokushima.

The gardens of Tokushima castle, with stone bridge.

A crane in the gardens of Tokushima castle.

Steam engine on display in the park by Tokushima castle.

Back to the tourist office at the station, and the same lady. "Ah, Keith-san and Elaine-san." Accommodation booked, and down to the ticket office on the ground floor to sort out the train. Now we know how we're going to leave Shikoku. The question is, how close to Kochi City can we get?

The temples are starting to get spread out along the Henro route now. From where we've got so far, temple 22 at Aratano, it's twenty kilometres almost due south to Hiwasa and temple 23, then there's the long 76 kilometres down the coast to the tip of Cape Muroto and temple 24. In outline, Shikoku looks just a little like a humped animal seen standing side-on, head to the right. The Henro trail goes right around its outline. Tokushima is its nose, and the triangular peninsular down to Cape Muroto forms the forelegs. Go around Cape Muroto and you're climbing up the back of the forelegs towards Kochi city, right where the belly would be. Temples 25 and 26 are quite close together, and it's only about eleven kilometres around the cape from 24 to 26. Then temple 27 is nearly another 30 kilometres further, about half way up the back of the forelegs. We may or may not get that far, and we certainly aren't going to manage the forty kilometres on from there to temple 28, which is almost in Kochi City itself. Not in the time we have left. But we can get a bus or a local train from wherever we end up to Kochi, and now we're booked in there. This sounds like a plan.

Now it's time for supper.

I want to try the octopus pizza I missed out on a couple of days ago. So, back to Uoroman, the rather Spanish-looking Italian wine bar. The two tables are occupied, but we get seats at the bar as we did the very first time there. This time I'm quietly confident about how to make my order clear. Elaine asks for a small garlic octopus dish, garlic bread and a small salad. I point extremely carefully at the octopus pizza on the menu, which lists the dishes in both Japanese and English, and ask "Tako desu-ka?" Is this octopus? He says "yes", and I point again and say, this please. (In retrospect, perhaps I should have made it clearer that I was asking because I like octopus, not because I want to avoid it.) Our wine appears, and the green salad - no complaints there - and the octopus with garlic - excellent, and gloriously garlicky. Then out comes my pizza.

It's Rotus Root!

What do I have to do to get a seafood pizza in this town?

I've eaten the Rotus Root pizza. It's OK, but I've had it once and it isn't octopus and I've promised myself octopus. I call the waiter back. He confirms it is not octopus. He confirms it is lotus root. This discussion happens mainly in broken English, with the odd 'tako' thrown in for confirmation. In the end, he says, graciously, "Sorry, make mistake," although I hardly think it's his fault. I put the lotus root to one side, he goes back behind the bar and confers with the others. We get the impression there's something wrong with the English menu, and I start to look closely at the kana in the Japanese entries. I can't see the kana for "tako" on the pizza menu, although I can see them in the entry for Elaine's garlic octopus. Maybe they don't really do octopus pizza?

Still, someone on the other side of the bar is cutting up octopus and putting it on a pizza base, so this is definitely looking hopeful. While we wait, I battle with the menu's detailed description of what I thought I'd ordered. One word turns out to be 'Sicilian' and there's something that might be 'organic'. If I could only do this menu decoding trick quickly enough, I might be able to get octopus first time. I still don't see "たこ" (which would be 'tako') but I do see "だこ" ('dako'), which I don't think is the same thing. Gosh, written Japanese is difficult.

And then, here's the waiter with an octopus pizza! And it's an excellent octopus pizza. Worth the effort. I'm glad I ordered that and not the Lotus Root - although I'm really not at all sure I understand what's just happened, which is par for our course when eating out.

Well fed, and well satisfied, we pay and leave. As our waiter takes the money, I say "totemo oishii desu", very tasty, and "tako-ga suki desu", I *like* octopus, and he smiles broadly and we all bow to one another and we head back to the JR Clement and bed.

Tomorrow, we're back on the road.

20

THE ROAD SOUTH TO YUKI (SATURDAY APRIL 21)

Whoever schedules the Tokushima trains isn't on our side. Or maybe they're trying to tell us that proper Henro walk with their backpacks and we've been taking things too easy. We'd thought we might be able to manage to get as far as temple 23 in Hiwasa today, in one long hike, but do that we'll have to be pretty early at our starting point in Aratano, where we finished two days ago, and for that we need a reasonably early train.

But not as early as 6:50, which is the only early train on offer. We may be dedicated Henro, but we need our breakfast. The next train leaves at 10:10, and it will have to do. We'll see how far we get, break at a convenient station, and carry on tomorrow.

We buy some croissants for lunch, arrive early at the station, and sit down in our Henro gear watching the trains come and go. Tokushima is not a big station. Double tracks lead in and out of it, splitting up to pass by the three platforms and to provide sidings where trains await an eventual call to action. Trains pull in, passengers get out, engineers in bright orange helmets and with orange straps around blue working clothes pass by, inspecting wheels, couplings and so on, and cleaners get on and start to pass through the empty carriages.

"Have you noticed that the cleaners get on, but then the train pulls away with them still on board?" asks Elaine.

"It's as though JR kidnaps them. Somewhere there must be another station full of cleaners. I've never seen a cleaner get off a train. They must get through cleaners at a decent rate."

But the cleaners are another mystery that we never solve. Our train arrives, on time. An hour later, as we get off at Aratano, a Japanese Henro finds enough English to ask us if we're going to Byōdō-ji, which is a reasonable assumption, given it's only about two kilometres away. But, of course, we aren't. We're just going to pick up our trail again and head to temple 23, whose name, of course, we aren't able to remember. "No," we say, "twenty-three - ni-ju-san," and he doesn't seem to be able to find the words to express the doubt we can see in his face.

He heads off, clearly not sure we know what we're doing, and we see him looking back a few times as we follow him along the road. Eventually, he takes the turning off to temple 22, and we carry on, now back on the Henro path where we left it two days ago, past more of the same large rice paddies that we saw here before, with the same large sunlit houses reflected in them.

A lady in a small white car stops, winds down her window, hands us two juice poppers and drives off. She seems to have a number of these stored on her front passenger seat; maybe she cruises the Henro route generously distributing poppers to thirsty pilgrims.

The track wanders across the countryside, then becomes a narrow road, winding picturesquely through a forest. We pass a mechanical digger balanced precariously on the side of a hill, apparently clearing up after some sort of minor landslide, and a group of workmen having lunch by a sign that presumably apologises for the inconvenience caused by the work in progress; you can deduce this from the picture of a bowing workman in a yellow hard hat.

We come out onto a main road and follow that for a while, reaching a dark 300-metre tunnel through the hills, made amazingly noisy by the passing cars, and emerge to find a welcoming Henro hut. We have a late morning tea, eating our croissants with the juice from the lady in the white car. As we sit, the Henro we saw on the train passes us, drinking from an identical juice popper. He recognises us - we are fairly distinctive - and presumably works out that we did know what we were doing back there. He manages a "hello", points to his juice popper and says "same lady" and smiles. Then he carries on, striding out at a rate well beyond what we could manage, which will probably easily get him to temple 23 today.

We don't see any point in rushing. It's a lovely day, pleasantly sunny, and we don't need to get to anywhere in particular today. Temple 22 had been slightly inland; we're now passing through the small coastal hills and will end up reaching the coast itself at a small town called Yuki. We know nothing about Yuki other than that it has a train station, with a train back to Tokushima at 3:37, and that makes it a reasonable place to finish today's section of the walk.

It's a fairly gentle descent from the hills into Yuki, and we get there just before three o'clock. We know we must be nearing the coast when we see a yellow warning sign with a picture of two crabs and the "chūi" 'caution' characters we now know *do not* mean 'Henro path'. The station is at the back of the town, and is almost the first thing in Yuki we come across. Somewhere there must be a seafront, but it's some way from the station, so we just settle in and wait for the train.

Adjoining the station, we find some sort of visitor centre. There's a 'stick your head through this hole and take a photo of yourself as a crab' cut-out, a large tank of fish that reflects a distorted view of the open doors of the waiting room, and a lot of posters on what seems to be the general theme of 'this historical personality vs this one' - at least, they have a number of old photos of people with 'vs' between them. I wish I could really read Japanese. Yuki looks as if it might be one of those slightly run-down surfer towns you see in the US or Australia where nobody cares about the run-down part because they just want to live cheaply and surf. We'll see more when we come back tomorrow.

"Crabs crossing": warning sign on the way down to Yuki.

Railway staff at Tokushima station.

Rice fields by the side of the road.

Quite an elaborate Henro sign.

Reflections in the fish tank at Yuki station.

In the train back to Tokushima from Yuki.

The trip back to Tokushima is fun, at least while the train remains fairly empty. We sit right at the front and look out past both driver and conductor at the track ahead as the train twists through narrow cuttings between the tree-covered hills. It's a bit scary to rush along like this at fairly high speed along a single track, realising how much depends on the signalling systems and the schedule working properly together.

In the evening, we take the soft option for supper and try the JR Clement buffet. I put on my only clean shirt for the occasion, and we sit down to an interesting French-oriented Japanese buffet. The lobster croquettes are outstanding. So much so that I go back for more - freshly delivered, I notice - and bite greedily into one. Scalding hot lobster mush erupts from it over my chin and all over my clean shirt sleeve.

"I've been attacked by a lobster croquette! Gosh, whatever's in it is scalding!" I roll up my sleeve and dab at the injured arm with water. There's sympathy, but tempered slightly by a suggestion that most people might have been more careful with a freshly cooked lobster croquette.

I recover, slowly. We're brought two small steaks ("included in the buffet", says a large German-accented Maître d' proudly). The JR Clement buffet is no place for vegetarians. I have a large bottle of Kirin beer, and feel rather better.

It's been an easy day - vicious lobster croquette, stained shirt and scalded arm notwithstanding - but we were only walking for about three and a half hours, and we keep telling ourselves we could have reached Hiwasa and temple 23 easily if only there'd been a train at a suitable time. Of course, we could have, but obviously Kōbō Daishi wanted us to take it easy.

21

ALONG THE COAST TO HIWASA AND TEMPLE 23 (SUNDAY APRIL 22)

All we have to do today is cover the distance from Yuki to Hiwasa, which is only about thirteen kilometres, so we can go the pretty way, taking it slowly along the coast.

Downstairs again for the JR Clement breakfast; I have my selection down pat now. It's rather Western, because I'm trying to keep my salt intake down, but at least I eat it with chopsticks, which is a bit of a trick when it comes to scrambled egg. In a way, a pair of chopsticks is just like a fork where you can control the spacing between the tines, so you ought to be able to use them to eat anything you can with a fork. I would feel I'm blending in, except that I'm obviously not.

We collect a couple of the seaweed-wrapped rice triangles from the 7/11, and we're ready for the 8:47 limited express to Yuki. This rattles along the track, through the cuttings, the green-tinged sunlight from the trees cheerful through the windows. The conductor comes through, pausing on entry to each carriage to bow respectfully, and then carefully checking all the tickets. We reach Yuki in about an hour.

"We're now spending two hours a day on the train, back and forth. I quite like this train-walk Henro mode, but we're a seriously long way south of Tokushima by now."

"Exactly," says Elaine. "But this is the last day we go back to Tokushima. Tomorrow, we're back on the road properly. And I'm looking forward to being back in a proper traditional Japanese room again. Sorry you'll have to sit on the floor, though."

I'm sure I can handle sitting on the floor. It's just part of blending in.

This is our first proper look at Yuki. We walk out of the station past a group of Japanese who seem to be playing croquet on the sort of light-coloured dry surface the French would use for boules. We walk towards the sea, down streets lined with slightly run-down buildings.

I was wrong about Yuki. It isn't a surfer town, it's a fishing village, and one in a spectacular setting, with small islands rising steadily and somehow unexpectedly out of the water not far offshore. Unattended fishing boats are moored in the harbour and the walls on the harbour-side support an impressive number of clotheslines, bare of anything except a huge variety of multi-coloured plastic clothes pegs, which I assume are used to dry nets.

We walk around the small harbour, and the track takes us off to one side and up what looks as if it might turn into a steep path.

It does. What's more, it's steep enough to warrant steps made out of awkwardly-spaced logs. A lot of steps. It's more of a strain than I expected to get up to the top, although I think it's mainly psychological; I'd not expected that sort of calf-torturing climb and I think I'm over-reacting to the sight of steps made out of logs. It's clearly only to the top of a small hill behind the village, so it can't be too bad. And in the end, it isn't. It levels out to become a lovely wooded trail close to the coast which would have some great views if the trees weren't there. We come to what might be a path to a lookout, and we head down it.

It's worth the detour. The trees open up to a vantage point with a lovely view of the coast, the little islands, and the beach well below us. There's a rather dramatic structure that acts as a shelter of sorts, with an octagonal seat and a central pillar supporting an octagonal concrete roof. As a sop to considerations of public safety there are also some barriers that would stop you falling down the cliff if they didn't include a huge gap to allow you to do just that.

Marvellous.

We return to the path and follow it down as far as the beach, which is deserted apart from one shelter tent (one of those clever folding teepee contraptions) and somebody, perhaps another Henro, settled down and resting outside a toilet block.

The road runs around the coast, next to the railway line, from which it's separated only by a fine disregard for safety and a small concrete divider just the right height to trip over. It leads us to Kiki, which is another fishing village, this time slightly shambolic but wonderfully colourful. It has a building with a corrugated iron roof in orange with patches of yellow, and nets in various shades of brown through red hanging out by the harbour. We note the prominent tsunami warning signs: flee to "The Mountain Behind of The Old School", helpfully in English, next to a picture of someone running. Tsunami are taken seriously here, especially following the one that hit north-eastern Honshu, including Fukushima, in 2011.

Carrying on around the bay we find a Henro hut that looks like a wooden lookout post, giving us a fine view out to sea. Then the path turns upwards and leads us through woods again. I notice a niggle of discomfort from the second smallest toe in my left foot - what would be the 'ring' toe, if our culture had a tradition of putting wedding rings on toes. Normally I'd have ignored this, but I've learned better, and in my newly enlightened state I agree to stop so we can bandage what turns out to be a cut and generally rather worn toe.

The path winds back towards the coast, taking us past another harbour and a deserted rocky beach, and then rises to follow a road along the cliffs. At one point, we look down on a small cave at the end of another beach where the shallow water is a clear and sparkling light blue.

Playing a croquet-like game at Yuki.

Yuki harbour. Ready to dry the nets.

At Yuki harbour.

From the view point above Yuki.

Nets at Kiki, a little further on from Yuki.

Tsunami evacuation area sign at Kiki,

About two hours on from Kiki, the waves start breaking more strongly, although it isn't obvious why. We can see a large modern light-blue building, overlooking the ocean, that looks as if it might be a hotel. Behind it there's a huge concreted rectangle running right up the hillside.

"I suppose that's to help stop landslides."

"Reasonable. Having a landslide come through your dining room plays havoc with your TripAdvisor ratings." We walk past the entrance and peer in to the foyer. The outside may be a little slab-sided and unimaginative, but it looks pleasant inside. There appears to be a coffee shop, and we consider that for a moment before deciding to press on.

We stop a little further along at a Henro bench - on principle, we pause at all Henro benches and huts, because it feels ungrateful to just walk past - and then carry on as the road drops down to sea level and turns into a promenade along a beach on the outskirts of Hiwasa. There are a number of people walking around on the long stretch of sandy beach, but all are fully clothed and nobody seems to be swimming or even sunbathing. It is getting a little overcast.

We pass a building just back from the beach that houses the Hiwasa Sea Turtle Museum. This is supposed to be one of the must-see attractions of Hiwasa.

"We ought to have a look at the turtles."

"We should," agrees Elaine. "But we're just about in Hiwasa now, so we could do this now or go to the temple first and come back." She looks at the sign, almost entirely in Japanese. "I think it says there's something on at 1:40, which is in about fifteen minutes. I don't know what it is, but maybe we should go in here now."

I'd been trying to decipher some of the kana on the sign, without learning much. Elaine has an uncanny way of looking at something as a whole and focussing on the important part. I've become used to this; I just accept it's something she does and I can't.

So we go in.

Inside they're obviously used to passing Henro. There's a sign that says "Henro leave bags here". The 'here' turns out to be the office, and the staff are amazingly helpful, pointing to where we should put our bags and staffs and hats.

It's rather a good museum. It's colourful and modern inside, with what I assume are informative displays on the history and distribution of turtles. We can't read the details, but there's enough English to give the general idea. In the display areas a few small land turtles are passing the time in the slow way turtles do.

Then there's an announcement in Japanese and everyone starts to move outside, so we follow. This must be what happens at 1:40, and we realise that what happens at 1:40 is sea turtle feeding time. The turtle keeper is out in the open by a large set of separate blue concrete turtle ponds, and he distributes handfuls of lettuce to everyone to throw to the turtles, who mill around enthusiastically, every so often snapping a head out of the water to snaffle a floating piece of Turtle-lunch.

It's all very jolly, out in the sun throwing lettuce to sea turtles. We're really glad there wasn't a convenient train yesterday morning and we didn't try to get to Hiwasa in one day. By splitting the trip in two we've had a glorious walk along the coast, and had time to feed turtles along the way.

. . .

But we do need to get to temple 23, Yakuō-ji.

We're coming close to the main part of Hiwasa now, and as we approach along the promenade and turn right towards the town, we see a prominent building a long way up on a hill. A very long way up. A discouragingly long way up.

"Please tell me that isn't the temple."

But as we get closer, we can see another striking building lower down on another hill. This is a deep red, and looks like a cross between a pagoda and a rocket, as if someone took a pagoda, cut the roof off, and inserted a large cylindrical body between the base and the roof.

It turns out that this isn't the temple itself, but it is the pagoda associated with it. The rest of the temple is the usual dark wood, sitting comfortably among the trees and aged by the years. It's also popular, perhaps because this is Sunday. Troops of white-coated Henro are milling around, reciting sutras in unison. We squeeze in, and perform our usual limited set of actions. By now, I have at least managed to remember the basic "Na-mu dai-shi Hen-jō kon-gō", which a bit of Googling (it was worth the effort of getting the iPad connected to the internet) translates variously as something along the lines of "Praise Daishi, the Illuminating and Imperishable". I feel comfortable enough mumbling that, and the syllables bounce along nicely in rhythm.

The legs would have voted against it, if asked, but we struggle up the steps to that remarkable pagoda. The sweeping panorama over the town of Hiwasa and the river flowing through it to the sea make the effort worthwhile. We have a quick look in through the doors of the pagoda. It seems that inside is some sort of illuminated Buddha figure, but going in involves an awkward exchange of hiking boots for indoor slippers, and we decide to just look at the view instead.

Books stamped, we head over to the station. Hiwasa station is a bustling complex, mostly full of all sorts of gift shops, somewhat sea-turtle themed, and containing nothing that even remotely resembles a ticket office. We go around, twice. There is a JR shop at the end, but it's just another gift shop, full of sea turtles, and nothing at all to indicate that JR is also in the railroad business.

We go outside, and, in the way that we usually do things, I'm trying to compose the phrase for "where do I buy a ticket?", when I realise Elaine is talking to someone at a tourist information window. She's obviously got across what we need, because in a moment the slightly gangly-looking lad at the tourist window is outside and almost dragging her to the JR shop and over to the cashier. Evidently JR do run a railroad, and their gift shop sells tickets, although they don't make this obvious. Tokushima limited express, one way, so much, platform 2 - all sorted, two tickets and two limited express supplements. We pause on the way out by a display of Hello Kitty birthday key rings, one for every day of the year (366 different ones, even allowing for leap years), and go back to buy one for Holly. As we leave, there's the lad from information, worried we'd misunderstood what to do next and pointing us frantically in the direction of platform 2.

We get across that we know it's platform 2. "Hai, wakarimasu", yes, understand, and we sit down outside for a while, looking over at the missile pagoda on the hillside. Did some Japanese entrepreneur come to the temple and tell them 1000 years of tradition was all very well, but what they truly needed was an illuminated Buddha in a spaceship? Who knows? But it is definitely striking.

The express rushes back through a series of glowing green tunnels, formed by the trees, and dark black tunnels, which are actual tunnels, and we realise just how far we've covered on foot. It's an hour on an express train - admittedly Shikoku's version of an express train - and we've covered it on foot over a few days.

The pagoda at temple 23, Yakuō-ji, from Hiwasa station.

Inside the Hiwasa Sea Turtle Museum.

A sea turtle, waiting to be fed.

At temple 23, Yakuō-ji.

Hiwasa, seen from temple 23, Yakuō-ji.

One thing I've come to appreciate on this trip is that it is possible to go a long way on foot, something nobody does nowadays. We have clearly gone well past the limit of what makes sense for our Tokushima-based, JR-walk-JR, style of pilgrimage. But we had needed to get our backs and feet back into shape, and it's served us well for this last week.

For supper, one last visit to Fortuna. Flushed with the triumph of having finally eaten an octopus pizza at Uoroman, I want to get a proper seafood pizza from Fontana. I like seafood, and I like pizza.

So, in we go, greeted by the jolly lads at the desk with "buona sera," something I suspect they've been coached in by their Italian owner. I say "buona sera" back, and they all smile. We sit down and get the English menu. This time I point to the marinara pizza on the menu and ask:

"Kore-wa, marinara pizza, shifudo desu-ne?" (This ,marinara pizza, it's seafood, isn't it?)

He looks at me in an incredulous way, as if I'd said, "this vegan pizza, it's steak and eggs, isn't it?". "No" he says, and slowly works through what it is - tomato, oregano, garlic, etc. - exactly what I had last time. Surely not. 'Marinara' - the very word says 'sea'! Where I come from, a marinara pizza is seafood. In what part of the world is a marinara pizza nothing to do with the sea?

"Shifudo-ga arimasen? Sakana-ga arimasen?" (Not seafood? Not fish?) "No" definitely not. He looks down the list of pizzas in the English menu. 'Salmon pizza. Is fish.'

I have the salmon pizza - which I have to say I enjoy enormously. It's a pity it's a Sunday, so the boss isn't there. Otherwise we could have had an enlightening discussion about 'marinara' and 'frutti di mare' and other pizza nomenclature. But for the moment, it's just another puzzle to chalk up to unfinished business. (This puzzle has an embarrassing solution, explained in the end notes.)

Back in the room, Elaine has taken to heart the tsunami warnings we've seen, and has downloaded three separate earthquake and tsunami warning apps. Which would be more useful if her phone wasn't permanently in airplane mode while we're walking to conserve its battery, which is rather showing its age.

I suggest there are more plausible local threats, such as attack by a vicious lobster croquette, and show her where the hot filling splashed painfully through my shirt yesterday and now seems to have left some sort of scald mark. I still don't get the sympathy I deserve.

Still, overall, it has been a most satisfactory day.

22

A NEW BASE - HIWASA (MONDAY APRIL 23)

Finally, the time has come to leave our cosy little base camp in room 1506 at the JR Clement.

But first, breakfast, a last turn around the buffet, and packing. We've not needed to get everything into our backpacks for a while, and I find it hard getting everything into mine. The only thing I've acquired is the replacement lens, and while it's bigger than I'd wanted, it can't make that much difference, can it? And then when I finally hoist the pack up onto my shoulders, I realise I've forgotten how heavy it was. We can't weigh it, but I suspect it's now around eight kilos, maybe a bit more with the lens, and I don't expect that to feel so heavy.

Down to the 7/11 by the station for some cash and something for lunch. At the entrance, we realise we're blocking a lady trying to get in with her wheeled suitcase, and as we move aside she asks us if we know 'Ocha - Japanese tea?'. She doesn't have much English - 'tea' is about it, but she then pulls us around to the drinks section of the shop and insists on buying us two bottles of green tea. I continue to be amazed by this custom of giving things to Henro, but isn't it nice of her?

The train takes us back along our route of yesterday afternoon. We get out at Hiwasa, and head off to find our accommodation for the next two nights. We cross the bridge over the river and turn down a little alleyway, and there's what must be the place.

Actually, there's remarkably little to indicate this must be the place, except that it's more or less where the White Book says we should find "GH Oyado Hiwasa". It's an old traditional house with a dark wooden facade and large wooden sliding doors just a couple of steps up from the path through the alley, with flower pots on each side. Looking more closely, there's an anonymous green letter box and a bell with a phone number underneath it that - yes, we got it right - matches that in the White Book.

We ring the bell. A voice over an intercom says, in English, "please come in", and when we push at the wooden door we find it opens for us.

Inside, there's a young Japanese who speaks particularly good English. We explain that we've arrived early, could we leave our bags, and we're planning to walk maybe as far as Mugi - the station two stops down the line, about 15km away - and then come back on the train. Yes, he says, we could do that. We could take the cliff walk, he says, much more interesting than following the main road. Then an older lady appears, who also speaks excellent English. At one point, she says, almost apologetically, to us, "I am going to talk to him for a moment in Japanese." Finally, Philippe, the owner, appears. It turns out that the lady is his wife, and the younger chap is their son. Continuing in excellent English, mother and son explain to Philippe what we plan to do. Immediately the discussion between the three drops into rapid French, only a little of which we can follow. "Au bord de la mer? On ne peut pas faire ça!"

Why can't we go along the coast? It isn't immediately obvious to us - or to the mother and son, apparently - but Philippe, who clearly has seen Henro come and Henro go, and occasionally Henro fall down, seems to have judged our walking abilities rather better than the other two thirds of his family. He reverts to English, and explains that, while the main road is level, the coast road, particularly at the Hiwasa end, has a challenging series of ups and downs that will take a very long time. He means will take *us* a very long time.

However, he has a compromise to suggest. The main road is

boring, but if we take it as far as the concrete works (he says this as though nobody could possibly miss the concrete works) we can then turn off to the left and take route 147, the 'sunshine road', which eventually meets up with the coast path, but has missed the ups and downs at the Hiwasa end.

So, we head off, happy to have left our backpacks behind once more, and saunter down the main road. Philippe is quite right about the concrete works; even we can't miss it, especially as the turn to the left is clearly marked as route 147. The 'sunshine road' rises up in an ominous sort of way, but is much quieter than the main road, and much more wooded. There's a sign banning motorcycles of more than 125cc from early evening until morning, which seems rather civilised.

After about two kilometres we realise we're crossing the coast path, and now we can see the Pacific Ocean coast of Shikoku. This is seriously spectacular scenery, densely wooded undulating hills rolling down to where their dark greens stop at the wave-splashed blue of the ocean. The join between land and sea is usually a patch of dark grey, steep, bare rock, but in places is a level stretch of either sand or lighter rocks. Tiny rocky islands are scattered quite close to the coast, and there are larger islands further offshore, their profiles clear against the paler blue of the sky.

The coast road itself has equally spectacular moments; it's a wide, well-maintained road, and occasionally sweeps high across a valley on top of towering concrete supports, curving across to disappear into the trees on the other side. It feels like too much road for its traffic, which appears to consist entirely of noisy motorbikes, many well over 125cc, more than a few of them large Harley-type chromed tourers. This is a road hikers can enjoy for the views, and bikers can enjoy for the turns. Fortunately, there aren't too many bikers out today.

There are numbered signs indicating viewpoints, and a set of four 'observation points' at intervals of about three kilometres. We stop at the first of these, where we find two other Henro - a German chap and a French girl - who've spread themselves out comfortably and are taking a long break enjoying the view.

We walk on. The scenery doesn't change much, but as we go we see one large offshore island slowly draw behind us, which shows we're making progress. The second and third observation points prove to be small and nothing particularly spectacular, but the fourth is much better equipped. The first and fourth have toilets, for which we're grateful. At the forth I slowly and painstakingly, with a couple of guesses at the kanji, decode a small and innocuous sign by the tap:

この水は飲めません

I think it says 'kono mizu-wa nomemasen' (don't drink the water), and I can't help thinking that there must be a more internationally-recognisable symbol that could have been used instead, if only in the interests of illiterate aliens like ourselves. We don't drink the water, but we do open up our seaweed triangles and have lunch. In the far distance, we hear what might be gunshots - about three, at roughly ten-minute intervals. Do people hunt around here? If so, what? Boar?

We're grateful we're only carrying our messenger bag and my camera. The Henro hats keep the sun off, but the Henro jackets do get warm, and we're perfectly happy to finally stroll down into the small town of Mugi. There doesn't seem to be a lot to Mugi, but it does have a station, which is all we ask, and we've timed things nicely to catch the 4:05 back to Hiwasa.

Taking the train back, and the time it takes for the journey, again makes us realise how far we're managing to walk. We've covered about 18 kilometres, and the spectacular coastline was easily worth the three extra kilometres over the direct route along the main road, but we still have another 60 or so kilometres to go before we reach Cape Muroto. It's going to be a while before we see temple 24.

The entrance area at Philippe's Guest House Oyado Hiwasa.

Motorbike traffic on the Sunshine Road.

The Sunshine Road sweeps over the countryside.

At the first rest point.

The Pacific coast between Hiwasa and Mugi.

Looking out from the fourth rest point.

As we make our way over the roughly 500 metres from Hiwasa station to our lodgings, I notice my left small toe is hurting again. I had thought I was over that.

We get back to the narrow alleyway just as Philippe arrives on his bike. We now go through the formalities of actually checking in, and Philippe gives us a long explanation of the etiquette connected with shoes and houses. He obviously gives this to everyone he feels might need it, and indeed, there is one thing I'd not appreciated: you should step directly from outside shoes to inside shoes, without putting your feet down - if you walk around in the area used for outside shoes in socks or bare feet, who knows what you might pick up and deposit on the tatami mats? This is obvious when you think about it, but I suspect it's something most Japanese feel uncomfortable explaining to a foreigner, which means it's left to other foreigners like Philippe.

He also supplies an aside about tatami mats, which reveals why he doesn't want clumsy foreigners tramping the detritus of the outside world into them. They're almost impossible to clean, he explains - they're straw, so you can't use water; they vacuum them, and they brush them, but that's it. If you have to replace a tatami mat it's about ¥10,000 (about $100) and you have to replace all six in a room together because you'll never get the colours to match otherwise. He says they normally replace tatami mats about every ten years. Hearing this, I'm so glad I didn't end up bursting my blister all over the tatami mats back in Kuramoto.

The house, built about 100 years ago, has a wonderfully old and traditional feel to it, and the sort of complicated geometry that I like in a house. There are a number of narrow staircases, and perhaps four guest rooms all jigsawed into it in some way. Downstairs is a small kitchen guests can use; Philippe doesn't do meals, but some breakfast things - bread, tea, etc. - are provided. He shows us the furo, a one-person affair, and a tight fit even then, but a welcome prospect.

Our room is up one flight of stairs, slightly spartan but oozing character. All the walls seem to be made of sliding dark wooden panels, including a set over the windows, which we finally get to slide enough to let some light in. The stairs down to the furo have white panels with embossed reliefs of flowers and branches. It is somehow the most Japanese house we've been in so far.

We take it in turns to go down to the furo, and soaking in that is just the thing after an eighteen kilometre walk. Even the temperature is comfortably below my pain threshold.

When I check on my feet, back in the room, I'm not entirely surprised to find a big blister on my left small toe. When I unwrap the bandage from my small right toe, I realise the toenail is no longer attached to the toe, but is nestling comfortably in the bandage. It may be comfortable, but I'm not. Elaine is laying out the futons and, as I move out of the way, I stub my toe violently against the leg of the small, low, table.

"What have you done?"

What I had done was scream and lie down on the floor clasping my toe.

"I've stubbed my toe!"

"Which one?"

"The one that hurts!"

I explain about the suddenly-unprotected nature of my small right toe, and the unfortunate coincidence that it was the one I stubbed against the table.

"Oh, poor you."

Which is more or less what I was thinking.

Come the evening, we look for supper. Philippe has suggested two options: Tsukushi, which he describes as a very traditional Japanese establishment; or somewhere by the bridge he calls the 'chicken place'. He says the chicken place *does* serve other things, but it sounds as if it might do so rather reluctantly. The general impression I get is of an American diner with a thing for chicken. We decide we'll try Tsukushi, which sounds a little more authentically Japanese.

On our way out, we run into two other guests, both Australian, who introduce themselves as Chris and Nadine. I might feel bad about having just sacrificed a toenail to the pilgrimage, but Chris and

Nadine are in much worse shape. They're wearing some of the loose-fitting Crocs shoes that Philippe has for use in the 'outside area' of the house, and explain that they had to borrow those because their feet have swollen so badly they can't even get their hiking boots on. Chris admits ruefully that some of the problem may be the weight of their packs; his apparently comes to about 14kg, and they've already posted some things home. When I ask him what he has in his pack he says, "mostly camera gear, to be honest." I sense the presence of a serious photographer, and we must have a chat sometime, but as we watch them hobble uncomfortably back into Philippe's, it's hard to resist something of a virtuous feeling as we consider our trimmed-down loads. On the other hand, we didn't mention we'd been having enough trouble with our backpacks that we'd been leaving them at base camp and taking the train to avoid carrying them.

Hiwasa doesn't seem to have a lot of places to eat. In fact, we don't see any as we head to the street where Philippe's map places Tsukushi, and it's not even obvious there's anywhere to eat when we do get there. There is what might be a sort of shop front, but it appears to be closed. A hint is a Coca-Cola sign with the English word 'closed' on it. That's the only word of English we can see. It sounds as if there might be people inside, but it looks very shut. It isn't even clear this is the place. We look to see if there's anywhere else in the street that might be it.

"What was the name again?" I ask. I never remember names.

"Tsukushi."

"I think this is it. That banner there has a 'tsu' and a 'ku' and a 'shi', although they're so stylised I didn't realise they were characters at first. I reckon this is it, and it's closed."

"So it's going to be the chicken place, then."

"It's going to be the chicken place."

We find the chicken place easily enough, which is just as well, because we've not seen anywhere else to eat.

It is *not* an American diner. It is a couple of decidedly Japanese rooms, sparsely furnished with basic tables and - incongruously - on the walls, pictures of the big sandstone monolith of Uluru, in the desert, standing proud in the Australian sunset. They do have an

English menu. Each dish is indeed chicken, except for a sashimi set - although there is a sashimi set with chicken, for those who happen to like chicken. Elaine orders the sashimi, and I get a katsu chicken donburi. And beer. Each dish is really, really, good. This is a top-notch chicken place.

"So, how do you think we're doing?"

"Well, I've lost a toenail, and I have a blistered toe, but I don't feel too bad. And our feet do still fit in our boots, which not everyone can say."

"We can do an easy walk tomorrow. Train back to Mugi, then it's about 12 kilometres to Kaifu, which is the end of the JR line. That's not a lot, but it will eat into the 60km we have left to Cape Muroto."

It's a plan.

23

TO THE END OF THE LINE, IN THE RAIN (TUESDAY APRIL 24)

Rain is forecast for today, so it's probably just as well our plans don't involve walking more than the relatively short stretch from Muji to Kaifu. But first I have to deal with the blister on my left foot. With some trepidation, and making sure I'm well clear of anything remotely like a tatami mat, I unwrap its bandage. This time, it doesn't burst horribly; it just sits there, feeling tender.

At about 7am, I dress, borrow Elaine's sewing kit, and limp down to the kitchen, hoping that it's empty. It is. I feel rather shifty, sneaking down to boil a kettle, sterilising the needle with the boiling water, sitting on the step between the kitchen and the outdoor area with my foot outside, and lancing the blister with the needle over a piece of tissue paper. Boringly unspectacular, in the end, but it does relieve the pressure, and with luck that will fix it. Elaine comes down.

"I've boiled the water; do you want tea?" I ask, which somehow seems horribly unhygienic, given why I boiled the water in the first place. We have a sort of breakfast of toast, butter, and tea.

Back in the room, we go over the plan for the next few days, because we'll need Philippe to book our accommodation. Tomorrow we'll leave Hiwasa, take the train to Kaifu, assuming we make it that far today, and carry on down the coast. From Kaifu it's about 45km down to Cape Muroto and temple 24, so on any reasonable assessment of our walking speed that will take us three days. It's also complicated by the fact that accommodation is limited and scattered rather unevenly along this fairly deserted stretch of coastline.

"Even if we thought we could do it in two hops of over 20km each, there just isn't anywhere to stay 20km south of Kaifu," explains Elaine, who's been paying close attention to the White Book. "That would put us right in the middle of the most deserted stretch of the whole coast. There's no 'there' there, and there's certainly nowhere to stay."

"Three shorter hops are fine by me. I mean realistically, I've just been sticking needles in my toes, so 45km in two days might be asking too much."

"Exactly. We can't avoid at least one long walk, but we can do 10km tomorrow, which gets us to Ikumi Beach, where there are a few places, and then one long haul, 20km, to what looks like the only place to stay in the whole deserted stretch, Lodge Ozaki, and then an easy-ish day to Cape Muroto."

"But we do need Philippe to get us into that one option in the bleak stretch."

At that point, there's a call from the other side of one of the walls.

"Hey, next door, these walls are paper thin and we're trying to sleep!"

We hadn't appreciated that the layout of the house had butted Chris and Nadine's room up against ours, and we had forgotten that Japanese walls often actually are made of paper, and even the wood panels of this room probably aren't effective soundproofing. It does seem to be late to still be sleeping, but I suppose if your feet don't fit your hiking boots, you may as well get all the rest you can.

We pack, silently, for a walk in the rain that's still forecast for today. For the first time, out come the waterproof trousers, and reluctantly I leave my camera behind, taking just the messenger bag for lunch and bandages and the vital White Book. Then we go downstairs to wait for Philippe or one of his family to turn up.

. . .

Philippe himself appears just after 9 o'clock. He and his family apparently live in a separate house a couple of blocks away. We explain what we need booking, and he says he'll get his wife to do that for us. It sounds as though even Philippe prefers to have a native Japanese speaker handle bookings, just like our French acquaintance from the walk to temple 22.

It isn't raining yet as we head to the station, but the sky is turning grey in the way skies do when they're getting ready to bucket down on suffering pilgrims with punctured blisters on their feet. We buy tickets, and put on the rain trousers. This is the first time we've done this in practice, and although in principle these unzip to let you get them on over hiking boots, in practice that isn't working for me. Anyone watching would think I'd never done this before. They'd be right.

But by the time the train for Mugi arrives, we're kitted out and ready. The trip to Mugi is an impressive reminder of how far we managed to walk yesterday. We stop at the Mugi Lawson for a more extended breakfast of bananas, croissants and coffee and finally hit the road a bit after 10 o'clock.

The road is route 55 and it's pretty boring, especially in the rain, which has finally arrived. But we do find we make good time, walking in the rain; we're lightly loaded, we don't stop for photo opportunities (no camera, and no opportunities) and we're remarkably cosy and dry in our rain gear.

"This walking in the rain isn't as bad as I thought it might be." Living in England might have accustomed me to rain, but actually it made me seriously averse to getting wet outdoors. Rain may be necessary, but there ought to be laws restricting it to times when I'm asleep. But like this, properly clad, nothing of me that matters is actually getting wet. I can handle this.

We slowly overtake another Henro, an older Japanese with an orange backpack. We manage to say 'konnichi-wa', and I think he asks us where we started from, so we say 'Mugi' because anything else involves trains and is far too complicated. Communication is frustratingly limited. He says something with the number 78 in it, and I think that's his age, which is pretty impressive. We move on ahead, leaving him walking steadily along.

A little later we pass a bay that looks strikingly bleak in the rain and stop to try one photo on an iPhone, and he catches us up again. This time, I've remembered something I can say to someone who's walking the Henro path at 78:

"O-genki desu-ne?" You're healthy, aren't you?

He nods, looking pleased, and we manage to exchange a few more words, although it's a somewhat constrained chat. In the end, he indicates we should carry on ("speedu" he says), and we move ahead, expecting he'll probably catch us up again.

As it happens, he doesn't. We press on - the only thing to do in the rain - and after about three hours' walking, which doesn't seem all that long, we reach Kaifu. There isn't a lot to Kaifu, although there are some more modern buildings, and we stop at a large sort of chemist-oriented home-things supermarket to stock up on bandages and the like, then head to the station.

Kaifu is the end of the line. It's the southern end of the JR railway line that runs down from Tokushima. There is another, private line that runs a bit further, but this is as far as JR goes. And even JR doesn't run express trains any further south than Muji.

We're back in 'Spirited Away' again. There's a section in that movie on a small train that runs from the bath-house of the spirits through a water-filled landscape, and this little almost empty train shuttling between Mugi and Kaifu has echoes of that.

The staircase at Philippe's Guest House Oyado Hiwasa

Packing in our room at Philippe's.

Rainclouds over the coast between Muji and Kaifu.

Kaifu station in the rain.

Back in Hiwasa, Philippe tells us his wife was able to make all our bookings for the coming nights, so we're good to set off tomorrow. We review the contents of our backpacks. What can we do to lighten the load? I definitely don't need my down jacket any more, and I've hardly used the small telephoto lens I brought. The lens is only about 200 grams, but anything we can post home will help.

There's a Post Office just down the street. When I get there, I find Chris and Nadine trying to post home yet more of their excessive load. This is causing some communications difficulties, especially as they want to try to make sure whoever they're sending their stuff to has to sign for it. I can't help much, but I look up the Japanese for 'signature' on my iPhone, which gets the idea across better than just miming writing something. It all takes a while but, once they've finished, the post office staff are well rehearsed in posting a parcel to Australia, which makes things easier for me. And I don't care about signatures.

Of course, there's always something you'd not thought of. In this case, they find a cheaper alternative way of sending it and want to discuss the options. I think the difference is ¥500 in ¥3500 and I honestly don't care, but don't know how to say that. Falling back on Google Translate, I manage to ask "how long does it take?" and discover the cheaper option is also faster, so I go for that ("hayaku ii desu", 'fast is good') and they're pleased. On the way out I pause to get cash from the Post Office ATM, which is fortunate, because it allows the postmistress to find me and give me the pen I'd left behind - one I'm quite fond of. On reflection, I may not mention my having used Google Translate to Elaine.

Back at the ryokan, it's filling up. A Dutch lady appears in the guest kitchen and explains how glad she is to be able to rest here for a couple of days, because she's 'emotionally exhausted'. She'd realised that just putting one foot in front of another day after day had become something to endure rather than enjoy, and I can see how that might happen. I've been sitting in the kitchen reading through Philippe's visitor's book, or at least the few entries in English and some of the more tractable ones in French, and most are on the general theme of having arrived here in a general state of unable to carry on, and being revived by the help and hospitality. I particularly liked the phrase 'moments de zenitude' in one entry. More prosaically, there's an entry from an Australian who wrote that he'd been drawn here by the free WiFi.

A well-travelled Japanese chap who looks in his fifties appears and starts talking to Ken (Philippe's son) in French. After a few minutes, they switch to Japanese, apparently realising they share the same native language. He looks as if he's been on the road for a while, and Ken shows him to one of the ground floor rooms. I head back upstairs until it's time for supper.

We decide we'll give Tsukushi another try for supper. Maybe it's only closed on Mondays; we should have asked Philippe earlier but he's gone home now. We go down through the kitchen, where we find a merry little group assembled. Chris and Nadine and the Dutch lady are chatting with the Japanese chap, who not only turns out to speak excellent English, but who also used to work for the Australian Commonwealth Bank! We don't mention Elaine's ATM problems, but we do raise the question of supper, and explain about both Tsukushi and the chicken shop. The Dutch lady has already eaten something and doesn't want to go out again, Chris and Nadine make a non-committal note of the alternatives and, to our relieved delight, our Japanese ex-Australian banker says he'll come with us to Tsukushi.

It's still raining, so we slip on the rain trousers, borrow three umbrellas from a copious selection by the front door, and Elaine leads the way to Tsukushi.

Which still has a closed door and a Coca-Cola sign that says 'closed'. I don't think our companion even notices a 'closed' sign in English. He opens the door and goes in, and we follow, feeling that maybe that's what we should have done yesterday.

Inside is a single warmly-decorated, large but cosy room with a bar at one end, a number of low tables along one wall, and a conventional table with five comfortable chairs in the middle of the room. We sit ourselves down there. Scattered all over the place are signs and blackboards with what may be descriptions of dishes and their prices. Not one of them means anything to us.

At this point we finally exchange names. Our companion is Kobayashi-san, but he says when he was working in Melbourne he was known as Sean (or possibly Shaun). He explains that this place sells drinks and a large assortment of small dishes. Basically, it's a tapas bar. He asks if there's anything we don't eat, and we say we eat anything, although Elaine adds "not too much meat". He asks rather tentatively if we have any budget constraints, we say no, and put ourselves completely in his hands.

Sean calls over the fellow behind the bar, who's been watching all this with quiet interest - there isn't anyone else here yet - and there's a discussion we can't follow a word of, but it involves some serious pointing at blackboard items, asking questions and getting answers, but eventually they both seem happy. Three glasses of beer appear on the table, and an assortment of other good things starts to arrive. Eggplant, green beans in pods - probably edamame - a pile of sashimi, three prawns with huge heads, bits of cuttlefish, a dish of avocado.

It's all glorious, and we'd never have managed to order anything like this on our own. I realise that Elaine has been reversing her chopsticks correctly when picking food from the communal dishes, and that I haven't. The more you think about the reason for reversing the chopsticks like that, once you've eaten with them, the more you prefer not to think about it, and I mend my ways quickly. If Sean noticed he didn't say anything about it, which is rather the Japanese way.

Midway through the meal, we're joined by Chris and Nadine, who'd decided to try to find the three of us, and obviously weren't put off by Coca-Cola 'closed' signs. We end up having a very jolly evening. It emerges that one reason Chris and Nadine had been a bit unprepared for the Henro track was that they'd not originally intended to do it at all. They'd been in Germany intending to go to Spain to walk the Camino to Santiago de Compostela, but their visas ran out, so they switched to Shikoku as a last-minute plan 'B'. Nadine works in food, organising diets for cancer patients, and is vegetarian, which is tricky in Japan. Temples, which seem to be all strictly vegan, have been working well for them, and they'd stayed at temple 12, which we thought David Moreton had told us had had to stop offering accommodation. Evidently not. Chris had just retired from what sounded like a job in financial IT, and was reinventing himself as a professional photographer, which helped explain the weight of camera gear in his backpack.

Sean appears to have worked for most of the big Australian banks. mostly in Tokyo, but also in Melbourne for Westpac. He's actually 65, rather older than I'd thought he looked. He has an untidy growth of beard that he's been letting grow but isn't happy with it because it's turning out to be quite white. He retired just recently and is now walking all 88 temples in one go, having covered the whole route in piecemeal fashion over previous years. He's planning to be up at 6:30 in the morning because he plans to cover 35km tomorrow, intending to reach a place he knows and likes and intends to stay a couple of days. I'd noticed earlier, when he took his shoes off, that most of his toes were carefully wrapped in individual white bandages, so he obviously knows things about the care of Henro feet that I wish I'd known. He says he needs about an hour to bandage his feet in the morning.

Chris and Nadine try to order some more dishes, selecting them by picking an item from the menu at random and asking Sean what it is. If you're vegetarian and in Japan, the odds are rather against you in this game. Their first try produces something sensible, the next two don't, and Sean finally orders something on their behalf. Chris holds up an empty beer glass and catches the bartender's eye. A new beer appears on the table. I say "watashi-mo, imahitotsu'" and he brings me one too. Nadine looks accusingly at me: "in the post office you said you didn't speak Japanese." I have to explain that all I have are a few scattered words and phrases, of which "me too, one more" is one of the few useful examples. I've always claimed that in a foreign country, all you need to be able to say is "two beers, please", "another two beers, please", and "where's the toilet?", but Japan has been proving me sadly wrong here.

Sean needs to be up early tomorrow, and Elaine and I feel the need for a fairly early start, so we split the bill five ways and leave Chris and Nadine to finish off what's left. It's still raining outside, but not badly.

I'm woken at about one in the morning by a storm outside rattling the wooden shutters of the room. There's that nice cosy feel of being inside and warm and dry when it's anything but outside, but it makes sleep difficult, and eventually I'm forced to dig some earplugs out of my backpack. With earplugs, I can sleep through most things (and once slept through a fire alarm, but that's another story).

24

DAMN FINE ACCOMMODATION - IKUMI BEACH (WEDNESDAY APRIL 25)

We come down to breakfast in the small kitchen fairly early, at least by my lax standards, although not early enough to say goodbye to Sean, who seems to have left well before. I bring my camera down, intending to get some shots of the downstairs area, and end up comparing cameras with Chris. He's carrying a huge Canon camera with a suitably large lens mounted on it. It's a lovely camera, but it feels as if it could anchor a battleship, let alone a Henro. He has an additional telephoto lens which is even bigger. He picks up my little Olympus mirrorless camera with its compact 'pancake' lens and acknowledges that it's going to be a lot easier to carry. I tell him truthfully that I envy the quality of the images he'll get from his, but I don't envy him the weight. Nadine nods, ruefully, and Elaine finishes her breakfast and keeps well clear of this discussion of boys and their toys.

We say goodbye to everyone, collect our packs, and move off to get the 8:24 train to Kaifu. Once they get away from Hiwasa, Chris and Nadine are planning to try to get to one of the islands off the coast that we saw yesterday and stay there for a day or so. As we go, I notice that my small left toe is feeling a bit sore yet again, which is funny, because I'm sure it looked fine when I checked it earlier. We'll have a proper look when we get to Kaifu.

We expected to have to change trains at Mugi, on to the small 'Spirited Away' Mugi-Kaifu shuttle train, but no, the electronic sign in the carriage says, 'this train is bound for Kaifu' in alternating English and Japanese. But there is a long stop at Mugi, as we wait for another train on the other track. It arrives, people board and it starts to move off, but there's a lady still trying to get to it so she can get on. She seems to have left her run too late, but an official on the platform in a yellow crash-hat waves frantically by the side of the train, the train slows and stops, the doors open and she scrambles on. So, JR does know how to be flexible with its timetables! As the train leaves, we see the yellow JR crash-hat and another local chatting animatedly. Possibly this is the most interesting thing to happen in Mugi this week.

Once at Kaifu, I look at my foot. Now I see why it's feeling sore. The small left toe has a new, glaringly obvious, blister. How did that happen? All we can do is apply a Band-Aid and if necessary I'll lance it tomorrow.

We set off.

Today's walk isn't going to be all that far, 10km, maybe 12 at most, will get us to Ikumi Beach, but this is going to be the first real walking we've done for a while with full backpacks, and it already feels completely different; this is hard work. Suddenly, instead of just a camera and a messenger bag full of lunch, everything I brought to Japan for a month is clinging onto my back and needing to be carried for the next 10 kilometres.

Just over three kilometres past Kaifu, the White Book has a 'knife and fork' symbol, which according to the legend in the front indicates 'dining room, restaurant/cafe'. This one, however, is specifically labelled 'vending machine'. Unfortunately, we've already passed it, so we never know what makes this particular vending machine so worthy of mention. Maybe it's telling us that finding anything to eat is about to get much harder.

Shishikui is a small town that has the first of the two train stations on the extended private line that runs south from Kaifu. It also has a small shop that sells us some rice triangles for lunch and some extra Band-Aids, which I suspect I may need. There doesn't seem to be any shortage of vending machines, spoiling that theory about the one marked in the White Book.

We see our first surfers, making a slightly desultory effort on a beach with not much surf. We note with interest that they have an area where they've all taken their shoes off, which somehow is just what we'd expect Japanese surfers to do. It starts to rain, and we dig out our light ponchos - mine is particularly lightweight, and hard to put on, but it works.

We go through a long tunnel of about 600m, which does at least have a safety barrier between us and the traffic, and then a shorter tunnel, which doesn't, and we find we've crossed the prefecture line and have left Tokushima prefecture and are now officially in Kochi prefecture. (Shikoku has four prefectures, rather like counties, and the Henro trail goes through each in turn: Tokushima, Kochi, Ehime, and Kagawa.) To welcome us, the rain stops.

The Henro path diverges from the main road and goes through the fairly prosperous-looking village of Kannoura. All along the way we've been seeing tsunami warnings and pointers to safe areas, but on a concrete barrier that forms part of its harbour wall, Kannoura has gone one better. The barrier has drawings of emergency personnel and what we assume are emergency instructions in huge letters running the length of the wall. They're almost decoration, in the way old drawings might incorporate exquisite calligraphy. We're taken by Kannoura, which really is the absolute, unarguable, end of the line, because Kannoura station is the second and last on the private line running south from Muji. After this, public transport runs on roads and has wheels and is called a bus.

Our first sight of a surfing beach.

The harbour at Kannoura.

The sea wall at Kannoura.

Ninja on a bridge at Kannoura.

We pause for lunch in a spectacular setting just by the side of the cliff road, with waves crashing on the coast below. We sit by two blue-green statues on small plinths, one a Jizō with a clean new white bib, the other a goddess figure we can't identify. It's a nice place to sit, but we need to keep moving.

Not too long after, we reach the small surfing village of Ikumi Beach.

There don't seem to be many buildings in Ikumi Beach, but our night's accommodation is easy to find. By the side of the road, outside one of the houses, mounted high on a slightly rusted green iron structure, is a large plastic sign that might even light up at night, which says, "Beach guest house, minshuku IKUMI, Damn fine accommodation."

"Well, that's what we want. Damn fine accommodation."

The main part of the house looks shut, but a small separate building has an open door, and we look in. Someone comes out to meet us.

"Minshuku Ikumi?"

"Ah, no, but, owner is friend. Wait please."

And they disappear into the main house and come back with a thinnish fellow with a weather-beaten face, a slightly greying moustache and goatee beard, and a jolly smile. And a pretty good command of English.

This turns out to be Ten, who runs Minshuku Ikumi. He's expecting us, and leads us over to the slightly chaotic house, shows us a selection of house slippers alongside a clutter of random pieces of surfing paraphernalia, takes us upstairs, shows us a small kitchen and points in the general direction of the toilets, and we follow him into a room large enough for a whole surfing family. The room not only has two futons and room for two more, but a pair of bunk beds over against one wall. Presumably, in high surfing season, this would provide cheap accommodation for quite a number of surfing buddies. For tonight, it will do us splendidly.

We leave our things in the room and take a quick walk to the beach. Ikumi Beach clearly *is* the sort of surfing village that I'd originally thought Yuki might have been. The beach is deserted, bare and windswept and overcast at the moment, and behind it are some surfing equipment shops and a large beach hotel that looks as if it might have had a heyday once upon a time.

Back at M. Ikumi, Elaine investigates the bath.

"It's incredibly hot. But I think we're the only people here, so I felt OK running some cold water into it until the bath thermometer said 43 degrees."

"43 degrees?"

"That's what Philippe's fancy bath system was set to. It seemed a good number to pick. His was fine."

Philippe had a bath controlled from a central panel mounted in the guest kitchen. He would set the temperature in the afternoon and when the bath reached that temperature the control panel would make an announcement in Japanese, presumably to the effect that the bath was now operational. And the temperature had been fine, if a bit hot for my taste.

Ten's system is slightly less high-tech, as I find when I go down to try the bath. The bath thermometer is a small plastic floating pig with a thermometer built into it. And the pig and Philippe's expensive electronic sensors clearly have a serious difference of opinion about the meaning of '43 degrees'. This is hot.

Back in the room, I investigate the furnishings. There are six surfing magazines, two of which are in English. There's a DVD player with one surfing video, and copies of 'My stepmother is an alien', 'Night in the Museum', some Japanese movie about a ship sinking, 'Casablanca' and 'Gone with the Wind'. I suppose that's just what you want when there's no surf. I like this room. It's a huge contrast to the other places we've stayed so far, and they've all been splendid in their various ways, but this room has a feeling of friendly informality.

Supper turns out to be in the building at the side that we'd gone to originally. This is a glorious combination of office, dining room, and general store room, and must be where everything that comes into the house eventually migrates to. There's a large dining table with two huge meals prepared, and while we enjoy them Ten sits at what might be a desk but is actually a table football game with a cover on it. His English rattles along. He tells us he's been running this place, which we think he says he rents, for somewhere over 10 years, and before that he ran a hamburger bar in Shishikui. He seems happy just to be somewhere he can surf. He explains that before Golden Week his guests are mostly Henro, but after Golden Week it gets too hot for walking and then the surfers start to appear. He tells us we've been lucky to have had just one day of rain so far. He gives us stickers that say 'Minshuku Ikumi', 'Damn fine accommodation', 'Live aloha'. He's proud of the 'Damn fine accommodation' line, which he says he got from watching the Twin Peaks episode in which special agent Cooper says, "That's damn fine coffee!"

And we sleep damn well in Ten's damn fine accommodation.

Ten at his soccer table.

Statues at our lunch spot on the way to Ikumi Beach.

The view down from our lunch spot.

At Ikumi Beach, by the surf club.

Damn Fine Accomodation - the sign for Ten's minshuku Ikumi.

25

THROUGH THE GOROGORO-ISHI
(THURSDAY APRIL 26)

This will be the day of our long walk down the coast, through the section known as the 'gorogoro-ishi'. The name means 'roaring rocks' and refers to when pilgrims used to have to walk along the dangerous rocky seashore, and the White Book warns that even today the section can be a problem for pilgrims, with its lack of stores and vending machines.

It's also short of places to stay, and the next accommodation on the road south from here at Izumi Beach is the rather isolated Lodge Ozaki, about 20 kilometres away, which is about as far as we can reasonably manage in a day. We have at least learned our limitations. Fortunately, Elaine - or more accurately, Philippe - or even more accurately, Philippe's wife - managed to get us booked in there. All we have to do is reach it.

And it's in the interests of our reaching it that I sneak into the little kitchen opposite our room, boil a kettle, and stick Elaine's sterilised sewing needle into the blister on my left small toe. It's a satisfyingly undramatic operation, no tatami mat injured in the process, and the patient returns to our room ready for the long haul to Lodge Ozaki.

In the small building where we had supper the night before, we find Ten seated at his table-football desk, watching the BBC news on the TV. French president Macron is visiting the White House, and the two Koreas are about to have talks. A generous breakfast is spread out for us on the main table.

"Remember," he tells us, "you have 16-kilometre stretch to walk with nowhere to buy food. Even no vending machine." He and the White Book are on the same page here. "Buy food, drink, at store in town, here."

We're ready to go soon after 8 o'clock. We say goodbye to Ten, tell him it really was damn fine accommodation, enjoy his smile, and head off down the road. We get some water from the vending machines near the surf beach and start to look out for the store Ten told us about. At first we think we must have gone past it, as the few buildings start to thin out, but in the end we see it on our left. It's not big, but it has some rice balls, a few bento-type boxes, and some bananas. We feel ready to face the desolation of the gorogoro-ishi.

It's a pleasant day to walk, with a little cloud covering the sky and taking the edge off the sunshine. The Henro path occasionally offers small detours from the main road, usually to take in small shrines or to pass Henro huts, and we take one of these through a lovely little village. Some of the buildings have seen better times, but there's a colourful red bridge over a small stream, and for the first time this trip we see low cloud filling the gaps between the hills, which is how hills ought to look from a proper Japanese village.

There's also a wonderfully eccentric shrine, reached up a flight of steps lined with red and blue vertical banners that we can't read, with buildings arranged around a small yard filled with a colourful collection of tables, potted plants, more banners, and ornaments, all in a charmingly organised jumble. There's nobody there, but on one of the tables is a large dog, following us disinterestedly through half-closed eyes, lying on top of a pile of cushions topped off by a red and white Disney blanket.

To the side of the shrine, there's an extremely comfortable Henro hut, with rugs on the floor, a small electric heater, a table neatly stacked with books, and signs, pictures, and a calendar all neatly arranged around the walls. It looks a real home from home.

Back on the main road, a bit over an hour after leaving Ten's place, we come across a single vending machine set back from the road, with a hand-written notice in front of it that reads, in English and Japanese:

"Warning: Next vending machine in 10km."

It has a small red Henro figure drawn at the bottom.

We must be entering the gorogoro-ishi.

The well-appointed Henro hut at the small shrine.

Low cloud between the hills, and a red bridge.

The guardian of the small shrine, on their Disney blanket.

The small, charming, and slightly jumbled shrine.

The last vending machine for 10km.

Until now the road has held back a little from the coast, but now it runs directly alongside the ocean. To the right of the road are steep tree-covered hills, to the left is a short grassy slope down to a grey rocky beach, with the waves breaking gently onto the rocks. You can imagine that walking along those rocks would have been difficult, before the road was built, and in bad weather, with the roar of the sea pounding the coast, faltering pilgrims would have regretted not waiting for calmer times.

And we follow this for most of the morning. It's spectacular, but it's also a long road. Comfortingly, there are numbered signs by the side of the road showing the kilometres left to Cape Muroto, and the numbers keep going down. Two days ago, these were starting with a six. Now it's a four, and eventually we reach the first that starts with a three. Thirty-nine kilometres is still a distance, but we've got two days.

Occasionally we can see a large bird above us in the sky. It's hard not to see this as a vulture, on the lookout for weakened pilgrims.

We have a quick lunch at a small lay-by with some seats and a large sign that has a picture of the coast with some distances marked, a cheerful drawing of what could be a can with two hands, one holding a flower, and a lot of writing in which 'gorogoro' appears a number of times. We assume it's telling us something useful, but have no idea what.

We set off again, south down the coast road.

We see another Henro coming the other way. He stops, and seems to be taking a photograph of something among the trees that rise up above the road. We pause, he points, and Elaine spots it first.

"It's a monkey! Up there, in the branches. There, there where I'm pointing!"

And then I spot it too. A small, red-faced monkey darting between the branches, occasionally pausing to look down at us. There's more than one. Even when you know they're there, they're some distance away, and hard to find, and you wonder how this other Henro noticed them. Eventually they disappear off deeper into the trees, and we all carry on as before.

Slowly we realise the hills are no longer so close as they were. There are paddy fields starting to appear now, filling the widening plain between the hills and the road, and finally we spot a vending machine. I'd assumed that somewhere we'd see the pair for the last vending machine we saw, one that also said 'last vending machine for 10km' but in the other direction, but if there is such a twin, we missed it. Still, we've made it across the treacherous gorogoro-ishi, that desolate stretch where the poor pilgrim can't find a machine that will sell bottled water, and we have survived. It's an achievement. It would have been more of an achievement a thousand years ago, and in bad weather, but still.

The road bends inland, and the signs for the Henro path lead us off the main road and take us a short cut across a river and into a small port town up ahead. At least, they would if the bridge across the river wasn't blocked off. Just why isn't clear, but there's a pretty intimidating barrier across the road and we can't see any easy way over it. Elaine, of course, takes this as a sign of personal map-reading failure, whereas of course, it's actually a barrier across the road. We backtrack a bit, sidetrack a bit more, and eventually get back onto the main road and follow it into the town. Finally, we manage to cut across to rejoin the Henro short-cut through the back of the town and down to the port. At one point, we realise we're at the other end of the blocked off bridge, and it looks as if it's been closed because it's blocked by garbage collection trucks. This is surely implausible, but we have no way of finding out more.

The port is seriously picturesque, with the green-tinged blue of the water meandering past a complicated series of breakwaters that presumably are precautions against tsunami, or at least aggressively rough seas. Leading out of the town, the main road is bounded by a high ocean wall with a walkway along the top of it, and you wonder how often this gets tested by the sea. Another large bird hovers over us as we walk along the wall. If it is a vulture, it's too late. I don't think Shikoku has vultures, but I'll check sometime.

A sign warning about excessive speed.

The coast along the gorogoro-ishi.

Trees on the coastline along the gorogoro-ishi.

A monkey among the trees.

The harbour at Sakihama.

Along the sea wall at Sakihama.

Lodge Ozaki is about three kilometres south of the port, but the White Book is a bit unclear about the exact location. The Henro path in the book splits, with one part following the main road, one apparently making a detour slightly inland, and Lodge Ozaki seems to be right in the middle of the two.

"There doesn't seem to be a shrine or anything on the inland branch, so maybe that's what you take if you want Lodge Ozaki," says Elaine, speculatively. "Let's try that way."

The inland branch is taking us into a small village, but we don't see anything that looks as if it might be Henro accommodation. However, Henro accommodation isn't always obvious, as we've noticed, so it isn't clear if we've gone wrong or not. The village looks pretty deserted, but finally we see someone working in his garden.

"Sumimasen. Lodge Ozaki?"

He nods, points in the general direction of somewhere in the distance, realises this is going to be hard to explain, puts down whatever he was doing, and beckons us to follow him. He leads us down one street, over to another, takes a cut through what is obviously the village cemetery, and finally brings us out on the main coast road. He then points down the road and says "Ozaki."

There is only one building in that direction, so presumably that's it. We walk down the road. There's a sign, and, given that I know the answer already, I can make out the hiragana characters for "O-za-ki".

"The sign says Lodge Ozaki. I can make out the characters."

"It's also got the right phone number," says Elaine. So much for having taught myself to read Hiragana.

The door seems to be open, so we walk in.

It looks empty.

Deserted.

"Sumimasen?" we say to the empty room.

A young fellow appears from somewhere in the back. He looks at us enthusiastically, says something we don't understand, realises we haven't understood, goes back, and returns with a piece of paper. On it is written:

"Tonight supper will become lunch. Sorry."

In all honestly, the meaning of that could be a little clearer.

"In room," he says helpfully. And points at the paper again. We may have reached the limit of his English.

"Do you know how to ask what's in the room?"

"No. It isn't one of my few phrases."

He disappears again, and comes back with something in his hand. Elaine realises what it is.

"It's a bento box. Oh. Maybe we get a bento box in the room. Maybe that's what supper is going to be."

"Maybe. That might sort of make supper like lunch.."

"I think,", says Elaine, "that whoever normally runs this place is away, and he's been left in charge. So there isn't a proper supper, but we get some ready-prepared Bento box in the room."

"In room," he says, waving the bento box happily, having realised he's finally got the idea through to us. Carried away with a successful communication, Elaine decides to go for broke.

"I wonder if we can get beer with the bento. Not now, with supper."

"OK. Ah. Biru-ga arimaska? Is there beer? In room?"

He seems to think this is an odd question, but nods, "Hai", yes.

That settled, he shows us the register, which we fill in, leads us upstairs and opens a door to reveal exactly the sort of room you'd like to stay in right by the coast. It has two doors, and looks as if the divider between two smaller rooms has been removed to make one big room. And those two rooms were right at the front of the house, with balconies looking out onto the ocean. I could sit and look at that for the rest of the day.

He points out a small fridge, and opens it. It is almost completely full of 550ml bottles of Asahi beer. I like this room more and more. And this does explain why he thought the question about beer was a bit odd. Of course there's beer available.

Elaine mentions her favourite Japanese word, 'furo', we remember 'sentaku' for laundry, and with a bit of pointing to downstairs even that gets negotiated to everyone's satisfaction.

We both make use of the furo, Elaine organises our laundry, we consider a walk on the beach, shelve that idea in favour of just sitting with a beer and looking at the view, and wait for supper.

. . .

At 6pm there's a knock on the door, and it's the lad from downstairs with our bento boxes. He seems to have done a fine job. The bento is fish-based, a nice temperature, and smells appetising. All it needs is beer, and that's in the fridge.

A few minutes later, there's another knock at the door. I open it, and a different but slightly familiar Japanese face smiles at me. I say "hello" and he looks at me as if I ought to know him, then gestures at his freshly shaven chin. It's Sean Kobayashi! He's caught up with us. He explains he knew we were here because he saw our names in the book when he registered. He suggests we eat together downstairs, we invite him in instead, offer him a beer - in a tea cup, because we can't find any more glasses - and we settle down to what turns out to be a most pleasant, long chatty meal, in which he passes on lots of hints about other places to stay further down the track. We won't get there this year, but we've already been talking about when we might be able to come back and continue. Maybe next year?

We finally say goodnight to Sean, and settle down to bed. There's a bit of noise from the lorries on the road, and I wake occasionally, but it's worth it to stay in such a splendid setting.

26

THE DEEP SEA, CAPE MUROTO, AND TEMPLE 24 (FRIDAY APRIL 27)

Last night we'd been told breakfast was at 6am, and we'd looked up the time of sunrise: 5:20am. Given the view from our room, if I have to get up in time for early breakfast, I'm going to make the extra effort to be up to see the sunrise, and the alarm on my phone has been set to make sure I don't miss it. Sunrise over the Pacific. It will be the first time I've seen it from Japan.

I sit out on the balcony, watching. There's a low bank of cloud in the distance, just over the ocean, and although the sun isn't above the horizon yet, some slightly higher clouds are already reflecting its red light. Then something bright inches over the horizon, a large yellow ball glowing in the gap between the low cloud bank and the sea, inching up slowly until it disappears into the clouds.

But the trick to a dramatic sunrise is to arrange the cloud banks properly, and today as the sun rises above the lowest bank it lights up the higher layers in a variety of oranges and reds, and the water below reflects a broad irregular line of light from the shore to the horizon, leading your eye to the risen sun. It's stunning, and I'm glad I set my alarm for it.

It's only as I start to get ready for breakfast that I realise.

I've just seen the sun rise over the land of the Rising Sun.

. . .

Sean is already at breakfast when we get down, and it's being served by the lady who runs the place, who explains in good English that she had to be away last night and was everything OK? All fine, not problem, we tell her, ignoring the slight confusion over the written note, which, with hindsight, was clear enough once you knew what it meant. Breakfast is excellent and dishes just keep on coming. I'm pleased to see that Sean breaks up his fish by holding a chopstick in each hand and hacking it into pieces, because that's what I've had to do, but I'd worried it was both inelegant and probably some sort of dreadful faux pas. At the end, there's even a bowl of yoghurt and some fruit, something that's fairly rare in Japan, and we really appreciate it. We say goodbye to Sean, who once again has set himself a challenging day's walk, pack and move off ourselves.

We're about ten minutes down the road when Elaine realises she's left her headband in our room. I wait with the backpacks while she goes back for it. She's gone rather longer than I expected, but eventually I see her coming back down the road.

"Sorry to be so long. I couldn't get in at first. It seemed it was completely deserted. They've all gone. Eventually I remembered there was a back door down by the laundry and sneaked in that way. I got up to our room and there was my headband."

Elaine has successfully burgled Lodge Ozaki.

It's now just about 8am, and we're on the move. There's a distance marker by the side of the road that says 20km to Cape Muroto. Well, we did twenty kilometres yesterday, and we're starting earlier today, thanks to the sunrise. We can do this.

The road is pretty much the same as it was for most of yesterday, rocky beach to our left, green hills to our right. For most of the journey it hugs the coast, although occasionally it bends inland a little. We pass a pair of 'husband and wife' rocks, two separate vertical rocks that have been joined by a rope in a symbol of union. It's a charming idea.

We had a filling breakfast, but haven't really got anything yet for lunch, and are feeling like a coffee break. There aren't many buildings along this road, certainly no convenience stores, and nothing that looks to me like any sort of café either. But Elaine has well-honed instincts here, and notices a small building on the other side of the road, with two vans parked outside it.

"I think that might be worth a look."

"You think it's a cafe? I can't see any sign of it."

"Maybe. I think there is a very small sign outside. There. Can you read any of that?"

We go over the road.

"There's some kanji, they mean nothing to me, then it says 'ka-ki-mi' - I don't know what that means either - and then, oh, it says 'kō-hī'. That's coffee. Maybe it is a café. How did you know?"

"Instinct."

We go in, and it is indeed a café. It's a jolly little place with a group of the local ladies sitting around, one chap on his own at a separate table, and now us. Now that we're inside, it could be an English village café. We sit down at a table, we're brought water, ask for kōhī, and it comes in charmingly elegant cups and saucers. After a few minutes, the lady behind the counter comes to us with two beakers of what turn out to be, not tea, but a pleasant, if rather salty, thin soup of some sort. It's a civilised and slightly unexpected pause along the Henro trail.

But, we realise we have to keep going. About half an hour further on, the Henro path detours through a small village, and we stop at a little store to look for something for lunch. We do buy *something*, but aren't exactly sure what it is we've bought. It's a packet of two things that look vaguely cake-y, and some sausage-shaped things that say 'banana', in English, but which don't appear to be bananas. As we go, the owner presses a packet of crisps on us. We may have something for lunch.

We pass a rather slow-moving Henro in blue trousers. We don't often pass anybody, so this is a notable event. I suggest that maybe his feet hurt; Elaine thinks (and she's probably right) that he's a rather older Henro making slow but steady progress.

Sunrise at Lodge Ozaki.

The Rising Sun.

Lodge Ozaki.

Husband and Wife rocks.

We're diverted away from the main road by workers doing something or other that involves diverting people away from the main road. We sit and eat one of whatever we've bought, as a sort of morning tea - it's some variety of bun with bean paste. We leave the rest for later. Looking behind, we see 'Stanley the slow but steady Henro' in his blue trousers negotiating with the road workers to be allowed to go the direct way. It looks as if they're letting him do so.

We carry on, get back onto the main road, and a bit further along we overtake 'Stanley' again. He smiles as we go past. Elaine was right; he is rather older, but he does look fit.

The distance markers to Cape Muroto keep dropping. We're managing something like three kilometres an hour, so by midday we've covered about twelve kilometres and the distance markers are now saying about 8km to the Cape. We see signs about 'Deep Sea World', which sounds interestingly like the Sea Turtle museum in Hiwasa. The signs say we're about one and a half kilometres from whatever it turns out to be, so we'll find out fairly soon.

Half an hour later, we come to a road leading off to our left and signs to both 'Deep Sea World' and to 'Searest Muroto'. There's more about Deep Sea World but nothing we can read. Searest Muroto describes itself as a spa, which isn't something we're particularly interested in. At least one of these two must be popular - there are signs to a car park, and we can see that there's a second road leading off to the left a little further down. On zero evidence either way, we decide the second will be the one for Deep Sea World.

It isn't. It leads to a large modern building marked 'Searest Muroto'. We follow the road round, through the car park, which is already playing host to a tour bus (evidently it is popular) and on to another even larger building.

Which is also marked 'Searest Muroto'. And that seems to have exhausted the list of buildings that we can see.

"We can go in," I suggest. "At least they ought to know where Deep Sea World is."

"At the very least, there's probably a toilet. That would be a good start."

We go in.

It certainly looks as if it should have toilets. It has a large reception area, with a front desk and smartly dressed staff. There's a restaurant over to one side. What this looks like is a hotel. Maybe it is a hotel.

Elaine spots the toilets and gives them priority. I go over to the front desk. This is the sort of fancy place that will speak English at the front desk.

"Sumimasen. Eigo-ga wakarimaska?" Do you speak English? There's a shaking of heads. I'd hoped someone dressed so formally at the front desk of a pricey Japanese hotel might speak English. This is going to be trickier than I thought.

"Deep Sea World desu-ka?" Is this Deep Sea World? Not that I think it is, but it's a start. There's a nod. Oh. But it's Searest Muroto. Is Deep Sea World the same thing as Searest Muroto? How do I ask that?

"Searest Muroto-wa, Deep Sea World desu-ka?" Which sort of means 'Is Searest Muroto Deep Sea World?'. They seem to think this is a silly question, but they nod.

I am beginning to think Deep Sea World may not be a museum.

"Kore-wa, nan desu-ka?" This, what is it? That's the question you're told to ask when you point to something on a menu and want to know what it is. It's a silly question, because you almost certainly aren't going to understand the answer. The people at the desk look puzzled, which is understandable, then they look under the desk and come up with what I think must be the only thing they have that's in English.

It's a list of instructions for visitors to the spa. Which I suppose must be what this is. They include a peremptory 'swimsuits must be worn', and there's also a list of prices for various options, one of which is 'hire of swimsuits'.

Elaine comes back, and I tell her what I've found out.

"This is Deep Sea World, which is just another name for Searest Muroto, and it's a spa."

"It's not a museum of life in the depths of the ocean?"

"It's a spa."

We consider the restaurant, briefly, but decide we can find somewhere in the grounds to eat what's left of whatever it was we bought back at the store.

Outside the building, we notice a huge sign we'd walked quickly past on the way in. It extols, in English, the virtues of spa treatments that use deep sea water. So this is a big complex devoted to pampering people who believe deep sea water has semi-magical properties. We can see three separate buildings on a large site, and there are actually three drives leading to the main road. There is also a small shady table out in the grounds with a toilet block nearby, and here we have lunch. The sausage-shaped things with 'banana' embossed on them turn out to be rather long banana cakes, and the rest of the bun with bean paste is still a bun with bean paste.

We see that the White Book gives the times for some bus services around here, and 'Deep Sea World' is listed as the final destination of many of the routes. We've clearly ended up at one of the centres of economic activity in Cape Muroto, without realising it.

. . .

On the basis of the distance markers, we'd assumed we still had six or more kilometres to go to the tip of Cape Muroto, which is roughly where we'll find temple 24, but we can see Deep Sea World on the map in the White Book, and it looks as if we're only a couple of kilometres away. Carrying on another four kilometres, following the distance markers, would have you well out into the ocean and exploring the Deep Sea for yourself. This will probably resolve itself eventually, one way or another.

We walk on, pleased to realise we're almost there, and fairly soon we see a sign pointing to a path on the left that says 'Kōbō Daishi's bathing pool, 5 min walk'. Obviously, we have time to see this. The path is concrete studded with stones a few inches apart - presumably for grip - and snakes through some dramatic rocks, with an increasingly distinct yellow hue. It's a landscape made for rock pools, and soon we're looking down on a decidedly spectacular one that makes me want to try it out. This must be it. Oddly enough, we can see no sign to indicate that this is what we're looking for.

That's because it isn't. A little further on, there's a shallow, greenish and uninviting pool with a sign saying this is Kōbō Daishi's pool. Why would he pick this one? There's also a helpful board explaining that over the last 1000 years the ground has risen by about five metres, so I guess things have changed since his day, and we're not seeing it at its best. If Kōbō Daishi were here now, I'm sure he'd be using that other pool.

The track continues, and we realise from the signs it's actually a well-organised discovery track right around the tip of Cape Muroto, taking in a variety of different environments. We've been in the 'birth of new land' zone, and now we move into the 'sub-tropical vegetation' zone, which is just what it says; the bare rocks are replaced by thick undergrowth and trees, including an incredibly tenacious tree that wraps its roots around boulders and hangs on for dear life, which presumably helps it survive amidst uncertain geology and the occasional tsunami. This is a great little track, and one thing that stands out is the flawless English used in the explanatory boards.

Two Henro, and what they now know is not a Henro route indicator.

The pleasant pool I had assumed was Kobo Daishi's.

The pool that really was Kobo Daishi's.

At the end of the sub-tropical section, we decide to leave the remaining 'deep ocean' zone for later, turn back to the main road, and find that we've emerged, as Elaine expected, right at our accommodation, Muroto-sō. Once again, the telephone number on the sign outside is the main - actually the only - give-away.

We go in. I struggle out of my boots and backpack, we ring the bell on the desk, and a lady appears who seems to expect us. Presumably not many Western Henro are booked in for this evening. She has a few words of English, although not many. She takes us up to a decent-sized and comfortable room with a view out over the road to the coast. This will do nicely. Elaine asks about the furo, naturally, and we think she says it will be ready by 4:30. That gives us time to get to temple 24, which should be just up the road. First though, a cup of tea - there's a pot in the room - and a bit of tidying up. Elaine goes out, then comes back almost immediately.

"I've got a puzzle for you. Come out and look at this."

I follow her down the corridor to where the toilets are to be found. There are two.

"All right, given those two symbols, which would you use?"

男 or 女 ?

Ah. This reminds me of a time in England, when I went off to the toilets in a pub and had to return to my friends at the bar and ask, "am I a duck or a drake?" (I thought I knew, but not to the degree of certainty required under the circumstances, and the old trick of just waiting to see who came out didn't work because nobody did.) I'm wiser about aquatic fowl now, but can't read Japanese gender kanji.

I get the iPad and work through a number of images on Google. The one on the left is male ('otoko') and the one on the right is female ('onna'). That settled, we can go back to getting ready.

The room has two Western chairs! They do dig into the tatami mats, but these aren't exactly pristine anyway, and it has to be said that not all six match perfectly. Not everyone has Philippe's standards. Neither Ten (whose tatami mats didn't match either) nor the lady here asked us for out passports either. Clearly some things get a little slack here as one heads south. It may be the Japanese equivalent of heading north in Queensland.

Temple 24 is a little way back up the main road, and then a climb up to the top of a hill. We head out of Muroto-sō, past a lookout platform - and a large concrete whale's tail, whose function isn't entirely clear. There's a path leading up to the temple. Very much up. Lots of steps, but at first they're cement steps, not logs, and then just uneven stones. But it's still about 165 steps to have to climb - I counted - and we've walked a long way today with full packs, even if we don't have them now. But at last we're there, at temple 24, Hotsumisaki-ji.

Our first temple for three days. It's nice to be back. And perhaps because it's a while since we've gone around a temple, we spend a while here. There's a lot to see; it covers a large area, with a huge imposing wooden gate with a giant blue-green Kōbō Daishi statue just outside, a number of separate buildings including a large pagoda, and numerous other statues and red-bibbed Jizō. We see 'Stanley' arrive in his blue shorts and he smiles at us and we smile back.

As we're leaving through the main gate, a very tall Henro appears, completely out of breath. He says - between gasps - that he's Danish and he's walked 45km today. He's 20, and fit, but all the same, that's walking! It seems he thought he was booked in at the temple that night, but his phone isn't working, and he's presumably been rushing to get there by closing time at 5 o'clock - which he's managed with an hour to spare. He mentions other Australians. He's come across Chris and Nadine, and says they made it to their island, which is a relief to hear.

Before going down, we make a detour to look at the lighthouse at the top of the cliffs. It's unusual in that it's a squat construction, with just a single storey circular base and something too short to be called a tower that has the lamp immediately above it. I suppose it's high enough at the top of the cliff and doesn't need to be more of a towering construction. But it feels odd to be able to look down on a lighthouse. On the fence surrounding the lighthouse is a white heart shape with a gold plaque that reads, in English and (presumably) in

Japanese, 'Katsura Lover's Sanctuary. Here I declare this land as "Lover's Sanctuary" to import the joy and magic of encounters, blissful marriages, and raising a happy home. I send my blessings to your encounters and wish you a wonderful future. Bridal Mother.'

Couldn't have put it better myself.

Back at the minshuku, baths - a bit on the warm side for me, but that's what I expect - and down at 6:30 for supper.

Supper is held in a large room with a big TV showing Japanese news, loads of bookcases full of what look like complete series of manga stories, a snooker table - of all things! - and a couple of large dining tables. The meal is memorable for two things: a) there are a huge number of dishes, even by Japanese standards, which just keep coming; and b) we have no idea what any of them are. Although most of them appear to be fish.

There is definitely a fish theme to the meal. There's a plate with a whole fish, a second plate with something that is almost but isn't quite a salmon steak, with two scallop-like things that are a real exercise to get out of their shells with chopsticks, and a sort of chowder ("from deep sea, 300 metres down" says the lady in charge), with an unrecognisable but highly flavoured piece of fishy something in it, and a bowl of what might be sea snails. Elaine passes her might-be-sea-snails to me, and I tackle one. You pull at them with a toothpick, and if you're lucky whatever it was can be squeezed out of its shell. But all of it is spectacularly good. It feels as if a whole fishing fleet has worked all day just to provide this.

As we leave, the lady running the place, who gives the distinct impression of being something of a fish enthusiast, asks us if we like fish. We say yes, and she looks relieved. Would we like fish or, or... beef... tomorrow, she asks tentatively, as if she feels she ought to ask, but her heart isn't in it. We say fish, which is absolutely true, and she looks relieved.

Upstairs, we lay out the futons and, just as we put the light out I say, "I can hear a mozzie!"

A mosquito is about the only known thing that can stop me sleeping. I draw the duvet completely over me as a shield and wake up in the middle of the night, not only bitten several times but also sweltering from trying to keep under the duvet. Elaine wakes as well, also bitten. She opens the window, although it pretends to have a fly screen, and I swap my duvet for a lighter one, finally having remembered the furnishings had included two heavy and two light duvets and realising I'd made the wrong choice. The cooler combination works, and cocooned safely away from the mozzie I get some proper sleep.

In the morning, I explained to Elaine the deep problem I'd experienced that night.

"I woke up a): wishing for a mozzie spray, and b): feeling that spraying for a mozzie wasn't exactly a Buddhist thing to do, and c): feeling that anyone who'd eaten so many fish species for supper couldn't really take that attitude, and d): remembering I'm not actually a Buddhist anyway. You see, I wasn't only suffering from mozzie bites, but also from deep philosophical uncertainty."

"You've always been happy to fill the bedroom with mozzie spray in the past."

Ah, yes, but if Kōbō Daishi had had a can of mozzie spray, would he have used it?

The entrance to temple 24, Hotsumisaki-ji.

Temple 24, Hotsumisaki-ji.

The slow but steady Henro arrives at temple 24.

The lighthouse at Cape Muroto.

Supper at Muroto-sō.

27

OUR LAST DAY AS HENRO - TEMPLES 25 & 26 (SATURDAY APRIL 28)

Today has to be our last on the Henro trail, at least for this trip. We can make it to temples 25 and 26, which are close to where we are now, but then it's another 30 kilometres or so from temple 26 to temple 27, and we've run out of days. We'd booked in here at Muroto-sō for two nights, and it looks as if that was an excellent choice; this place makes a good base, and it's fun, especially the meals, at least on the basis of last night's fishy extravaganza. Because of Golden Week, we've had to book ahead for the next few nights, tomorrow in Kochi City and then in Takamatsu, so we now have a fixed schedule for the few days we have left in Japan. But we're sorry to have to stop.

Breakfast is another grand spread in the large room downstairs, and we try to follow some of Japanese breakfast TV. There are reports from the North/South Korean summit, something the Japanese are particularly interested in, given the traditional antagonism between Japan and Korea, but it's livened up considerably by a section where one of the presenters visits a woodland adventure park and tries out a spectacular flying fox ride. Breakfast TV seems to be almost the same in any language.

Before we hit the road for temple 25, we want to go and see Kōbō Daishi's famous cave, which we missed yesterday when we left the main road for the walk past his bathing pool. The young priest who would later be known as Kūkai, and after his death as Kōbō Daishi, trained here, meditating inside his cave. He said that the only things he could see from the cave were the sky and the sea, and a combination of the characters for 'sky' and 'sea' make up the name 'Kūkai', which he adopted after his meditations. Presumably he also took time out to make use of the pool on the other side of what is now the main road.

The cave is actually two caves, both at the bottom of the cliff-face, one where he lived, and one where he meditated. Unfortunately, when we get there we find both are closed at the moment due to rock-fall risks, which seems particularly sensible given the amount of overhanging rock, but is a bit disappointing. From a distance, we can peer into the dark interiors and imagine a solitary life inside.

We turn around, and follow the main road, route 55, on past our temporary base at Muroto-sō. The section of road just after we round the tip of Cape Muroto reminds me of some of the less urban parts of California - a few scattered buildings, but mostly wide roads and palm trees. But some of the smaller, narrower, streets are clearly Japanese, with dilapidated run-down buildings, particularly with rusting corrugated iron, right next to new, pristine dwellings, which doesn't appear to bother anybody. And always the criss-cross of wires above all the streets.

The Henro path follows route 55 most of the time, with occasional diversions through the centres of villages and small ports. Some of the boats we pass at their moorings are particularly colourful, and give rather a jolly feel to the walk. The general design of a port in this part of the island seems to concentrate on huge breakwaters forming sheltered harbours with such an intricate route to the ocean that it isn't always obvious just how the boats do get out. Presumably the point is that huge waves can't find their way in.

We pass the occasional tsunami shelter, open steel constructions with about four floors, on top of which people will presumably be safe from a tsunami roaring through the lower levels.

"It's a good idea," says Elaine, "but how many people could you fit at the top of these?" Certainly, they don't look as if they could take everyone living nearby.

Monument in front of Kōbō Daishi's caves.

Kōbō Daishi's two caves.

Restocking the vends, on the side of route 55.

The open steel construction is a tsunami shelter.

Temple 25, Shinshō-ji, is in the middle of what looks like a reasonably large town. As we near the temple we're stopped by a lady on a bike, who's been riding along talking to herself non-stop. She tells Elaine something long and totally incomprehensible, then rides off, still chattering to herself.

"Did you follow any of that?" I ask.

"Not a word."

We carry on. Temple 25 suddenly appears at the end of a side street. More accurately, looking down the side street we can see its entrance arch, and through it a huge flight of steps that lead up to yet another more elaborate arch, past which is presumably a temple. We struggle up these steps - I count 115 - with a long pause at a bench about 12 steps from the top.

"I think that lady might have been telling me there were a lot of steps up to the temple," says Elaine. We'll never know.

Shinshō-ji is compact, but its elevation - those 115 steps - gives it lovely views out over the town. We can see out over the modern buildings to the harbour with its substantial breakwater, and over to the uniform blue calm of the ocean. The small temple grounds are crowded; there's a conducted tour group, so their driver tells us, all chanting sutras in unison. The driver watches from the back, then joins in at the end as they start looking round for him. We get our books stamped at the office, and watch as another Henro carefully lays out a freshly-stamped scroll and dries it with a hair dryer. Bizarrely, behind him appear to be a set of Wanted posters with black and white photographs of what are presumably some of Shikoku's most sort-after disreputables.

The town has a Lawson shown on the map in the White Book, and we zig-zag our way to it through the backstreets. We buy lunch triangles and croissants and coffee, but this is a Lawson without seating, and we have to eat these sitting at a nearby bus stop. Given how far we've walked, which is about four kilometres, we suspect this town might just be the zero-point used by the distance markers we were following yesterday, counting down the kilometres to Cape Muroto. It is a real urban conurbation, having a temple and a Lawson and a harbour and all, and by local standards the overall built-up area is substantial. The White Book doesn't label it clearly, but it looks as if this is actually Muroto City.

Steps up to temple 25, Shinshō-ji.

Boats in harbour, seen on the way to temple 25.

Pilgrims at temple 25, Shinshō-ji.

Going down the steps, temple 25.

Drying a scroll at temple 25.

Temple 26, Kongōchō-ji, our last for this trip, is only a few kilometres further on. We follow the Henro path out of the town to where it crosses the main coast road at a colourful point marked by a rather gaudy car dealership, a convenient shelter, and a positively glorious flowerbed glistening in the sun with yellows, reds, whites and purples. We sit for a while, just because it's colourful, pleasant and bright. And it has some shade.

Then we need to move. The Henro path is following a smaller road running parallel to the busy coast road, but slightly inland. There are bus stops, which will be useful when the time comes to return to Muroto-sō and its promise of more deep sea fish for supper. We're passing rice paddies that stretch from the road to some hills in the distance, and it looks as if the temple must be up amongst those hills. We start to try to estimate how high up it's going to be and how much of a climb we're in for. The Henro path profile in the White Book shows a climb similar to that up to temple 24 yesterday, which was steep but didn't last too long. We should be OK.

We can see that we're close to the point where we have to turn off this road, so we pause at what must be the nearest bus-stop and take a photo of the time table. It's on the right side of the road for a bus back to Cape Muroto, so any bus should do, which is just as well because the times are about all we can decipher. (I can see the characters for 'bus', but that isn't what the unbiased observer would call particularly useful.)

About 50 metres on from the bus stop we turn off to the right, past more paddy fields, and finally the path reaches the hillside and heads off into the woods. Then it starts to climb. It starts off as a concrete strip, then steepens into steps of irregular stones. It's hard going, and takes us several rest stops, but finally we come out into the open, and we've reached our final temple. There's a car park, just to remind us that there are easier - but less satisfying - ways of getting up here, and a tempting small café that advertises ice-cream, but we press on up the final steps to the temple proper.

Kongōchō-ji sits in the sun in a large open area surrounded by trees, with a view out to the ocean, and has substantial temple buildings in what seem a lighter wood than most. It's a bright and lovely place, and a splendid temple to end at.

We perform our usual, somewhat minimal, routine of washing hands and face, ringing the temple bell, putting in our offerings and our name slips, and mumbling our few words from the sutras. In front of one of the halls is a stone basin filled with sand into which visitors have placed lighted incense sticks. In the middle of the basin, looking slightly out of place but practical, is a tin that once contained pineapple slices but now houses the flame used to light the sticks. Elaine puts in money for a couple of sticks, lights them, and places them in the sand.

At the office, the monk stamping the books appears to have a cold and is watching baseball on the TV, but he performs the stamping and adds the calligraphy as elegantly as any of the others. We put the book away rather sadly. We won't be doing this again for a while.

Just by the temple gate there's what might be a small tea room. There was the café by the car park, with its promise of ice-cream, but if the proper temple has a tea room we feel we should go there. It has a number of long tables, one decked with plates of small vegetable snacks, and a blonde-haired chap dressed in black is sitting at it, his backpack parked outside. Another of those ubiquitous small Japanese ladies is standing at the side of the room, and as we come in she bustles around quickly and puts two cups and a pot of tea on the table in front of us.

The black-clad blonde turns out to be Danish. We tell him we met a Dane yesterday who'd walked 45km to reach temple 24.

"Ah, so he made it. I thought it was crazy, but he was going to do this. A 45km walk all in one day."

He displays a more relaxed attitude. He says he slept in a Henro hut last night, "But it was by the road and too noisy to sleep well. Tonight, I will stay at this temple. You need to sleep well if you're walking."

We ask him what the deal is with this tea place, thinking it will be time to pay and head back, but he has no idea.

"I came in and sat down and was brought tea, and I think I will find out later about paying."

The lady comes across and I try to ask: "ii deshita, ikura desuka?", that was excellent, how much? But she ignores my bad grammar, waves her hands across each other, and says something I assume means 'no charge'.

"Honto-ni?" I'd learned that was how you said 'really?' and I've always wanted to use it. She nods, and we say lots of 'arrigato's, wave goodbye to our Danish friend, and head back down the hill the way we came.

The Henro path runs back past the same paddy fields, and reaches the road where we can get the bus. At the junction with the road, there's a Henro hut, and we look in. This is an elaborate Henro hut; it has a small annexe that turns out to house a Western toilet and a shower. It also has a guest book, with the recent entry: 'Thank you so much! I have so much trouble with squat toilets'. Then we hike the 50 metres down the road to the bus stop. We make a careful note of this bus stop. When we come back, and it's pretty clear we will, this is where we stopped walking, and where we're going to be starting again.

. . .

Back to Cape Muroto and our room at Muroto-sō, for laundry and the bath. Just one of us has the bath, as it turns out. I go first, shower, dip one foot in the bath and pull it back extremely quickly, stifling a yell. I shower again, this time with hotter water, trying to accustom myself to higher temperatures, then return to the bath and dip in the other foot. It's actually painful. Torquemada could have got the Pope to confess to Protestantism with that bath. I go back to the room.

"You were quick."

"Yes, you may manage that bath, but I couldn't."

She goes to see. She survives the inquisition, but only just.

"I didn't stay in long. Your whole body goes pink."

I bet that's how they cook lobsters.

Supper isn't lobster. We'd recognise lobster, and tonight's supper consists entirely of fish we don't recognise. There's one small fish - "river fish", says the lady enthusiastically - and a large whole red fish that might be a red emperor but probably isn't. There's a strongly flavoured sashimi that we think might be bonito. We find it far too strongly flavoured at first, then realise it's served with orange slices, and that the orange juice seems to moderate the taste nicely.

"These are splendid; it's a great meal, particularly the red what-not, but I wish I knew what these were."

"I think," says Elaine, "that she has an arrangement with the local fishermen. Anything weird they catch they bring to her and she serves it to the guests. Oh, coelacanth, believed extinct - let's see what that's like as sashimi."

"It works though. I'd come back here."

Maybe we will.

The corner with the flowers and the car dealership.

The entrance to temple 26.

Ringing the bell at temple 26, Kongōchō-ji.

Incense sticks at temple 26.

Muroto-sō serves up another seafood feast.

28

LEAVING SHIKOKU, AND RETURNING

The next day, we said goodbye to Muroto-sō, walked to the bus stop over the road, and took the bus to Nahari, where we could get a train to Kochi City.

Now, we were no longer Henro, no longer pilgrims. We were tourists. We spent a couple of days in Kochi City, taking in Kochi castle - one of the few remaining Edo period castles - and staying at a very modern high rise hotel that had a list of rules that included "kindly refrain from going out of your room with nightwear and slippers" and "refrain from inviting gangsters, extremist organisations or other members". We happily complied with both.

With the idea of visiting the art island of Naoshima, in the inland sea that separates Shikoku from the main island of Honshu, we took the train north, right across Shikoku, to the city of Takamatsu. Our first attempt to reach Naoshima was frustrated by fog, and we ended up instead going around the lovely Ritsurin gardens in Takamatsu, where we drank tea in an Edo era tea house with a wonderfully peaceful view of the central lake.

We did make it to Naoshima, on a rainy day that limited what we could see, not that a day would be long enough anyway, leaving Elaine intent on returning. The last of the 88 temples are all in the Takamatsu area, so she will get her chance, eventually.

And then we flew from Takamatsu to Tokyo and from there back to Sydney.

We did return to Muroto-sō, the next year, making it our starting point as we continued on the Henro track. We took the bus from the same bus stop over the road, got off at the bus stop near temple 26, Kongōchō-ji, and started walking again. In the roughly three weeks we had available, we walked to Kochi City, and then on as far as temple 37, Iwamoto-ji. I found I particularly enjoyed walking through Kochi province along the ocean road. Elaine is still encouraging me to write up my diary properly for this section, and I intend to at some point.

At this rate, limited mainly by the amount of time Elaine could take off from work, it was looking as though another three years of walking in March/April would complete our 88-temple pilgrimage. The next year, we had flights booked back to Kochi, ready to take the train back to temple 37. We had accomodation booked close to the southernmost point of Shikoku, near temple 38, Kongōfuku-ji, which we intended to reach in time for my birthday at the end of March.

But that year was 2020, and Covid-19 turned the world upside down. As I write this, in September 2021, we are still unable to leave an Australia that has been relying on closed borders to keep the virus at bay, and we are not sure when we will get back to Japan to continue in the footsteps of Kōbō Daishi.

But we will.

29

SOME RANDOM NOTES AND EXPLANATIONS

We finished this part of the journey with a large number of unanswered questions. Some remained mysteries. But I did eventually find out a little more about some of them.

When we got back, I spent a while on Google, fount of all knowledge, and there is apparently a well-known Japanese dolls' village in Shikoku, called Nagoro, where most of the population has left and been replaced by over 300 dolls, most made by one older lady. But Nagoro is well off the Henro route, so the doll's village we passed through wasn't Nagoro, although the style of the dolls looks remarkably similar. Obviously, somebody knows what's going on, but so far, I don't.

Embarrassingly, I discovered that the answer to "where in the world is a marinara pizza nothing to do with seafood?" is "in Italy". There, 'marinara' is a traditional Italian sailor's pizza, and is essentially a margherita without cheese. It's named after the people who ate it, not after what's in it. It's an Australian misconception to think it has seafood on it. That's why Italian seafood pizzas are always called "frutti di mare" - I'd always wondered about that.

On reflection, I think the only thing wrong with Uoroman's English menu was that it had odd spacing, with the Japanese for a dish, then a large gap before the English translation, and then, almost immediately, the Japanese for the next dish. So, when I pointed to the English for the octopus pizza, the waiter thought I was pointing to the Japanese for the next dish, which was the Lotus root pizza. I suspect that when I said 'octopus' (in English) he heard 'lotus'.

The little coastal town of Mugi has a Wikipedia entry, but the only thing that ever seems to have happened in Mugi is the 'Cyprus mutiny' of 1830 when Australian convicts took over the ship (the 'Cyprus') they were on and tried to land at Mugi but were turned away by the Japanese authorities.

SeaRest Muroto, aka Deep Sea World, really is a major spa facility. It was founded by makeup artist Shu Uemura, who believes uncontaminated water from the ocean depths has serious therapeutic benefits. I found an on-line article at travelandleisure.com that said that before the opening of the spa, Cape Muroto was best known for the Shingon Buddhist pilgrimage. That may or may not reflect the priorities of the modern visitor to Cape Muroto.

And for anyone tempted to try the pilgrimage themselves:

The White Book - 'Shikoku Japan 88 Route Guide' - is essential if you're planning to do the pilgrimage. It's published by Buyodo Co. Ltd., and is available in English from various booksellers, such as Amazon. The maps in it are excellent, although there are places where the map layout reflects the fact that the original Japanese edition was designed to be read from back to front, like all Japanese books. You'll get used to that.

There is a lot of information about the Henro pilgrimage on-line, and there is a particularly useful and helpful Facebook group called OHenro San, which you can ask to join if you're serious about wanting to do the pilgrimage.

30

A BRIEF APPENDIX: TRYING TO LEARN JAPANESE

Elaine and I approach foreign languages in completely different ways. This isn't surprising, since we approach almost everything in completely different ways. She thinks you learn a language in order to communicate with someone else who speaks it, no matter how ungrammatically. I think you learn a language in order to understand how the language works, what its underlying structure and grammar are, and then you use that to communicate.

I find my way more intellectually satisfying.

But, annoyingly, her way works much better in practice.

I'm fascinated by how things work in general; I like understanding the underlying structures in things. She wants to be able to order lunch. She will cobble words together into some sort of phrase, backed up by a waving of hands and a pointing to things, and will get across what she needs, while I'm stuck trying to remember just what the subjunctive form of the verb is, and whether that's what I ought to be using anyway. Her German, which she learned while working in Munich some years ago, is what she describes as 'fulfilling needs German'. My German, which I was supposed to learn at school but didn't, is much stronger on grammar, but a bit of a dead loss when it comes to actually fulfilling needs.

. . .

On our previous trips, almost entirely in the bigger cities, we could manage without knowing Japanese. We picked up a few phrases, like 'Ohayō gozaimasu' for 'Good morning', but there were enough people who spoke English, or there were signs in English, or at least menus with pictures of food you could point to, and you could survive perfectly well with almost no knowledge of the language. And, indeed, it was clear that people had even managed the Shikoku pilgrimage with pretty minimal Japanese.

But it always seems rude to me to go to another country and expect them to speak your language; you should at least do them the courtesy of trying to learn some of theirs. And for someone interested in the underlying structure of things, Japanese is a treasure trove of the unexpected, particularly the way the written language works.

If you're only used to English, or other European languages, the first thing you notice about Japanese is that it doesn't use anything like a European alphabet. English has a nice, simple, set of 26 characters. The French use the same set, more or less, but add a few flourishes in places, like Orléans, with its accented é. Even the Greeks and the Russians use an alphabet; even if the actual letters are different and their capital cities are Αθήνα and Москва, they're using a single, simple set of letters each with a sound you can learn. Alphabets have vowels and consonants, and you have to combine these to get sounds you can actually pronounce.

The Chinese don't use an alphabet. They have a set of thousands of different characters each of which represents a word or phrase. The technical term is 'logograms' - word pictures. Just basic Chinese literacy requires you to learn somewhere between two- to three-thousand separate characters, and everything is written using these.

I had originally thought Japanese used the same system as Chinese, and was written entirely in this sort of logogram character. But it isn't that simple.

It's written in a mixture of three quite different sets of characters:

kanji, hiragana, and katakana. Strictly, none of these are alphabets. In a Japanese sentence, you will often see all three sets being used. And, because that isn't complicated enough, there's also a fourth set (roma-ji), which actually is an alphabet ('our' roman alphabet, in fact), but which isn't strictly a part of Japanese, although a lot of Japanese learn it.

Kanji is a set of logograms. In fact, they *are* the Chinese characters, imported into Japan in the 5th century. People who can read Chinese can make a guess at the meaning of something in Japanese written in kanji - although they'd probably get the pronunciation completely wrong. But these are the 5th century Chinese characters and Chinese has moved on since then. And knowing Chinese doesn't help at all when it comes to hiragana and katakana.

The two 'kana's, hiragana and katakana, look a bit like alphabets, but are actually syllabaries. Each has about 46 characters, each of which represents a syllable. This is actually a sensible idea. Each character can be pronounced, because each one includes a vowel. Although it isn't as flexible as an alphabet, it is more regular. Japanese has five vowel sounds, just like English, a,i,u,e and o, pronounced 'ah', 'ee', 'oo', 'ay' and 'oh' . You can then combine each of these five vowels with any of the nine consonants k,s,t,n,h,m,y,r and w. You can also have the vowels on their own, which in theory gives you 50 separate sounds. In practice, there are five combinations that aren't used (yi,ye,wi,wu and we), and one extra, which is just an 'n' sound. That's your 46 basic Japanese sounds, and there is a separate kana character for each.

What's odd about the kana is that both hiragana and katakana are used for exactly the same set of sounds, but are completely different character sets.

For example, the vowels on their own, a,i,u,e and o, are written as あ, え, う, え, and お in hiragana, and as ア, エ, ウ, エ, and オ in katakana. The combinations ka,ki,ku,ke, and ko are written as か, き, く, け, and こ in hiragana, and as カ, キ, ク, ケ, and コ in katakana.

	a	i	u	e	o
	ア あ a	イ い i	ウ う u	エ え e	オ お o
k	カ か ka	キ き ki	ク く ku	ケ け ke	コ こ ko
s	サ さ sa	シ し shi	ス す su	セ せ se	ソ そ so
t	タ た ta	チ ち chi	ツ つ tsu	テ て te	ト と to
n	ナ な na	ニ に ni	ヌ ぬ nu	ネ ね ne	ノ の no
h	ハ は ha	ヒ ひ hi	フ ふ fu	ヘ へ he	ホ ほ ho
m	マ ま ma	ミ み mi	ム む mu	メ め me	モ も mo
y	ヤ や ya		ユ ゆ yu		ヨ よ yo
r	ラ ら ra	リ り ri	ル る ru	レ れ re	ロ ろ ro
w	ワ わ wa				ヲ を wo
	ン ん n				
g	ガ が ga	ギ ぎ gi	グ ぐ gu	ゲ げ ge	ゴ ご go
z	ザ ざ za	ジ じ ji	ズ ず zu	ゼ ぜ ze	ゾ ぞ zo
d	ダ だ da	ヂ ぢ ji	ヅ づ zu	デ で de	ド ど do
b	バ ば ba	ビ び bi	ブ ぶ bu	ベ べ be	ボ ぼ bo
p	パ ぱ pa	ピ ぴ pi	プ ぷ pu	ペ ぺ pe	ポ ぽ po

Table of Katakana and Hiragana symbols. The vowel sounds, a,i,u,e,o ('ah','ee','oo','ay','oh') form the columns, and each row corresponds to a consonant. Each box shows the katakana characters for the resulting syllable, followed by the hiragana equivalent, and then the romaji transliteration of the sound. Characters can be followed by smaller versions of some characters to produce other sounds, but these are not shown here.

Although they represent the same sounds, hiragana and katakana are used differently. Hiragana are used, amongst other things, for native Japanese words for which there aren't kanji. Also, Chinese verbs don't have different forms (unlike English with 'move', 'moves', 'moved', etc.), so the one logogram can be used in all cases. Spoken Japanese does, so written Japanese appends endings in hiragana to the basic kanji for the verbs to handle this.

Katakana are used mainly for words imported from other languages and often appear on menus. That means it can be quite useful for Westerners to learn katakana. If you see a word like, for example, ラメン, it can be useful to know these are the katakana characters for 'ra','me' and 'n' - in other words, ramen noodles. Sometimes a bit of imagination is needed, for example, スパゲッティ turns out to be 'su-pa-ge-tte-i' or 'spaghetti'.

Since they could do exactly the same job, it isn't obvious why Japanese should need both katakana and hiragana. What's more, any word that can be written in kanji could also be written in, say, hiragana. In fact, children learn hiragana first, and then, to help them with the kanji they have to learn, children's books will often have the hiragana written above the kanji in discouragingly small print (when this is done, it's called furigana).

So you might think that Japan could manage nicely with just one of the kanas, say hiragana. Why struggle with having to learn all those kanji - children have to learn about two thousand - when you could just learn the 46 hiragana characters? I put this once to a Japanese friend, one who'd spent a lot of time in the West, and he thought a while, and said:

"I think it's just more macho."

Which is probably true. Interestingly, Japanese is usually written without spaces between words, and having the different types of character does help delineate words. It also brings home just how important the space character is in English writing.

To be fair, we may be puzzled as to why Japanese has both hiragana and katakana characters for the same sounds, like both あ and ア for 'a', but then, we have both 'A' and 'a'. We have two versions of each letter, and half of them are only used at the start of sentences and proper names. We're just so used to our capital letters that we don't even think of them as a separate version of the alphabet. So, let's not get too taken with how much more rational our system feels to us.

As if that isn't complicated enough, Japanese actually has more sounds than are represented by the 46-odd kana characters. There are little modifiers that can be added, so, for example, a small round circle at the top-right of one of the 'h' sounds, 'ha','hi','fu','he','ho' makes it a 'p' sound, 'pa','pi','pu','pe','po'. So in katakana, ハ is 'ha' while パ is 'pa'. (Oh, yes, and the 'h' sounds really are 'ha','hi','fu','he','ho' with the 'u' sound being 'fu' instead of 'hu'. Just because.) Two small lines at top right turn 'h' sounds into 'b' sounds, 't' sounds into 'd' sounds, 's' sounds into 'z' sounds and 'k' sounds into 'g' sounds. So, again in katakana, カ is 'ka' while ガ is 'ga'.

And there are even more complex combinations involving smaller versions of characters acting as modifiers that can produce other, less usual sounds. My name 'Shortridge' is written in katakana as ショトリッジ with the first pair of characters producing the 'sho' sound, and the last pair coming close to the awkward 'dge' sounds at the end. It can be useful to be able to write your name in katakana; ask a helpful Japanese to show you how. (On a visit to one rather out of the way town our daughter Holly had to be taken to a local clinic, where reception pushed a form at me and pointed to a line for her name, and wouldn't accept it in Western script. Holly turned out to be fine, by the way, and the doctor we eventually saw did speak usable English.)

I know this isn't correct historically, but it's as if the Japanese originally took over the Chinese set of characters (the kanji) fifteen hundred years ago, and then wondered what to do about verb endings and new words. Instead of inventing new kanji for them, they decided to invent hiragana so they could write them by sound instead. And then when they started borrowing foreign words like 'spaghetti', they didn't want to use hiragana for them, so they invented katakana instead. I find this a useful way of looking at it, but it isn't actually how hiragana and katakana developed, which is complicated (at one time, hiragana was regarded as 'women's writing', which might explain our Japanese friend's 'macho' comment).

Interestingly, the invention of both katakana and hiragana is traditionally credited to Kōbō Daishi, whose trail we are following on the Shikoku pilgrimage.

And what about that fourth set of characters, romaji? Why did I say the Japanese vowels, a,i,u,e and o, are pronounced 'ah', 'ee', 'oo', 'ay' and 'oh', since that isn't the English pronunciation for those letters?

Once Westerners started coming to Japan, they discovered that they needed a way of writing Japanese sounds in a way they could handle - using a Roman alphabet. Someone had to decide on what Roman letters to use for what sounds. And at this point, you have to remember that the different languages that use Roman letters pronounce them differently, and English is actually something of an outlier here. Some of the earliest foreign visitors to Japan were Portuguese, and it's the southern European vowel sounds that are being used by romaji.

A few different systems of 'romanisation' for Japanese exist, but there is one that has become the standard. It's handy, but it can be confusing. The important thing to realise is that romaji isn't supposed to be a way of writing Japanese in English, it's a way a writing Japanese in a set of Roman characters, and it has its own set of conventions about how those are pronounced. You actually have to learn how to pronounce romaji, just as if it were a foreign European language. It helps to think of it as Spanish, or Italian, but it isn't exactly the same as any European language.

So, for example, the Japanese word for 'I go' is written in hiragana as:

いきます

And this is transliterated into romaji as 'ikimasu'.

Now if I pronounced that as if it were an English word, I'd get something like 'ick-im-ass-oo'. But the way it's supposed to be pronounced is more like 'ee-key-mahss'. That final 'u' simply isn't pronounced. This catches out a lot of people using phrase books that just give the Japanese in romaji, without attempting to indicate the English pronunciation. Just like 'ikimasu', many Japanese verbs end with a silent 'u' when written in romaji, and that's just plain misleading if you're trying to pronounce the language. But that's how romaji is. Japanese writing just isn't simple, even when it's written with English letters.

A couple of other things about pronunciation and romaji:

A vowel with a bar over it indicates a long vowel.

Double consonants indicate a slight pause. 'Gakko' (school) is 'gah-koh'.

There's no letter 'L', but the 'R' sound is somewhere between an 'R' and an 'L'. When I hear a Japanese say 'Elaine' I hear it as 'Eraine' but it's really somewhere in between.

Japanese don't have a 'V' sound, and 'V's in imported words end up as 'B's. So a convenience store is called a 'konbini'.

You don't actually need to get into the written language to start trying to learn some Japanese, although you're almost certainly going to have to use romaji at some point. I just found it fascinating.

Or, seen from another point of view (Elaine's): "If you hadn't spent so long trying to understand how the writing works, you might know more of the useful words."

I ended up going to Shikoku with a seriously mixed amount of knowledge of Japanese, all of which I had found interesting, not all of which turned out to be useful. Early on, encouraged by the idea that it might help with menus, I tried to learn most of the katakana characters, although I never really got enough practice, despite buying a set of flash cards. Then I tried to pick up some of the basics of the language itself.

Everyone has different ways of learning a language. At first, I never found the time to take proper classes in Japanese, but after our first trip to Japan I did buy copies of the Pimsleur Japanese course on CD. Pimsleur doesn't work for everyone, but I've found theirs are the only CD-based language courses that work for me. You spend a lot of time going over and over the same thing, because repetition is the best way to get something stuck in your head. This means you go through a lot of CDs to learn not a huge lot of Japanese, but there's some chance that you'll remember what you do cover. I was going to say, 'it works for me', but actually nothing with foreign languages really works for me. It did help, though.

One big plus is that you hear the words over and over again and you know how they're really said. A big minus, for me, is that there is basically no explanation of the grammar, or why the sentences go together the way they do. As I said, I like to know how things work.

But I persisted, and worked through the first Pimsleur course before we went back to Japan the next time. However, being in the big cities we really didn't need mush Japanese.

Moreover, Pimsleur seems to be intended for American businessmen. And it does seem to be businessmen rather than businesswomen. Early on, you spend a lot of time on useful phrases like: "Watashi-no tokoro-de nanika nomimasen-ka?" ("Wouldn't you like something to drink at my place?")

It also seems to believe that you can use dollars anywhere in Japan to buy things; there's a deal of practice asking about the price of things in dollars.

And my favourite snippet of foreign language learning comes in one lesson that introduces the Japanese word for 'alone' ('hitori' - literally, 'one person'), using a dialogue where a man asks a woman if she is alone (hitori'). She replies that, no, she is with her husband, and the man says, reluctantly, that in that case, he will return alone ('hitori-de').

Clearly, all this is essential vocabulary for the American in Tokyo on business, but not of real use to a couple on a pilgrimage in one of the more rural parts of Japan.

As a language, the way Japanese works is quite different to any European language I know of, which is why literal translations sound so much like stereotypes out of some comic book: "Honourable chopsticks exist, question?"

Bear with me for a couple of examples.

A useful phrase, for me, is:

"Watashi-no namae-wa Keith desu" (My name is Keith)

Japanese uses particles attached to the end of words to indicate their role in the sentence:

-wa indicates this is the topic of the sentence.

-no indicates possession.

"Watashi" is the Japanese word for "me" or "I", and "namae" is

Japanese for "name" (although it's pronounced nah-my). "Desu" (pronounced dess - one of the most common silent 'u's that romaji puts in to confuse you) is effectively the word for "is".

So, in "watashi-no namae-wa Keith desu", "watashi-no namae" is "me-possessing name", in other words "my name" and the -wa says this is the subject of the sentence. So "(watashi-no namae)-wa" says this is a sentence about my name, and the "Keith desu", essentially, "Keith is" says that my name is Keith.

-ka at the end of a sentence makes it a question.

Here's a useful question:

"O-namae-wa nan desu-ka?" ("What is your name?")

The O- prefix is there for politeness. Japanese are famously polite, and are polite about all sorts of things, particularly people's names. But not just names. Chopsticks (hashi) become o-hashi. This O- is what often gets translated into the comic-book "honourable". "Nan" is Japanese for "what" and the "ka" at the end makes this a question. And "O-namae-wa nan desu-ka?" is, essentially, "name-concerning, what is?"

Note that nowhere does the sentence make it explicit that it's *your* name that's being asked about. We might think a sentence that amounts to "What is the name?" is lacking in context, but it seems perfectly natural to a Japanese speaker.

Context is important in Japanese sentences, but is often understood from what's gone before, or just from the circumstances.

Pointing to something you don't recognise on a menu and asking "nan desu-ka?" ("What is?") can be useful, so long as you think you might understand the answer. Or you might say "Kore-wa nan desu-ka?" which breaks down as "this-concerning, what is?", in other words, "What is this?".

Verbs, unsurprisingly, work in surprising ways.

"Ikimasu" (remember not to pronounce the final 'u'!) means "I go", but it also means "You go", "He goes", "We go". It doesn't change no matter who is going. This is handy, because you don't have to worry about learning all the different forms for the verb like you do in, say French or German, or indeed most languages. (English, which usually just sticks an 's' at the end in one place - "I laugh", "You laugh", "He laughs" etc. - is much easier than most European languages as far as this goes. It gets its own back with its incredibly inconsistent pronunciation.)

Strictly, the verb is "iku" (to go) and the -imasu form is the present tense. The negative form of the present is -imasen, so ikimasen is "I don't go".

And Japanese verbs really only have one form for the past and one form for everything else. So "ikimasu" not only means "I go" it can also mean "I will go", and you have to work out which it means from the context, again. You need the context a lot, which is why Japanese has a nice easy way - using the -wa particle - to set the context for a sentence. And the -ga particle can set the subject of a verb, in case that isn't clear either.

Japanese verbs make up for this by having a variety of extra forms we don't have in English, including a specific form for "I would like to", and one for "let's". So "tabemasu" is "I eat" (or at any rate, somebody or some people eat), "tabetai-desu" is "I want to eat" (rather impoilte), "tabetain-desu-ga" is "I would like to eat" (much more polite) and "tabemashō is "Let's eat." There are more.

Negatives in Japanese can get complicated, particularly when you get to forms like "I don't want to", but for that you need to do your own Japanese course, preferably with a human teacher who can explain all this stuff.

Elaine and I finally found a splendid human teacher in our area, but we only managed a couple of lessons with Tomoe-san before we left. We tried to concentrate on what we thought would be the trickiest part of our pilgrimage, namely booking accommodation for the next night or nights. We imagined we might have to do this over the phone, and this was a seriously intimidating prospect.

"ashita heya-ga arimasu-ka?" ("Do you have a room for tomorrow?")

Elaine, merely wanting "satisfying-needs Japanese" is happy to just write this phrase down. I need to know that it breaks down into "ashita (tomorrow) heya (room) -ga (subject) arimasu (exists) -ka? (question)", and that you're really saying, "tomorrow, does a room exist?" which is the way Japanese phrase a "do you have?" type of question. Both our approaches are fine, but they satisfy different needs - hers that we get a room tomorrow, mine that I feel I understand the way the language works.

As it turns out, we never used this. Getting rooms booked for the next night was easy, because people who ran accommodation were used to being asked to ring ahead, and understood what was needed almost without being asked.

Where we needed much more help turned out to be understanding menus. We covered this all too briefly with Tomoe-san, who taught us to point at a menu and ask "nan desu-ka?" but who also pointed out that the tricky bit was going to be understanding the answer. And she was absolutely right.

ABOUT THE AUTHOR

Keith Shortridge was born in England, but spent much of his early childhood in Malta. He has degrees in Physics and Astrophysics from the University of London, and spent most of his career helping develop astronomical instrumentation. He lives in Sydney, with Elaine - a professor of Physics - and their children, Holly and Tom. Until Covid-19 struck, he was attempting to spend his retirement travelling as much as possible. This is Keith's first book.

www.ingramcontent.com/pod-product-compliance
Lightning Source LLC
Chambersburg PA
CBHW042042290426
44109CB00001B/1